£ 37.50

CORPORATE VISION AND RAPID TECHNOLOGICAL CHANGE

The impact of technological change on market structure can be much more drastic than that of traditional sources of competition such as price. However, to date the economic analysis of technological change has tended to overlook important insights from organisational behaviour.

In *Corporate Vision and Rapid Technological Change*, these two traditions are brought together. The authors present an economic analysis of technological change and market structure which incorporates organisational strategy towards technology change and corporate structure. In a radical departure from conventional theory, it is argued that the relationship between technological change and market structure cannot be properly understood without appreciating the role of firms' strategic vision. It also shows that the direct measurement of the rate of technological change – as opposed to indirect measures like patent counts or R&D expenditure – is essential if changes in market structure are to be understood.

The first four chapters set out the theoretical background to this argument. The remaining chapters develop this theory through case studies of some of the most innovative and fast moving industries in the world, including software, micro electronics and biotechnology.

Dr Peter Swann is Senior Research Fellow at the London Business School. From 1990–92 he was co-ordinator of the ESRC/DTI Research Initiative on New Technologies and the firm. He is also Managing Editor (Europe) for the journal *Economies of Innovation and New Technology*. **Dr Jas Gill** teaches economics at the University of Brighton. He has extensive research experience in technological innovation.

CORPORATE VISION AND RAPID TECHNOLOGICAL CHANGE

The Evolution of Market Structure

Peter Swann and Jas Gill

London and New York

First published 1993
by Routledge
11 New Fetter Lane, London EC4P 4EE

Simultaneously published in the USA and Canada
by Routledge
29 West 35th Street, New York, NY 10001

© 1993 Peter Swann and Jas Gill

Typeset in Garamond by
Ponting–Green Publishing Services, Chesham, Bucks
Printed in Great Britain by
Biddles Ltd, Guildford and Kings Lynn

British Library Cataloguing in Publication Data
A catalogue record for this book is available from
the British Library

Library of Congress Cataloging in Publication Data
Swann, Peter.
Corporate vision and rapid technological change: the
evolution of market structure / Peter Swann and Jas Gill
p.   cm.
Includes bibliographical references and index.
ISBN 0–415–09135–7
1. Technological innovations – Management.
2. Corporate planning
3. Industrial management.
4. Technological innovations – Management – Case studies.
I. Gill, Jas (Jasvinder,(1955– . II. Title.
HD45.S9   1993
658.5'14–dc20   93–14949
CIP

ISBN 0–415–09135–7

CONTENTS

FIGURES

TABLES

ACKNOWLEDGEMENTS

Most of the research described in this book derives from an ESRC/DTI funded project entitled, *The Speed of Technology Change and the Development of Market Structure*, which was a part of the ESRC/DTI Research Initiative on *New Technologies and the Firm*. Most of the research was carried out at Brunel University, where the project was based. We are grateful to the ESRC and the DTI for their financial support.

We are grateful to the following for their permission to use material in this book.

To Harwood Academic Publishers GmbH for permission to reproduce (in Chapters 2 and 4) material from a paper by one of us: 'Rapid Technology Change, Technological Visions, Corporate Organisation and Market Structure', by P. Swann, *Economics of Innovation and New Technology*, 2(1), 3–25, August 1992. That paper is Copyright © Harwood Academic Publishers GmbH.

To Dataquest Europe, of Denham UK, for permission to quote and use some of their data in some of the figures, tables and text of Chapters 5, 6 and 7 (on microprocessors, memory chips and standard logic).

To A. Golding for permission to reproduce data from his D.Phil. thesis, The Semiconductor Industry in Britain and the United States: 'A Case Study in Innovation, Growth and the Diffusion of Technology', (University of Sussex, 1971) in Tables 7.1 and 7.2.

Figures 8.3, 8.4, 8.5 and 8.6 draw on data the survey, 'World Class PC Celebration', *PC World*, 5(11), October 1987. This data is reprinted with the permission of *PC World*.

Figures 8.5 and 8.6 draw on data from pages 2.91 to 2.203 of the book *The Computer Industry Almanac 1989* by Juliussen and Juliussen. Copyright © 1988. Published by Brady, a division of Prentice Hall Computer Publishing. Used by permission of the publisher.

Table 7.1 draws on data from page 41 of the book *Innovation, Competition and Government Policy in the Semiconductor Industry* by R. Wilson, P. Ashton and R. Egan. This is a Charles River Associates Research Study, published by Lexington Books, D.C. Heath and Company, 1980. The material is used with permission of Charles River Associates.

ACKNOWLEDGEMENTS

Table 6.1 is adapted from page 631 of the article by M. Gort and S. Klepper, 'Time Paths in the Diffusion of Product Innovations', *Economic Journal*, 92, 630–653 (September 1982). The material is used with permission of Blackwell Publishers.

Table 7.3 is adapted from pages 113–15 of the book, *The Semiconductor Business: The Economics of Rapid Growth and Decline*, by Franco Malerba, Pinter Publishers, 1985. This material is used with permission of Pinter Publishers Ltd.

Figures 6.4 and 6.7 draw on data from various issues of *Integrated Circuits International*. This material is used with permission of Elsevier Advanced Technology.

Figures 6.4, 6.7 and 7.1 draw on data from various issues of *Electronics*, and Table 7.3 draws on data from the article by M. Payne, 'The American Challenge on Chip', *Electronics*, 44(2), 74–8 (20 January 1969). This material is used with permission of *Electronics*.

Chapter 8 makes use of two simulation models, originally developed by one of the authors in conjunction with Hilary Lamaison and Mark Shurmer (Swann and Lamaison (1990a, 1990b), Swann and Shurmer (1992)); we would like to thank them for their work on the original data collection and experimentation with these models.

We would like to thank the following companies, institutions and individuals who provided useful data relevant to Chapters 6 and 9. In Chapter 6 (memory chips): Elsevier Advanced Technology Publications; Macintosh International; and the Department of Trade and Industry. In Chapter 9 (biotechnology): Elsevier Publications; Longman and Macmillan (for providing their publications on industrial developments in biotechnology); Nature Publishing Co. (for back copies of Bio-Technology); and Elsevier Science Publications Ltd (for back copies of Trends in Biotechnology). The following companies provided market and technical data on their HIV diagnostic kits: Abbott Laboratories, Amersham International, Baxter Healthcare, Behring, Diagnostics Pasteur, DuPont, IAF Biochem, Mast Diagnostics, Mercia Diagnostics, Organon Technika, Pharmacia, Roche, Sanofi and Wellcome.

We are grateful to the following for supplying data relevant to the biotechnology case study in Chapter 9: Vi Rawlinson (Manchester Transfusion Centre) for market and technical data on HIV kits used by the UK Blood Transfusion Service; John Parry (Virus Reference Laboratory) for technical reports and discussions; and John Clewley (Virus Reference Laboratory) for material on PCR based HIV diagnostics.

Much of our understanding of the semiconductor and software industries (Chapters 5, 6, 7 and 8) has been built up by reading a very large number of issues of the following excellent trade magazines: *Byte*, *EDN* (formerly *Electronic Design News*), *Electronic Design*, *Electronics*, *ICI* (*Integrated Circuits International*), *Microprocessors and Microsystems*, *PCBW* (*PC

Business World), PC Magazine, PC Week, Practical Computing. It is obviously impractical to reference every detail that has been learnt from this trade press.

Finally, we would like to record our thanks to the following for comments and discussions on various different parts of the work described in this book, though none of them are responsible for remaining errors: John Barber, Benjamin Coriat, Paul David, Ken Flamm, Peter Grindley, Mike Hobday, Henry Keil, Greville Kroll, Leslie Libetta, Claude Menard, Stan Metcalfe, Jane Millar, Simon Moores, Jerry Silverberg, Roger Silverstone, Ed Stein-mueller, Paul Stoneman, Tracey Taylor, Steve Woolgar; to industry analysts, marketing executives and editorial staff at: Dataquest Europe (Denham UK), Inmos, Lotus User's Group, *PC Magazine* (UK), *Practical Computing*, Siemens, Texas Instruments, 4-5-6 World; to participants in seminars at London Business School, MERIT (University of Limburg), PREST (University of Manchester) and the University of Lancaster; and to participants in the Conference des Grandes Ecoles (Paris, 1991), EARIE (1990), the ESRC Industrial Economics Study Group (1990), and the ESRC/DTI New Technologies Initiative Co-ordination meetings (1988–92).

1

INTRODUCTION

1.1 AIMS AND OBJECTIVES

The central aim of this book is to examine the role of strategic visions of technologies and markets in influencing the links between rapid technology change and market structure. Our thesis is that the connections between technological change and market structure cannot be fully understood unless the role of strategic visions is appreciated. We argue that this perspective offers a way of resolving some of the puzzles that have arisen in the theoretical and empirical analysis of the relationship between technology change and market structure. If this argument is accepted, it is then apparent that strategic visions play a central role in corporate strategy and industrial policy.

The book has two subsidiary aims. The first is to bring together insights from two rather different traditions: the economic analysis of technological change and market structure, and the organisational analysis of technology change and corporate structure. Indeed, we argue that the concept of corporate vision is instrumental to this synthesis.

The second aim is to show just how important the direct measurement of rates of technology change is to understanding the development of market structure. Indirect measures (such as R&D inputs or patents) are very useful for large-scale comparative work.[1] For the purpose of our analysis, however, such measures tend to hide the details of the technological trajectory followed and as a result it is hard to check whether technology change is compatible or incompatible with a company's vision. We show in five case studies that it is possible (if time consuming) to document rates of change directly.

1.2 INTERCONNECTIONS

The interconnections between rapid technology change, firm organisation and the development of market structure have been the object of extensive study, both in the fields of economics and of organisational behaviour. Schumpeter (1954) showed how competition from a radically different source, or using a radically different production technology, or indeed in the form of

1

a radically different product, would be much more disruptive to existing market structures than the traditional price competition. A sequence of later writers have developed and extended this basic insight to explore how rapid technology change interacts with market structure.

Throughout this literature, two broad hypotheses persistently surface which, while by no means an exhaustive summary of the literature, are especially useful to frame the subtle dynamic forces at work here. The first might be termed *persistent dominance*: well-anticipated technological change usually leads to further concentration because those incumbents with greatest market power are best placed to develop and exploit new technologies. The second might be termed organisational inertia: all organisations, especially large ones, find all change disruptive if it cannot be handled using existing routines, and find technological change disruptive if it is incompatible with widely held organisational views or visions of where the companies' techno-logical strategy is heading.

On a first pass through this literature, one is tempted to make a crude generalisation which, although an oversimplification, is quite interesting. Much of the economics literature seems to embody persistent dominance, while much of the organisation literature is concerned with organisational inertia. Given the starting concerns of the two disciplines, this is not perhaps surprising. Moreover, it is a simplification, because with the diffusion of organisational analysis into economics (e.g. Williamson, 1975, 1985: Aoki, 1986), not all economic analysis generates persistent dominance. Likewise, with the diffusion of market and competitive analysis into organisational behaviour (Tushman and Anderson, 1986; Willman, 1992), organisational inertia is not always seen as the dominant force.

The combination of these two forces, persistent dominance and organ-isational inertia, makes for a very interesting dynamic (and path-dependent) interrelationship between technological change, firm organisation and market structure. This book is a contribution to that analysis.

1.3 VISION, TECHNOLOGY CHANGE AND THE ORGANISATION

The central focus of this book is on the role of what we shall call the firm's strategic vision of where technologies and markets are going. Metcalfe and Boden (1990, 1991, 1993) talk of the *strategic paradigm*, and we shall use the two terms interchangeably. There is some overlap here with Rosenberg's (1976b) use of the term 'technological expectations', though these do perhaps have passive overtones, whereas in the absence of strong technological determinism the firm can have some active role in shaping the future of the technology. The vision is the strategic plan of top management for future technologies and future markets. We argue that this plays a central role in determining an organisation's ability to adapt to the challenge of technology and market change, not just because of its importance in R&D and investment strategy, but also because if a strategic vision is well implemented, technology change – even if rapid – will not seem so disruptive as it can be implemented using existing organisational routines.

It is argued that the vision plays a pivotal role in the dynamics of technology change and market structure, and that a fuller economic understanding of those dynamics requires a thorough analysis of those visions. While radical change is taken to be disruptive and incremental change less so, we argue here that the very terms 'radical' and 'incremental' are conditional on a vision of where the technology is going. A firm that anticipates a change in technological direction may consider it incremental; one that does not may find the same change radical. If a vision correctly anticipates a marked change in the future path of a technology, then radical becomes incremental.

In short, the whole balance between organisational inertia and persistent dominance can rest on the completeness and perspicacity of the firm's vision and, indeed, on how thoroughly it is implemented.

This is an important component of a fuller economic analysis of these issues. In Chapter 4, it will be seen that a model incorporating such elements can generate a wide range of dynamics.

1.4 THE FORMATION OF VISIONS

Chapter 3 discusses the concept, formulation and implementation of visions in detail. However, we have to address one important preliminary issue at the start. If we take a technological determinist stance, where technology unfolds of its own accord along an as yet unknown path, then it is clear what is meant by the accuracy of a vision: it is simply the accuracy of a forecast made by a forecaster who cannot influence the outcome. And as with forecasts, we can define *ex post* and *ex ante* accuracy. This is analytically convenient (Chapter 4) but unrealistic.

If we take a 'shaping' view of technological development, however, then the meaning of *accuracy* is much less clear. Indeed, the nature of each firm's vision influences the market-determined path of the technology. If n different firms each have different visions and as a result start marketing n different technologies in line with those visions, then none is wrong in the first instance. In due course, however, we would expect one or more to emerge as dominant designs (or *de facto* standards), and those firms whose products do not lie in that group can be said (*ex post*) to have had the wrong vision at the start. Yet this immediately suggests that accuracy is inherently path dependent: we know from the popular *de facto* standards model (see chapter 8 on this) that the outcome of a market race can be greatly influenced by small changes in timing, design, marketing and other aspects of strategy.

Indeed, a market outcome which makes one firm's original vision wrong might switch to one that makes it right as a result of one other firm changing its vision. Moreover, the character of the standards model is such that there may be an optimum vision which will turn out to be correct in that technologies produced by the firm that implements that vision win the standards race, while a slightly more ambitious (or slightly less ambitious) vision will not just be slightly wrong, but spectacularly wrong.

1.5 MEASURING TECHNOLOGY CHANGE

Some very thorough studies of technological change have achieved a comprehensive coverage of a wide range of industries by concentrating on an easily measurable index of innovation, such as patents, R&D inputs or the remarkable SPRU database that counts significant innovations (Robson and Townsend, 1984).

Some commentators have cast doubt on the value of R&D as a measure, since anecdotal evidence (at least) and some econometric evidence finds only a low correlation between R&D input and innovative outputs. Many comment that in any case R&D is a very specialised form of innovative activity, and much innovative activity requires no R&D input at all (at least not by the current innovator). Many pragmatists, however, would argue that in a world of patchy and incomplete data, R&D expenditure is always a useful measure of something even if it is not perfect.

We would take a similarly pragmatic view of patent statistics. We know that the value of a patent is subject to a very high variance, that different industries have different propensities to patent and that patenting propensities may vary over a product life cycle. Conditional on some additional data about the patent, however (i.e. whether it is renewed, citations, and industrial classification), it is possible to reduce that variance. Again, our view would be that patent data are always a useful measure of something even if not a perfect measure of innovations.

The innovation count data (as in the SPRU innovations database) is in many ways preferable to the others, though what it gains in precision it loses in comprehensiveness.

However, for our present purposes, none of these sorts of data is really sufficient. The point is that if we are to examine whether technological trajectories are consistent with corporate visions we need to place both in a product or characteristics space. This is hard to do with R&D data, patents or innovation counts, because these indices do not in themselves indicate whether, and to what extent, the innovations undertaken in the market are consistent with corporate visions. It is only really possible to do this by locating the innovations in a characteristics space, and that requires information which R&D data cannot hope to measure, which patent numbers cannot convey (though patents themselves can do, if not in detail) and which innovation counts pass over. For that reason we needed to measure the rates and directions of technology change in product spaces.

4

For three of the case studies this has been easy enough, even if rather time consuming (microprocessors, memory chips and standard logic chips). For the biotechnology product examined, it is possible to chart the rates of change in some technology parameters but less easy to chart the more subjective measures. In the software case, it is relatively easy to chart technology change in the form of upgrades but harder to locate different categories of software package in a common characteristics space.

Other studies that have attempted to do this have found comparable difficulties (e.g. Saviotti and Trickett, 1992), but further efforts in this direction are needed if we are to unpick the connection between rapid technology change, visions, and market structure.

1.6 STRUCTURE OF THE BOOK

The organisation of the book is as follows. Chapter 2 gives a brief survey of some of the existing literature on the interrelationship between technology change and market structure. The first part of this surveys relevant economic and organisation theory. The second part summarises some of the empirical studies that have been conducted. The chapter also provides a business policy motivation for the analysis to follow.

Chapter 3 then discusses the concept of a technological and market vision, the formulation of visions and their implementation, and more general questions concerning what we shall call vision policy. Chapter 4 shows how the vision policy and firm organisation interact with rapid development of technology and evolution of market structure. We shall see that a number of organisational characteristics (speed of learning, absorptive capacity, etc.) are critical in determining ultimate market structures.

Chapters 5 to 9 discuss the five case studies that we have conducted to illustrate these issues. They are historical cases covering a number of years and refer to microprocessors (Chapter 5), memory chips (Chapter 6), standard logic (Chapter 7), PC software (Chapter 8), and a biotechnology product, HIV diagnostics (Chapter 9). Writing this book has seen a continuous cycle between case and theory: our starting conceptual framework has been revised continually in the light of case material and, conversely, new questions have been asked of the cases in the light of theoretical developments.

Finally, Chapter 10 draws conclusions from the case studies and shows that the framework developed here has a number of important implications for business strategy, business policy and industrial policy.

2

EMPIRICAL AND THEORETICAL MOTIVATION

2.1 INTRODUCTION

It is now widely recognised that the causal relationship between market structure and innovation runs in both directions. There is a very large body of literature on the question of how different market structures will generate different patterns of innovation. At the same time it is well recognised that the innovative activities of different firms will impact on market structure, although the body of economics literature on this is not as large. This latter linkage can happen either because innovative activity influences performance (and hence structure) or because of the connection between innovation and entry: often innovations by incumbents may act as a barrier to entry, but at the same time, especially in the formative stages of a market, innovation may come from new entrants.

While the two causal chains – from structure to innovation, and from innovation to structure – can be separated conceptually, and sometimes empirically, any discussion of one almost inevitably has to make some reference to the other. In econometric studies, this will be to take proper account of simultaneity in estimating each equation. In theoretical studies of strategic innovative behaviour, the two are interconnected because, for example, it is the knowledge of the feedback from innovation to concentration (via entry barriers) that provides the strategic incentive for incumbent monopolists to innovate. More generally, one causal link becomes part of the explanation of the reverse link.

Of course, the two causal linkages are interconnected because of the closed system dynamics that they generate.[1] If concentration has a positive effect on innovation, and if innovation reinforces concentration, then in response to an exogenous increase in innovative activity we find a virtuous circle[2] of continuing positive feedback, with increased concentration and increased innovation. An early exponent of this success breeds success hypothesis in this particular context was Phillips (1956, 1966, 1971). Conversely, if concentration has a negative effect on innovation (Blair, 1948, 1972), and innovation has a negative effect on concentration, then in response to an exogenous increase in innovation we find a spiral of reduced concentration and increased innovation (Geroski, 1991; Geroski and Pomroy, 1990). Note that in either case (continuing positive feedback or continuing negative feedback), an exogenous increase in innovative activity leads to further increases in innovation.

Alternatively, if one relationship is negative and the other positive, we find that innovation and concentration follow a jointly cyclical pattern, and, as is well known from the economic analysis of hog cycles, these fluctuations can converge on an equilibrium level of innovation and market structure, or may show growing instability. This model, and especially its dynamics, are described in a little more detail in section 4.2.

Despite this inherent interconnection, our interest in the present book will concentrate on one linkage: the effects of innovative activity on the relative performance of different firms and hence on market structure. The reasons for focusing on this linkage are twofold. First, of the two, it has received much less study in the literature. Second, and more important, the main contribution of our work is to demonstrate how corporate visions for the future of technologies and markets can play a central role in determining whether rapid innovation is concentrating or deconcentrating. That thesis is primarily of relevance to our understanding of how innovative activity influences market structure, and less to the reverse linkage.

Our argument, to be developed in succeeding chapters, is that the effect of a particular innovative activity on the performance of a particular firm depends on its accumulated corporate competence, but also on its corporate vision. When we know how the competence and visions of different firms compare, we can assess the effects on relative performance and hence market structure.

We shall argue that it is the confluence of vision and competence that is critical here. In some of the case studies, we shall argue that it is difficult to explain the relative success of different firms simply by reference to their accumulated competence. Referring to some of the debate in the philosophy of science[3], we could argue that just as theory guides data collection so current visions determine the future accumulation of competence – as well as the constructive exploitation of presently accumulated competence.

In this chapter, therefore, our purpose is to review some of the most relevant literature that informs the various steps of our argument. Section 2.2 surveys empirical economic literature on the linkage between innovation and market structure while section 2.3 briefly surveys some of the relevant economic theory on this linkage. Section 2.4 surveys some of the organisation literature on how firms cope with rapid innovation and briefly discusses the idea of competence, while section 2.5 provides a brief account of some of the main ideas in technological paradigms, trajectories, visions and technological forecasting. Finally, section 2.6 attempts a synthesis of these different strands, to prepare the way for subsequent chapters.

2.2 TECHNOLOGY CHANGE AND MARKET STRUCTURE: EMPIRICAL ECONOMICS

As noted above, we shall not attempt to survey here the very extensive literature exploring the influence of market structure on innovative activity. See Baldwin and Scott (1987), Kamien and Schwartz (1982), and Cohen and Levin (1989) for excellent surveys of some of this literature.

The literature about the reciprocal relationship between innovation and market structure can perhaps be categorised along two axes: first, whether it is empirical or theoretical; second, whether it is essentially economic or organisational in orientation. This is an over simplistic categorisation because a number of contributions are of both theoretical and empirical substance, and because there has been an increasing (and healthy) mutual permeation between the economics and organisation literature. Nevertheless, it is a useful device for organising what follows. This section is concerned with empirical economics, the next with theoretical economics and section 2.4 with organisation literature.

In the empirical economics literature, two polar positions have emerged. Thus at one end it is argued that rapid technological change under difficult imitation conditions tends to increase concentration. Phillips (1956, 1966, 1971) was one of the first to expound and analyse this hypothesis. At the other end, Blair (1948, 1972) has argued that recent (post Second World War) innovations have tended to reduce minimum efficient scale and so have been deconcentrating. Here we shall review some of the other economics literature that has examined this question from an empirical point of view. This review draws heavily on the excellent surveys by Scherer (1980), Kamien and Schwartz (1982), Baldwin and Scott (1987), Acs and Audretsch (1991), Geroski (1991) and Hay and Morris (1991).

Concentrating

Phillips (1956) and Horowitz (1962) were among the first to explore the reverse feedback from innovation to market structure. Phillips (1966) examined this with data on eleven industry groups and found that when the technology permits product change and differentiation, the scale of surviving firms is large and concentration is high. In his book on the aircraft industry, Phillips (1971) found that relative success in innovation was an important determinant of the growth of firms and of growing concentration.

Mansfield produced another early study of the relationship between innovative activity and subsequent firm performance, and again his conclusion was that innovative success could lead to faster firm growth and hence to greater concentration (Mansfield, 1962). Mansfield's (1968b) study of the steel and petroleum industries found that successful innovators grew much more rapidly than previously comparable firms for a period of five or ten years after the innovation. Mansfield (1983, 1984) examined some major process innovations in the chemical, petroleum and steel industries, and found that process innovations were more likely to increase (than reduce) economies of scale and hence would be a force leading to greater concentration. Among product innovations, on the other hand, the picture was less clear cut. In steel and petroleum, product innovations were more likely to increase concentration. In the chemical industry, on the other hand, as many product innovations led to a reduction in concentration as led to an increase. And in the pharmaceutical industry, product innovations were more likely to reduce concentration.

This positive feedback is an example of a more general tendency that 'success breeds success', or what has been termed the Matthew effect.[4] This manifests itself as a positive autocorrelation in firms' growth rates. Thus, for example, in a study of 2,000 firms in twenty-one UK sectors over the period 1948–60, Singh and Whittington (1975) found that firms with above average growth rates in the first six years also tend to show above average growth performance in the second six years.

Branch (1972–3, 1974) studied this two-way causal relationship and found strong evidence that R&D success (measured by patents) did lead to increased profits and growth but weaker support for the hypothesis that higher profits lead to greater R&D expenditure. Later studies by Grabowski and Mueller (1978) and Ravenscraft and Scherer (1982) lend support to Branch's findings. A recent study by Fitzroy and Kraft (1991) also finds that innovative success promotes faster sales growth.

It is recognised that innovation can generate barriers and so lead to sustained concentration. Thus, Comanor (1964) found that expensive and risky R&D would act as a barrier to entry in the pharmaceutical industry. Stonebraker (1976) found that the risk of losses (through failure) to industry entrants was positively correlated with industry R&D intensity (R&D spend/total sales). Freeman (1965) found that R&D was a barrier to entry in the electronic capital goods industry. Firms had to have strong development capacity to assimilate the inventions of others and to gain access to existing technology through cross-licensing, know-how agreements and patent pools.

R&D is a barrier to entry in the Mueller and Tilton (1969) analysis of industry dynamics over the product life cycle. At an early stage of the life cycle, neither absolute nor relative size may be essential for innovative success, but at a later stage (of technological competition) the large industrial research laboratory operates at an advantage, and if large R&D programmes are maintained, this will build a barrier to entry. Pavitt and Wald (1971) also conclude that small firms have their greatest opportunities in the early stages of the life cycle, when scale economies are lowest, but as the technology matures the opportunities for small firms decline.

Grabowski (1968) found further evidence to support the success breeds success hypothesis. In a study of the chemical, pharmaceutical and petroleum industries, Grabowski found that one of the main determinants of a firm's R&D intensity was its prior research productivity (measured by patents per scientist or engineer employed).

Other literature casts light on this concentrating hypothesis in a different way. Menge (1962), for example, argues that rapid style changes in the car industry would impose greater costs on small producers than on large producers, and hence would be a force for concentration. This is one example of firms using rapid technology change as a device to raise rivals' costs (Salop and Scheffman, 1983). In his study of diversification, Gort (1962) found that the industries into which and from which firms would diversify were usually R&D-intensive. If this is taken to imply that R&D-intensive firms are at an advantage in making such diversifications, then a form of success breeds success may carry across from one market to another.

Following from Phillips' in-depth study of the aircraft industry, a number of other industry studies have lent weight to the argument that rapid technology change and high imitation costs are a force for increased concentration. These include Dosi (1984) and Malerba (1985) on semiconductors, Katz and Phillips (1982) on computers and Altschuler *et al.* (1985) on the automobile industry. Auerbach (1988) also examines whether there has been a uniform trend towards increasing monopolisation in four key industries, steel, cars, semiconductors and food retailing.

Deconcentrating

Blair has taken an opposite view of the effect of technology change on market structure. In an early paper (Blair, 1948), he argued that the previous ubiquitous trend towards increasing plant size and market concentration was being halted by certain fundamental shifts in technology. His later major study (Blair, 1972) comprehensively reviewed the impact of technology advance on scale economies. He argued that while from the late eighteenth century through to the 1930s technological change had been a force towards increased concentration, the position was changing as newer key technologies were having the opposite effect, reducing plant size and capital requirements for optimal efficiency. Over the earlier period advances in steam power, materials and methods of production and transport had acted to increase scale economies, while in the latter period developments in electricity, plastics, trucks, materials and production methods had served to reduce scale economies. Another study by Hamberg (1967) has reached similar conclusions.

Relatively few econometric studies have provided evidence in support of this perspective. One is that of Geroski and Pomroy (1990), which estimated a dynamic model of market concentration from data on seventy-three UK industries over the period 1970–9 and found that innovations were deconcentrating. In another paper, Geroski (1990) found a negative effect of concentration on innovative intensity, and the two studies together imply a negative feedback model where innovation reduces concentration which further increases innovative activity. This is a very interesting contrast to the positive feedback models described above.

A study by Mukhopadhyay (1985) using a similar regression to Geroski and Pomroy (1990) found that over the period 1963–77 concentration fell in US industries of high and medium R&D intensity. As the Mukhopadhyay study used innovative inputs (R&D) and Geroski and Pomroy used innovative outputs (innovation counts) it is interesting that their results are similar.

Geroski and Pomroy (1990) note the evidence in studies by Pavitt *et al.* (1987) and Scherer (1984: Chapter 11) that small firms introduce a disproportionately large percentage of major innovations. They note that this does not strictly imply a deconcentrating trend, but does suggest that small firms prosper at the expense of larger firms. This is probably especially true in new markets at an early stage of their life cycles (Acs and Audretsch, 1987).

This last argument has roots in the analyses of innovative activity over the product life cycle, and the notable contributions of Mueller and Tilton (1969), Gort and Klepper (1982), and Gort and Kanakayama (1982). Innovative activity and entry appear to be positively correlated, and both of them fall as the product life cycle matures. Acs and Audretsch (1989) put this in a slightly different way. Building on the theoretical arguments of Nelson and Winter (1982), Winter (1984) and Gort and Klepper (1982), they argue that the entrepreneurial regime (occurring first) tends to promote the entry of new innovative firms, while in the technological regime (occurring later) such firms are deterred from entering.

Related to this is the work of Utterback and Abernathy (1975) which found that most product innovations tend to occur in the early stages of the product life cycle, while most of the innovations occurring towards the end of the product life cycle are process innovations.[5]

We noted above the research of Mansfield, some of which supported the innovation-is-concentrating thesis. However, Mansfield (1983, 1984) found clear evidence that product innovation in pharmaceuticals was deconcentrating, though innovation in steel and petroleum was concentrating, and the evidence from chemicals was mixed. In a case study of metal working, Carlsson (1984) found clear evidence that innovation was deconcentrating, and Carlsson (1989a) showed that the implementation of flexible technology[6] led to a striking decrease in both plant and firm size in that industry. The study by Piore and Sable (1984) on flexible specialisation adds some more prescriptive support to this argument.

2.3 TECHNOLOGY CHANGE AND MARKET STRUCTURE: ECONOMIC THEORY

Again, a comprehensive review of this literature is beyond the scope of this chapter, but some of the main themes will be summarised here. Excellent surveys are available in Kamien and Schwartz (1982), Baldwin and Scott (1987), Tirole (1988: Chapter 10) and elsewhere.

Much of the economic theory that analyses how rapid technology change impacts on market structure tends to imply persistent dominance, or success breeds success, and so supports the thesis that rapid technology change is concentrating. We review some of that literature first, and then turn to those components of economic theory that support the perspective that rapid technology change is deconcentrating.

A well-known and early theory of how technology change reinforces social structures is that of Marx: 'The bourgeoisie cannot exist without constantly revolutionising the means of production'.[7] But we should perhaps start with Schumpeter (1954), who saw to the heart of the matter. There are, by common consent, several Schumpeterian hypotheses. One part at least endorses the success-breeds-success hypothesis. Large firms and firms with market power can take advantage of such scale economies as there are in R&D (though these are uncertain, to say the least) and have the retained profit with which to finance R&D programmes. In addition, the companion Schumpeterian hypothesis notes that successful innovation reinforces market power, and the prospect of a (temporary) monopoly position consequent on innovation is one of the chief attractions of such innovative activity. Size and market power facilitate some aspects of (and components of) innovation, and innovation reinforces size and market power.

There are, however, Schumpeterian hypotheses that lend support to the hypothesis that technology change is deconcentrating, and we return to that below.

An important, and unjustly neglected, study by Downie (1958) provided a detailed economic analysis of why we should expect a systematic tendency for technical change to increase concentration. Firms which already have relatively low costs will be able to reduce their average cost faster than those that have relatively high costs, and so competitive price reductions by the low cost firms will drive out the relatively high cost firms. A similar mechanism has been used in some of the evolutionary models of technical change and market structure (see, for example, Nelson et al., 1976; Nelson and Winter, 1978).

The positive feedback in this model is observed in more recent theoretical studies. For example, Flaherty (1980) has shown that equality of market shares is not a stable equilibrium in a model of homogeneous firms undertaking investment in cost-reducing process innovations. Any slight perturbation gives one firm a cost advantage and a higher market share, and that leads the firm to make greater investment which in turn offers it a further cost advantage.

The simulation models used by Nelson and Winter (1982) exhibit a rich diversity of possibilities, but the tendency towards increasing concentration is still dominant. The rate of increase in concentration depends on the rate of technological change, the technological regime, the ease of copying or imitation, among other factors. With rapid technological change and difficulty in imitation, the tendency towards concentration is most pronounced, confirming the arguments of Phillips (1971).

A wide range of other theoretical literature tends to find this persistent dominance, or success breeds success result. One very influential and striking example of this is Dasgupta and Stiglitz (1980a, b). In this model, only one firm engages in R&D and the incumbent is better placed to exploit an innovation than any entrants. More generally, the analysis of patent races finds a strong though not invariable tendency towards persistent dominance. For an excellent introduction to this literature see Tirole (1988).[8]

A different strand of model which also (in one sense) predicts persistent dominance is the standards model (Farrell and Saloner, 1985, 1986; Katz and Shapiro, 1985, 1986; David, 1985, 1987). Positive feedback here comes from the assumption that the attraction of a particular product is partly a function (directly or indirectly) of the user base; so as one consumer adopts that product, it becomes more attractive for subsequent consumers. We shall see in Chapter 8 that incremental innovation in the software market tends to be concentrating when it builds upon this positive feedback by ensuring compatibility from one generation of the product to another.

In a deeper sense, however, it could be argued that the emergence of standards is not a concentrating trend in that open standards facilitate entry to markets by removing the proprietary rights around leading designs.[9] Nevertheless, it can be argued that closed (*de facto*) standards do tend to favour the incumbent.

Similar first-mover advantages apply to producers of pioneering brands, even outside a standards context. For example, Schmalensee (1982) argues that even when competition sets in, pioneering brands have the advantage of appearing less risky than new brands, as the pioneering brands are known while the new brands are not. As one would expect, this issue has been analysed in the marketing literature (see, for example, Urban *et al.*, 1984). Another area of the economics product competition, that of product proliferation, suggests that rapid product innovation that takes the form of proliferating slightly differentiated brands will also act as a barrier to entry, and hence will reinforce concentration in a market (Schmalensee, 1978).

One further strand of the literature that finds rapid technology change to reinforce concentration is that which looks at how the cost of R&D increases with speed. This suggests that rapid change is likely to be concentrating because development costs will increase as the speed of development increases (Scherer, 1984: Chapter 4). Wyatt (1986) likens the research process to searching along the branches of a tree. If speed is not a consideration, the firm follows one research line at a time until it finds the best line and the overall number of research lines followed – and hence cost – is minimised. On the other hand, if speed does matter, then the firm will operate several research lines in parallel, and while that strategy will lead to a faster discovery of the successful research line it will also lead to higher costs as more lines are pursued.

It would be wrong, however, to imply that all economic theory presumes in favour of persistent dominance. There are parts of the patent race literature (e.g. Reinganum, 1985) in which drastic innovations give the entrant a greater incentive to innovate than the incumbent. Gort and Klepper (1982) suggested that many major innovations would emanate from new entrants, and would tend to occur in the earlier stages of the product life cycle, while many minor incremental innovations would be introduced by existing producers and would occur throughout the life cycle.[10] In a simulation model of innovation in different technological regimes, Winter (1984) found that in the entrepreneurial regime, new entrants were responsible for about twice as many innovations as incumbents, while in the routinised regime, established firms were responsible for the vast majority of innovations. As Mueller and Tilton (1969) and Gort and Klepper (1982) point out, this tends to result in net exit and increasing concentration when a technology matures. A study by Rogers (1982) found that the Mueller and Tilton model fitted the experience of the semiconductor industry very well.

2.4 ORGANISATION, COMPETENCE, STRATEGY

While much (but not all) economic theory tends to dwell on the possibility of persistent dominance, a first look at some of the organisation literature suggests a concern with what we shall call organisational inertia. A central idea here is that radical innovations can present severe difficulties for established firms (Daft, 1982; Tushman and Anderson, 1986) and are easier for the small and new firm to exploit (Rothwell and Zegveld, 1982).

In fact, rather than the dichotomy, radical versus incremental, Tushman and Anderson (1986) use the slightly different classification of competence-destroying and competence-enhancing innovations. The former occur when mastering the new technology requires fundamentally different competence from the firm's existing competence, while the latter can be mastered by firms using their existing technological competence. (A similar perspective was taken by Abernathy and Clark (1985).) Tushman and Anderson argue that competence-destroying innovations are initiated by new firms, while competence-enhancing innovations are initiated by existing firms. Tushman and Anderson point out that competence-enhancing innovations need not be minor, and indeed can represent 'order of magnitude' improvements in a technology, but the key is that they do not render obsolete those skills that were used to develop the previous generation of technology.

Competence-destroying innovations would appear to have a clear economic implication. We would expect them to lead to greater market turbulence (Audretsch, 1992), and that in the long run they would lead to major changes in industry structure (Chandler, 1962, 1977; Mensch, 1979; Auerbach, 1988) and a redistribution of power and control within the firm (Barley, 1986).

The organisation literature has for some time suggested that large incumbent firms are slow to adapt to the challenges of competence-destroying innovations. Thus Burns and Stalker (1961) and Stinchcombe (1965) suggested that organisational structure may reflect such inertia. Burns and Stalker advanced the influential distinction of *organic* and *mechanistic* organisations. The latter had a clear organisational structure and were best suited to stable and predictable market conditions, in which they could exploit scale economies. The organic form, conversely, was the best for rapidly changing conditions, especially where new problems and requirements could not be broken down and distributed within an existing mechanistic structure.

Hannan and Freeman (1977, 1984) suggested in more detail a variety of reasons why established firms may exhibit structural inertia. These include internal pressures such as sunk costs, limits on the information received by decision makers, existing standards of procedure and task allocation. Moreover, they argued that any organisational restructuring disturbs a political equilibrium and this may cause decision makers to delay (or even postpone) reorganisation. There are also external constraints leading to inertia, including exit costs and limits on the availability of external information. For these reasons, Hannan and Freeman argued that the ability of established firms to adapt to a rapidly changing environment was limited. Indeed, this may mean that old organisations become moribund, as they cannot adapt fast enough. McKelvey and Aldrich (1983), among others, advanced an evolutionary perspective on the development of organisational forms in the face of rapid technology and (more generally) environmental change. Child (1984) reviewed the theoretical analysis and practical experience of organic system design.

These ideas have filtered into the economics literature, too. Nelson and Winter (1982: Chapter 5) argued that large complex organisations depend in large measure on tried and tested innovative routines, and are poor at improvising co-ordinated responses to novel situations. These routines can be seen as a truce in intra-organisational conflict, and Nelson and Winter note that such a truce is valuable and should not be broken lightly. In short, when routines are in place, it is costly and risky to change them radically. (See also Willman (1992) for an excellent review of these issues.)

Yet, as Pavitt (1991) and Mowery (1983) have pointed out, many large firms have shown great resilience to innovations that appear to be competence destroying. Pavitt notes that a typical characteristic of these firms is that they are multi-divisional and operate on a broad front in their technological activities. This offers the opportunity of particular success in technologies which depend for their development on a wide accumulated competence across disciplinary, functional and divisional boundaries. But this characteristic also presents several problems for the firm, including:

- the management of synergies across divisions and development of technologies that do not fit tidily into existing divisional structures;
- the management of co-specialised assets (Teece, 1986); and

15

- the tension between corporate centralisation (to exploit synergies) and decentralisation (to promote rapid decision taking).

As Mansfield (1968a) notes, the exploitation of synergies depends on inter-divisional communication about diverse experience, perhaps through the exchange of personnel and experience (Aoki, 1986). Cohen and Levinthal (1989, 1990) recognise that this is part of the absorptive capacity of the firm. As they point out, that absorptive capacity does not just refer to the firm's interface with the external environment, but also to the transfers of knowledge across and within sub-units of the firm. Nelson and Winter (1982) point out that an organisation's absorptive capacity does not depend so much on the individuals as on the network of linkages between individual capabilities. And as Simon (1985) points out, it is learning and problem solving from diverse knowledge bases that is most likely to yield innovation. To keep aware of new technological developments and the competence to deal with them, firms must sustain their multiple technological bases (Dutton and Thomas, 1985).

Teece (1988) points out that, because success in innovation requires responsiveness to user needs, a number of interfaces must be crossed in the process of technological innovation. Each of these interfaces could become a potential barrier to innovation unless some gatekeeping functions are put in place. Roberts (1979) argues that three gatekeeping functions are particularly critical: the technical gatekeeper, the market gatekeeper and the manu-facturing gatekeeper.

Teece (1988) argues that a firm's core business depends on the underlying natural trajectory embodied in the firm's knowledge base, and hence there is a path dependency in the firm's core competence. Teece argues that organ-isational routines serve to buttress this path dependence, and hence to determine the technological paths followed by the firm. We shall return to the theme of trajectories in the next section but it is important to recognise that the degree of technological determinism depends on this degree of organisational buttressing.

Utterback (1978) has argued that older vertically integrated firms will have a greater commitment to old technology because they are likely to have made large upstream and downstream investments related to these specific techno-logies. This is a similar argument to the switching cost concept that underlies the economics of standards (Klemperer, 1987, and see previous section).

Williamson (1975) has extensively analysed the advantages to the M-form company in its ability to exploit R&D activities,[11] but it is also recognised that such organisational forms are likely to get into serious difficulties in a rapidly changing environment. Kay (1988) argues that such forms tend to ignore important information because it does not fit into existing classifications, and the structure comes under stress as it is referred up the hierarchy. Hayes and Abernathy (1980) suggest that the restricted and short-term orientation of divisional profit centres can lead to a neglect of future technological opportunities.

Finally, we should note that there is some recent and exciting work in strategic management in the area of dynamic capabilities and competence (Teece, Pisano and Shuen, 1991). Unlike other analyses of strategic interaction, this recognises that the scope for short-term strategic re-orientation is limited, and that the fundamental units of analysis are competence and capabilities rather than firms and products. As noted before, Teece sees current competence and routines bounding the possible technological paths followed by the firms, and hence the ongoing accumulation of capabilities.

2.5 TRAJECTORIES, PARADIGMS, TECHNOLOGICAL FORECASTING AND VISIONS

Dosi was an early exponent of the idea of the technological paradigm and technological trajectory, (Dosi, 1982) and his remains one of the most influential works in this area. For Dosi, the paradigm is a package of generic knowledge: it defines the technological opportunities for further innovations and some basic procedures for how to exploit them. The trajectory, on the other hand, is the activity of technological progress along the economic and technological trade-offs defined by a paradigm (see also Nelson and Winter 1977; Saviotti and Metcalfe, 1984; Dosi, 1988a).[12]

The concept of a paradigm is similar to the concept of a focusing device as described by Rosenberg (1969, 1976b) or a technological guide-post (Sahal 1981, 1985). Georghiou *et al.* (1986) refer to a corridor along which a technology can develop. The central idea is that innovative activities are inherently selective and cumulative. Firms do not survey all technological possibilities before making technological or product choices. Rather, they restrict their search to areas where they can build on their existing technological capabilities (see also Teece, 1988).

Viewed from this perspective, the trajectory that the firm follows appears well determined by past experience and by the inherent character of the technology. An alternative view is that technology trajectories are under-determined from a technological and even a historical point of view, and that there is strong element of social agency in the path selected.

The concepts of paradigm and trajectory really embody three components: one is accumulated competence, the second is technological intrinsics and the third is technological and market vision. The approach we take here does perhaps differ from these earlier studies in that we consider that (at least at certain critical points of technological development), the trajectory can be shaped, in part at least, by the technological and market vision of the firm. Thus to anticipate an example that will be discussed at length in chapter 5, the path of microelectronics technology at the time of the introduction of the microprocessor was clearly constrained by the intrinsic character of the technology and the accumulated capabilities of the principal firms, but was ultimately shaped by the unusual but compelling vision of one (or perhaps two) new firms.

In fairness, it must be recognised that the authors noted above are aware that radical events can shift a trajectory outside the bounds set by accumulated capabilities. For example, Teece (1988) notes that some fundamental break-throughs (paradigm shifts) do not build upon incumbent firms' competences. He also notes that if these shifts cause the institutional locus to lie outside the incumbent firms, and if the new knowledge is difficult to copy, then collaboration (perhaps via licensing) becomes prominent. He notes that this has been particularly relevant in biotechnology where new incumbents have experienced the threat of new technological breakthroughs but also embraced the opportunity via collaboration.

In the same vein, Dosi (1988a) notes that the boundaries placed by techno-logical paradigms do not imply that traditional economic inducement mechanisms are inoperative. Indeed, these fundamental mechanisms will continue to shape both the rate and direction of technological change, but within the boundaries of the paradigm. Chapter 3 sets out a simple economic model which captures the determinism and freedom of the technological trajectory.

A number of writers see the paradigm as a more strategic issue. For example, Pavitt (1991) notes that just as large firms must learn to define appropriate divisional objectives and boundaries, so they must form appro-priate technological expectations (or 'visions') about the future capabilities of a technology. In a series of papers, Metcalfe and Boden (1990, 1991, 1993) show how the articulation of a technological paradigm or 'vision' is central to the firm's technology strategy. These visions both act as a guide-post, or enabler, but also as a constraint.

In a number of case studies of firms where senior management backs risky innovative projects in the face of resistance from the finance executives, Lonie *et al.* (1993) find that a product champion with vision can be decisive in ensuring that senior management strategically, overrides financial criteria. We shall return to some of these strategic ideas in chapter 3.

A number of empirical studies have mapped *ex post* technological trajec-tories. Among these we note those by Dosi (1984) on electronics, Saviotti and Metcalfe (1984), and Gardiner (1986) on airplanes and automobiles, Saviotti and Trickett (1992) on helicopters and Walsh (1984) on chemicals. We also present some technological mapping in our five case studies (Chapters 5–9).

However, our argument above was that there is scope for an element of vision to shape the precise character of the technological trajectory. For that reason, it is of considerable interest to try to map *ex ante* visions as well as *ex post* trajectories. This *ex ante* mapping is much harder to achieve, but, as we shall see in the next chapter, it can to some extent be done from press pre-announcements by the major participants in an industry.

This immediately leads us into a literature that addresses the question of technological visions but appears to have developed somewhat in isolation from that described above. This is the field of technological forecasting, in which some important standard works are Bright (1968), Wills *et al.* (1969), Jantsch (1972), Jones and Twiss (1978) and Martino (1983). At first sight the term 'forecasting' suggests that this is essentially reactive or passive, rather like macroeconomic forecasting, where the forecasts and strategic plans of any one agent can have little effect on the object of forecast. In that sense, it has more in common with the concept of technological expectations used by Rosenberg (1976a). Just as the formation of macroeconomic expectations is often classified as either adaptive or rational, so also can be the formation of technological expectations. In short, such forecasting techniques may simply extrapolate from past trends, or they may be based on some model of the system generating the technology.

Yet if expectations or forecasts shape strategic plans, they can in turn shape the technology about which expectations are being made. In this book we use the term 'vision' to capture this proactive and strategic concept, to distinguish it from the more passive 'forecast' or expectation.

Indeed, there is a sense in which technological forecasts may become self-fulfilling. A very striking example of this is Moore's law (see Chapters 3 and 5–7), which was articulated in the mid-1960s, and suggested that the number of active components per semiconductor chip could be expected to double every year (Noyce, 1977). This was not exogenous science or technology: indeed, such a technological path could only be realised if sufficient investment in semiconductor fabrication technology took place to enable denser integration in chips. The articulation of the vision, and its incorporation into strategic plans, was part of its own realisation.

In saying this it is not suggested that any vision can be self-fulfilling. Chapter 3 sets out a simple model which explores the circumstances in which visions can be self-generating.

When visions are of critical strategic importance, the construction of visions is a key part of corporate strategy. The work of Metcalfe and Boden (1990, 1991, 1993) gives some very important insights into how these visions are formed in three case studies of major UK companies. Von Hippel (1979, 1980) showed how important the user or consumer could be in conceiving innovations, and hence as a source of visions. This procedure is applied particularly by Japanese firms as a means of constructing their visions (Cawson *et al.*, 1993). The construction of visions may, however, be a task for scientists and engineers (Bosworth and Wilson, 1993).

Visions become embedded in organisational structure, so that organisations can cope with change which is anticipated in the sense that they have a routine for it (Kay and Willman, 1993). When events precipitate a crisis in the corporate vision, a new vision, this will often lead to organisational restructuring (Webb and Cleary, 1993). In this way there is a clear mapping between organisational structure (including accumulated capabilities) and the visions that are compatible with that structure – and vice versa.

2.6 AN ATTEMPT AT SYNTHESIS[13]

In this last section, which reproduces part of an earlier paper (Swann 1992), we try to pull together some of the main themes that have been addressed here, to motivate the theoretical discussion of chapters 3 and 4, as well as the case studies.

The distinction between *radical* and *incremental* innovation is an important one (Mansfield, 1968a; Freeman, 1982) and generally well understood. While a stream of incremental innovations can serve to reinforce the position of existing market leaders (Nelson and Winter, 1982; Ettlie *et al.*, 1985), radical innovations can present severe difficulties for established firms (Daft, 1982; Tushman and Anderson, 1986) and are easier for the small and new firm to exploit (Rothwell and Zegveld, 1982).

Gort and Klepper (1982) suggested that many major innovations would emanate from new entrants and would tend to occur in the earlier stages of the product life cycle, while many minor incremental innovations would be introduced by existing producers and would occur throughout the life cycle. In a simulation model of innovation in different technological regimes, Winter (1984) found that in the *entrepreneurial* regime, new entrants were responsible for about twice as many innovations as incumbents, while in the *routinised* regime, established firms were responsible for the vast majority of innovations. As Mueller and Tilton (1969) and Gort and Klepper (1982) point out, this tends to result in net exit and increasing concentration when a technology matures. A study by Rogers (1982) found that the Mueller and Tilton model fitted the experience of the semiconductor industry very well.

Tushman and Anderson (1986) use the slightly different classification of *competence-destroying* and *competence-enhancing* innovations. The former occur when mastering the new technology requires fundamentally different competence from the firm's existing competence, while the latter can be mastered by firms using their existing technological competence. They argue that competence-destroying innovations are initiated by new firms, while competence-enhancing innovations are initiated by existing firms. Tushman and Anderson point out that competence-enhancing innovations need not be minor, and indeed can represent 'order of magnitude' improvements in a technology, but the key is that they do not render obsolete those skills that were used to develop the previous generation of technology.

On the other hand, some of the theoretical economic analysis of market structure and innovation (e.g. Dasgupta and Stiglitz, 1980a and b) finds a tendency towards *persistent dominance*. In the Dasgupta and Stiglitz model, only one firm engages in R&D and the incumbent is better placed to exploit and innovate than any entrants. This is in line with a tradition of analysis that saw technological change leading to greater concentration, because it led to greater economies of scale and barriers to entry. Indeed, rapid change which is not competence destroying – the order of magnitude improvement in technology – is likely to be concentrating because development costs will increase as the speed of development increases (Scherer, 1984: chapter 4) and Wyatt (1986). As a result, the first mover has a clear cost advantage over those who are trying to catch up if the speed of change is fast enough.

The work of Phillips (1966, 1971) in particular, and Mansfield (1968a, 1983, 1984) to some extent, finds some empirical support for this persistent dominance hypothesis. Not all economic analysis has reinforced this view, however. The work of Blair (1948, 1972) cast doubt on this as a uniform trend and suggested that some shifts in technology had been deconcentrating. A study by Geroski and Pomroy (1990) found further empirical support for this. The distinction between competence-enhancing and competence-destroying innovations plays a key role here. Competence-destroying innovations lead to greater market turbulence (Audretsch, 1992) and can in the long run lead to major changes in industry structure (Chandler, 1962, 1977; Mensch, 1979) and a redistribution of power and control within the firm (Barley, 1986).

These major changes in industry structure suggest that large incumbent firms are slow to adapt to the challenges of competence-destroying innovations. Burns and Stalker (1961) and Stinchcombe (1965) suggested that organisational structure may reflect such inertia. Burns and Stalker advanced the influential distinction of *organic* and *mechanistic* organisations. The latter had a clear organisational structure and were best suited to stable and predictable market conditions, in which they could exploit scale economies. The organic form, conversely, was the best for rapidly changing conditions, especially where new problems and requirements could not be broken down and distributed within an existing mechanistic structure.

Hannan and Freeman (1977, 1984) suggested in more detail a variety of reasons why established firms may exhibit structural inertia. These include internal pressures such as sunk costs, limits on the information received by decision makers, existing standards of procedure and task allocation. Moreover, they argued that any organisational restructuring disturbs a political equilibrium and this may cause decision makers to delay (or even postpone) reorganisation. There are also external constraints leading to inertia, including exit costs, and limits on the availability of external information. For these reasons, Hannan and Freeman argued that the ability of established firms to adapt to a rapidly changing environment was limited. Indeed, this may mean that old organisations become moribund, as they cannot adapt fast enough.

Nelson and Winter (1982: Chapter 5) argued that large complex organisations depend in large measure on tried and tested innovative routines, and are poor at improvising co-ordinated responses to novel situations. These routines can be seen as a truce in intra organisational conflict, and Nelson and Winter noted that such a truce is valuable and should not be broken lightly. In short, when routines are in place, it is costly and risky to change them radically.

Yet, as Pavitt (1991) and Mowery (1983) have pointed out, many large firms have shown great resilience to innovations that appear to be competence destroying. Pavitt noted that a typical characteristic of these firms is that they are multi-divisional and operate on a broad front in their technological activities. This offers the opportunity of particular success in technologies that depend for their development on a wide accumulated competence across disciplinary, functional and divisional boundaries. But this characteristic also presents several problems for the firm, including the management of synergies across divisions and development of technologies that do not fit tidily into existing divisional structures; the management of co-specialised assets (Teece, 1986); and the tension between corporate centralisation (to exploit synergies) and decentralisation (to promote rapid decision taking).

As Mansfield (1968a) notes, the exploitation of synergies depends on inter-divisional communication about diverse experience, perhaps through the exchange of personnel and experience (Aoki, 1986). Cohen and Levinthal (1989, 1990) recognise that this is part of the absorptive capacity of the firm. As they point out, that absorptive capacity does not just refer to the firm's interface with the external environment but also to the transfers of knowledge across and within sub-units of the firm. Nelson and Winter (1982) point out that an organisation's absorptive capacity does not depend so much on the individuals as on the network of linkages between individual capabilities. And as Simon (1985) points out, it is learning and problem solving from diverse knowledge bases that is most likely to yield innovation. To keep aware of new technological developments and the competence to deal with them, firms must sustain their multiple technological bases (Dutton and Thomas, 1985).

Pavitt (1991) also notes the central importance to large firms of defining appropriate divisional objectives and boundaries, and forming technological expectations (or 'visions') about the future capabilities of a technology. The concept of a technological trajectory has been advanced to describe the path or corridor within which a technology is expected to develop (Dosi, 1982; Georghiou et al., 1986; Nelson and Winter, 1982) while Metcalfe and Boden (1990) show how the articulation of a technological paradigm or 'vision' is central to the firm's technology strategy.

Key hypotheses

The literature surveyed above, in short, tends to emphasise one or other of the following observations. First, R&D activity has an element of fixed cost to it, there are economies of scale and the incumbent monopolist has more to lose by failing to innovate than the prospective entrant has to gain, so that, all in all, technical change is concentrating. Second, and alternatively, radical techno-logical change presents great difficulties for the organisation, it upsets existing structures and these structures give the large organisation an inertia that makes it difficult to change direction quickly; this argument then implies that rapid and radical change is deconcentrating.

Connected to these observations are two opposed though not incompatible hypotheses which we can call A and B. Hypothesis A asserts that incumbents accelerate the speed of change in an attempt to shake off actual and potential competitors. Hypothesis B works in the other direction. Rapid technology change puts severe strain on an organisation which was set up to produce earlier versions of the technology. For that reason it is the small and perhaps new firm with organic structure that is better equipped to cope with the organisational pressures of rapid technology change.

While these two hypotheses are opposed they are not mutually inconsistent. One group of firms, the incumbents, may be responsible for accelerating change in a particular direction, where the entry-deterring effect of accelerating change is greater than the organisational stress. At the same time another group, the new entrants, are responsible for accelerating change in another direction, where the relative importance of these two effects is reversed. In particular, we argue that technology change along a simple and widely recognised technological trajectory – such as miniaturisation of semiconductor components – is less disruptive to the organisation, so that the large incumbents have the edge in innovations of this type. On the other hand, technology change that departs from a recognised trajectory – for example, by radically redefining the product or proliferating extra product features – may be more disruptive, so that the smaller new entrant has the edge here.

Chapter 4 sets out a model which illustrates the *combined* effects of these two hypotheses, and this model provides the theoretical guidance for the case studies that follow in chapters 5–9. First, however, Chapter 3 explores the concept of a technological vision in more detail, its important strategic role and its critical importance in resolving whether rapid technology change is concentrating or deconcentrating.

3

THE STRATEGIC ROLE OF VISIONS OF THE FUTURE FOR TECHNOLOGIES AND MARKETS

3.1 INTRODUCTION

This chapter examines the idea of a *vision of the future* of a technology or a market. These visions are often widely articulated within the organisation and sometimes widely publicised outside, especially in markets with rapid technology change. Indeed an organisation's *vision* could be said to be an essential part of its technology strategy.

The concern in this chapter is less with the *ex post* factual accuracy of these visions; rather we shall concentrate on how the visions are articulated and publicised, and what their effects are on the subsequent development of the technology and market structure.

What is important here is that the vision defines the range of technological and market outcomes for which the organisation can be prepared. If the actual path of the technology strays too far from a company's vision, then that company may only be able to follow at a cost or time disadvantage. In such circumstances, and where most firms' visions have turned out to be incorrect, small organic firms may be at an advantage. Conversely, when a large organisation finds that the vision is accurate, that organisation will be well placed to take advantage of economies of scale that arise from having an organisational structure designed to cater for that vision.

Visions can be updated, of course, but that is not unproblematic at the level of the organisation, as firms become accustomed to organisational routines (Nelson and Winter, 1982), and visions become embodied in corporate or organisational structure (Metcalfe and Boden, 1993). To change the vision, and in a manner that will allow the economies of scale to be exploited, requires a corresponding change in organisational routines and structure.

Of course, this inertia is not necessarily inefficient. On the contrary, when the vision is correct, the mechanistic structure is a source of economies of scale. When a technology settles down, so that its path can be foreseen, it is firms of this type that will have an advantage. The organic structure is more or less an irrelevance at that stage. But when the technology is at an early stage, and trajectories are hard to predict, the organic structure will be able to adapt more readily to follow the emergent path.

By way of motivation, let us start by citing the example of one of the best known visions of the future in recent history. The popular account, which may be partly fictional, states that in the early 1950s, many observers suggested that the world's demand for computing power could be satisfied by a handful of large mainframes. Even when it become clear (later in the 1950s) that this vision had been wrong, some in the industry continued to argue that there would be no market for computers other than the large mainframe. Again that turned out to be mistaken.

In retrospect we tend to laugh at such examples, and use them to imply a lack of foresight on the part of computer industry executives at the time. One radically different view is that this statement illustrates the precise opposite. The companies knew perfectly well the potential market for minicomputers and ultimately microcomputers, and knew that these could undermine the market for mainframes, but feared that these were technologies that they could not control. Rather than give these futuristic products a level of credibility, these companies deliberately played them down. For 'no need for computers other than large mainframes' read 'there is undoubtedly a potential market for small computers, but we desperately hope it doesn't take off'.

The vision may have been 'wrong' in the sense of *ex post* factual accuracy, but it was 'right' in the sense of *ex ante* strategy. It was factually incorrect, but it was the right vision for traditional companies to declare; to give legitimacy to the technology they feared would not be. Good Schumpeterians should articulate visions in which their market power is maintained or increased; they should not admit the possibility of scenarios in which their market position is weakened.

3.2 TERMINOLOGY OF VISIONS AND EXPECTATIONS

It is useful here to classify visions of a technology according to two criteria:

1 are they tactical or strategic? (i.e. short term or medium to long term);
2 are such visions created for effects internal or external to the firm? (The external effects might be further sub-divided into effects on consumers/ users on the one hand, and effects on rival producers on the other, but this will suffice for now.)

Figure 3.1 illustrates the four categories and gives examples. By short term we mean no more than the lifetime of one generation of product; in semiconductors this may be as little as three years. By medium term we mean five- or ten-year plans. Long-term visions sometimes extend to a twenty-year plan. On our visits to companies in connection with this research, we were informed that one Japanese firm had a hundred-year plan for its core technologies. (I regret we were not able to gain information on any parts of this.)

	Tactical (pre-announcements)	Strategic (long-term visions)
Internal	Commit warring factions to a particular product - `it is in the programme ... it has been agreed'	Used in reorganising company to cope with future technology change – if vision is well understood, change is incremental
External	User: encourage buyer to wait for new product Rival: signal, or entry deterrent	Encourage user to plan future products and production around this vision of the future of the technology

Figure 3.1 Categories of corporate vision

3.3 TACTICAL USES OF PRE-ANNOUNCEMENTS

Tactical uses are statements about the intention to introduce a particular product, service or production process at some point in the near future. In that sense they are simple pre-announcements of particular products. We shall subdivide this later according to how precise the pre-announcements are.

Internal tactical use is probably very widespread. One of the more obvious examples is the use of a product pre-announcement to force a consensus (or at least a decision) on 'warring factions' within the organisation. Tactical pre-announcments can play a role in helping to establish organisational routines, which Nelson and Winter (1982) see as a truce in intra-organisational strife. For example, there is commonly a tension between marketing and design in many organisations, when marketing want a product to fill a niche at the right time, while design want a product with the minimal number of design faults. The pre-announcement can be used to force the hand of each party, as once the form of the product is public knowledge it is hard to alter it.

External tactical use may be of at least two sorts. One is the announcement which is designed to encourage buyers to wait for the better (or cheaper product) rather than buy the rival's inferior and expensive product today. This use of pre-announcements has been well studied in the context of standards races; see Farrell and Saloner (1986). This depends on credibility and it is arguable that pre-announcements may have been abused by some manu-facturers who promise their product earlier than it actually appears. Accurate pre-announcements would appear to increase the consumers' knowledge, and that would appear to have positive welfare effects (Fisher *et al.*, 1983). However, it is not difficult to show how pre-announcements can be used in a predatory way (Farrell and Saloner, 1985).

The second external tactical use is to signal to competitors or perhaps to deter entry. A classic example of this in semiconductor memories is given in Porter, 1980: chapter 4, 78–9), where firms appear to enter a pre-announcement auction to settle the prices they will charge for memory chips in two years' time. One firm declares a price, which is then undercut by a rival and the bidding goes on until the price will go no lower. As Porter notes, before any actual investments are made the lowest bidder has effectively won the battle. As Porter also notes, this is only the end of the story, of course, if the winner demonstrates a credible commitment (in its other actions), that it would actually sell memories at the low price. Without this, entry would not be deterred. Such commitment would probably take the form of investment in the necessary fabrication equipment to produce components at that cost.[1] This is an example of a more general possibility, discussed further below, that visions can to some degree be self-fulfilling.

3.4 STRATEGIC USES OF VISIONS

Strategic uses tend to take the form of statements, often public, sometimes not, of the following sort: 'We expect the following broad path of developments in the technology. Product a will appear next year, product b (twice as powerful) three years later and product c (twice as powerful again) three years after that. They will observe upward compatibility.'

The internal strategic use of visions of the future are as a long-term planning device. The principle is that if this vision permeates the organisation, change along that anticipated path is simply 'incremental' change, and the organisation can cope with that. On the other hand, if there is no clearly articulated vision, or the actual path of technology change is not consistent with an old and outdated vision of the future, then any change is likely to appear 'radical', and that is much more difficult to cope with. Indeed, as argued in Chapters 1 and 2, it could reasonably be said that the distinction between incremental and radical change has little meaning unless defined with reference to the organisation's vision of the future.

The external strategic use of visions is similar to the external tactical use in that the aim is to influence either the investment decisions of users or the entry decisions of (actual or potential) rivals, or perhaps both. The difference is one of degree. Users are not simply persuaded to wait for a particular model; rather they are given an expansion path and a preview of future technology on which to base their own visions of the future and investment decisions. This is especially relevant for a technology with high switching costs. A credible vision of the future may make an even greater disincentive to entry for the rival although a credible demonstration of commitment is harder too.

Of course, any firm may use 'visions' for a variety of purposes, and indeed any one statement may have more than one type of effect (a tactical announcement may be for internal and external user and external rival purposes), but nevertheless the classification is conceptually valuable. In this chapter we are primarily concerned with statements to achieve the objectives on the right of Figure 3.1 – the strategic use of visions – and we examine four cases in the microelectronics industry.

3.5 PARADIGMS AS A PUBLIC GOOD: DETERMINISM VS 'NON-DETERMINISM'

In the literature on paradigms, there is a sense in which they are seen as an economic public good, and also a sense in which they are deterministic. In fact, this representation has something of the 'straw man' about it, as we are not convinced that these authors take as inflexible a line as is sometimes claimed. Nevertheless, it is quite interesting to explore these two assertions a little further, and we shall see that they are interrelated.

Those who argue that paradigms are a public good would point out that they satisfy the first condition of a public good (consumption is non-rival) because once a paradigm has been articulated by one user, it could be transferred at low cost to another user. The paradigm does not necessarily satisfy the second important characteristic of a public good (non-exclusion), as the originators of a paradigm can exclude others from their vision, although in practice such visions frequently diffuse to other interested parties.

Turning to the issue of determinism, it is apparent that a philosophically watertight definition of the distinction between determinism and non-determinism is quite elusive. From a statistician's point of view, a deterministic relationship describing the behaviour of variable X is one in which all the causal factors are known and there is no random component to the behaviour of X. A non-deterministic relationship, conversely, is more commonly called a stochastic one – that is, where the behaviour of X does have a (possibly quite large) random component. Yet what is randomness? Some would argue that it is no more than ignorance of causal factors.[2]

A strong version of determinism in paradigms and trajectories is that they are completely determined by the internal character of the technology (or perhaps the technological system to which they belong). There are no degrees of freedom for the actual technological path to rebel from those technological constraints. A slightly weaker form of determinism might admit that social and economic forces could in principle shape the way the technology develops, but that only one path will be profitable, so that any who follow a different path will not survive. One version of this weaker form of determinism would admit path dependence in the following sense: the firm's ability to progress along a particular technological path depends on its accumulated technological competence (see, for example, Teece, 1988). A necessary condition for the firm to survive is that it follows the technological path that most naturally flows from its accumulated experience, and even that may not be sufficient. In any of these versions, the technological trajectory is fully determined by the intrinsic nature of the technology, the firm's accumulated

28

competence resulting from its technological history and the competitive nature of the markets in which it operates.

Critics of these deterministic interpretations of trajectories reject the argument that there are no degrees of freedom left for any other social or economic agency to shape the technological trajectory. The most explicit statement of this critique is in the work of sociologists on social shaping of technology, but it is implicit in much of the economics literature too.

We argue here that at least part of any technological trajectory is shaped by other social and economic forces. There is a role for the vision, whereas in the 'straw man' deterministic models described above, there is no active role for vision: it is simply the result of technological and competitive imperatives. For that reason, the view of trajectories taken here is not deterministic in the sense of the preceding paragraphs. However, we shrink from the label non-deterministic, for we do not believe the trajectory followed is subject to large random and unknowable forces but, on the contrary, that it is shaped by corporate visions that are (in principle at least) amenable to articulation and study.

The public good properties and deterministic character of trajectories are, it can be argued, inherently interconnected. If a trajectory is deterministic in the strong sense described above (it is determined exclusively by the intrinsic character of a technology), then it is quite reasonable to suppose that it is a public good. At the opposite extreme, if social agency has many degrees of freedom to shape a trajectory, then it is much less of a public good because it will not travel from one environment to another without losing value. Taking a middle position, if the trajectory is determined by accumulated technological expertise, then it must lose its public good character unless most companies have similar technological experience. This last may be a reasonable assumption for most long-term incumbents in a well-established market but at times of more radical change it is less acceptable.

The models introduced in Chapter 4 which analyse the role of visions in influencing the relationship between rapid technological change and the development of market structure can be constructed from a deterministic viewpoint or a less deterministic viewpoint, which admits the possibility of multiple and diverse visions. The former is analytically more tractable (e.g. Swann, 1992), even if less satisfactory, than the latter. But we shall see that in modelling terms the two can be made to look quite similar.

The models in which trajectories are deterministic penalise firms whose technological vision is out of line with the exogenous trajectory. A less deterministic model modifies this to take account of two cost penalties: one relating to the discrepancy between actual trajectory and vision, and the other relating to changes to the vision away from that indicated (though not dictated) by accumulated experience.

3.6 STRATEGIC VISIONS OF THE FUTURE IN MICROELECTRONICS

We now discuss, very briefly, four examples of strategic visions of the future in the microelectronics industry. For now, we concentrate on how the visions of the future are formed and how they are articulated. We shall return to each of them in later Chapters, to see the role they played in the subsequent evolution of market structure. (Case a is a recurrent theme in Chapters 5, 6 and 7; cases b and c are discussed in Chapter 5; case d is discussed in Chapter 6.)

The cases are essentially historical, one going back to the 1960s. There are obvious disadvantages and difficulties with such an historical approach – the problem of reconstructing the visions! The advantage, however, is considerable: examining a complete historical episode allows us to see the outcome in a way that contemporary cases would not. Moreover, the historical microelectronics cases have been very well studied and there are many secondary sources to draw on.

Whereas individual product preannouncements are discrete and reasonably quantifiable events, longer term visions of the future tend to be much harder to quantify.

Moore's law: the annual doubling in the number of components per chip

Perhaps the simplest and best-known vision of the future in microelectronics was 'Moore's law', named after a co-founder of Intel Corporation,[3] which asserted that the number of components per chip would continue to double every year [Noyce, 1977]. The functional capacity of any integrated circuit chip (e.g. microprocessor) is effectively proportional to the number of elementary components it contains. Petritz (1978) has noted that Moore's law is a product of three trends which made it possible to integrate a larger number of components into a single chip:

1 steady progress in the miniaturisation of components;
2 a steady increase in the ingenuity of circuit designers in packing more components (of given size) into a given area of silicon and in circuit 'cleverness' (realising the same logical function with fewer elementary components); and
3 a gradual increase in the size of chips that were viable to manufacture in bulk. For reasons too complex to discuss here, the probability of a chip operating successfully declines exponentially with its size [Wise *et al.*, 1980].

Moore's law is important because in chips there are two parts to marginal cost: one is the raw chips, the other is the testing, handling and packaging. The latter can easily dominate the former, so it is most economical to pack as many components as possible on to a chip.

In 1964, Moore plotted (on a log scale, base 2) the net effect of these three trends over the early 1960s and noted that, roughly speaking, the points lay on a line with unit slope. That is, the number of components per chip had roughly doubled every two years, and Moore forecast that this would continue. And indeed it did, although by the mid to late 1970s, the rate of increase was starting to tail off; it was suggested that the law should be amended to state that the number of components per chip doubles every two years, although the law can still be made to hold if wiring is included in the device count.

The fine detail is less important than the overall message: an exponential growth of functionality for given cost could be expected and producers and consumers alike should plan accordingly. Moore's law was soon widely accepted throughout the industry and was clearly the basis on which a large number of technology investment decisions were made.

In 1964, when Moore's law was first articulated, the principal type of integrated circuit was the standard logic component. These were logical building blocks comprising relatively straightforward combinations of elementary gates (NAND, NOR, etc.). At that stage the apparent consensus vision in the industry was that developments in standard logic would take the form of an increase in the number of logic gates per chip, and firms could plan on that trajectory. In the early days of these products, there would be a small number, five to ten, of these gates on any one chip, so that the function of any one chip was still fairly elementary and it could be used in a wide variety of applications. Manufacturers' catalogues in the late 1960s/early 1970s contained a hundred or so standard logic designs, but the point was that they were standard, and each design would be produced in fairly large volume so that considerable economies of scale existed.

By the late 1960s, however, it was apparent that this trajectory was running into difficulties. Packing more functions into a chip (with a given number of inputs and outputs) seemed unavoidably to mean that chips would become more specialised and less general purpose. That meant the potential market for any one chip would be reduced and manufacturers would have to proliferate a much larger number of specialist devices, which would inevitably undermine the all-important economies of scale. [While there were economies of scope from producing related designs, it was generally agreed that these were not sufficient to compensate for the lost economies of scale.]

In short, while Moore's law provided an opportunity, it also presented a problem for large incumbents. For as you pack more and more gates together, you make the resultant circuit much more specific and specialised in its function. Ultimately, the density of gates might mean that any one integrated circuit would only be of use to a few buyers. In short, the catalogue would have to grow to thousands of very specialised designs, and the economies of scale would disappear.

We shall see how this question was resolved in the next case.

31

1968–74: The 'problem' in standard logic, custom design and the emergence of the microprocessor

We saw above that while Moore's law provided an opportunity, it also presented a problem for large incumbents. For as you pack more and more gates together, you make the resultant circuit much more specific and specialised in its function. And ultimately the density of gates might mean that any one integrated circuit would only be of use to a few buyers. In short, the catalogue would have to grow to thousands of very specialised designs, and the economies of scale would disappear. Economies of scope existed, but were not comparable.

We have studied the trade press in the late 1960s, and there the large incumbents articulated this problem for LSI (large-scale integration), implying it was a problem for users and manufacturers alike. But in some sense it was not a problem for users as they still had the MSI (medium-scale integration) circuits, and an additional (albeit expensive) LSI option. The problem, on the contrary, was one for the large incumbents, as the economy of scale advantages they had enjoyed to date would be undermined if specialised (almost customised) components became commonplace.

By 1969, this 'problem' was well recognised and the predominant belief was that only memories were really amenable to being produced in standardised designs; every other form of LSI would have to be produced to the user's (or system house's) specification. Not everyone was of the same view: we shall see below that one company in particular took a different view.

Nevertheless, the principal vision emerging was one of low costs customising made available by very expensive CAD installations (Watson, 1969). The barrier to entry would remain in the form of the capital cost of setting up this CAD facility, and not in the form of volume production of any one design. At that time it was clear that a number of major manufacturers had extensive CAD investment plans.

One company even went as far as to plan local CAD centres. These would be professionally staffed custom design centres in those locations where there was a heavy concentration of potential customers, who would then have all the design tools available (Watson, 1969). To those unfamiliar with the technology, it is a little like the colour-matching schemes of the major paint manufacturers. The demand for ever more finely differentiated colours and shades of paint can better be met by local paint mixing facilities, than by ever wider ranges of 'off the shelf' pots.

The alternative vision, articulated by Intel, was that non-standardised control logic – and which was not amenable to standardization – might be treated instead as a huge read only memory, the function of which would be defined in software. This turned into the concept of a microprocessor. The key idea was to make the logic chip into a small scale von-Neumann computer (or at least the processor, if not the memory); then what the chip would do depended on what instructions were stored in the program memory. The same piece of hardware could perform quite different functions by altering the software.

In short, the hardware could be standardized, thus enabling chip manufacturers to reap economies of scale, while the customisation would be done in software where (it was believed at the time) economies of scope were almost as generous as economies of scale, then this trajectory offered a clear solution to the difficulties of the standard logic trajectory.[4] Other manufacturers were clearly aware of this alternative vision, but as Watson (1969) notes, whatever views people held of standardised LSI in the further future, the overwhelming consensus was that the immediate future lay with customisation. As is well known, however, this alternative vision turned out to be *right* as a forecast of future developments, and (most commentators would now agree) *right* in a value sense.

But even if the vision of local customisation turned out to be wrong as a forecast of the main future developments in the technology, it is (we argue) essential to understand it if one is to understand the relationship between the speed and direction of technology change and the development of market structure in the early 1970s (see chapter 5). The customisation vision was vital as it underpinned the product strategies of some of the main incumbent producers at the start of the 1970s. That explains (at least in part) why they had such difficulty in adapting to the radically different trajectory offered by the microprocessor. After the introduction of the microprocessor, circuit design became a matter of software design rather than hardware design. The replacement of hardware design skills by software design skills as the scarce resource posed a radical challenge for those companies that would compete in the new market.[5]

1973–85: The Intel vision of the microprocessor

By introducing the microprocessor, Intel took the technology in a direction that incumbents had not been prepared for. But having done this, Intel then articulated (quite publicly through the trade press and advertisements) a trajectory of ongoing improvements in microprocessor designs, with enhanced components and networks of supporting products, which it proceeded to deliver.

When the microprocessor market started to grow, the Intel vision of the future became accepted as something close to a consensus view of where microprocessor technology was going. That in turn led to a consolidation of Intel's market position. In Chapter 5 we map out the character of trajectories in this technology for some of the leading producers of 'own-design' microprocessors over the period, using the three main technology parameters defined in Swann (1986).

As we shall see in more detail there, the sequences of product introductions from 1971 suggest that most of the successful manufacturers followed a similar trajectory of steady improvements in processor power, bit size and, functionality, and reductions in cost. Intel's is the most striking example of this at work and ties in with its articulated vision, but similar patterns are observed for Motorola, Zilog and Rockwell. Some manufacturers, however, did not appear to follow this trajectory, and on the whole they were less successful.

1970–93: unrelenting density increases in DRAMs

As we shall see in Chapter 6, the implication of Moore's law for dynamic RAMs (read and write memory chips) has been a steady, indeed relentless, increase in the amount of memory packed into a chip. Indeed, the step from one generation to the next would tend to be a factor of four in the number of memory cells (from 4 kilobytes (4K) to 16K to 64K to 256K, and so on). But here there was no 'problem'. As noted before, memory is one of the few areas of chip design where design is very regular and standardised, and (to a first order of approximation) a circuit for a large memory chip is that for many memory chips placed side by side.

The potential for using memory chips of ever greater capacity was seen to be almost limitless, and hence the vision of the future for memory technology was perhaps the clearest of all. Moreover, the technology of production in this industry has increased its capital intensity very rapidly indeed. It is not then surprising that the rate of technological advance in this market has been as fast as any in semiconductors and, as we shall see, the effect has been to increase concentration (though subject to some subtle composition effects – see Chapter 6).

Some commentators argue that the growing concentration in memory production is simply a consequence of the ever increasing capital intensity, nothing more, and is not evidence of the arguments advanced in this book. To that we reply, why has capital intensity increased at such a rate? It is hardly satisfactory to say that this advance is simply exogenous. Rather, we would argue, it is because incumbents have undertaken massive investment with the confident vision that memory capacity will continue to rise very rapidly. With that vision, such investment is essential to remain in the race. But if the vision had not been held so confidently, would the level of investment have been so high, and would the degree of capital intensity have increased so fast? We would argue not.

3.7 SELF-FULFILLING VISIONS

We conclude this chapter by asking under what circumstances it is possible for a vision to be self-fulfilling, in the sense that if everyone believes it it will happen. This would not mean anything if trajectories were strongly deterministic; it is, however, much more important when technology trajectories leave degrees of freedom for visions to shape the actual outcome.

We say that visions are self-fulfilling if there is a *range* of visions that could be held and whichever of them is held will turn out to be right. If a model with visions has any equilibrium[6] at all, there must be one self-fulfilling vision. What is much more interesting is if there is more than one such vision. If such a range exists, there are then two possibilities: (a) the range of self-fulfilling visions is infinite; or (b) the range of self-fulfilling visions is bounded. Case (b) can in turn be subdivided: the range of self-fulfilling visions can be (i) contiguous, or (ii) it can be formed of several discrete blocks in parameter space. Figure 3.2 summarises this.

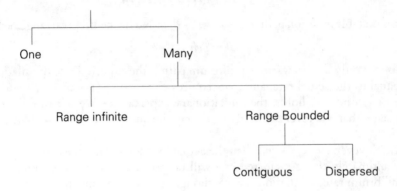

Figure 3.2 Self-fulfilling visions

We shall explore this possibility in two models. One is a very simple economic model of self-fulfilling expectations of inflation. The second relates to Moore's law, as described in the previous section, and asks whether Moore's law can be self-fulfilling.

A simple model of self-fulfilling expectations of inflation

The very simple model described here has a similar character to the Phelps–Friedman long-run Phillips curve,[7] and the basic hog-cycle model of demand and supply, though set up slightly differently.

Suppose that in any period t, suppliers bring a fixed quantity of a product to market, which they know is exactly what consumers will demand (D_0) if prices are stable and there is no anticipated inflation. The price at which this product is offered is increased in any period if there was excess demand in the previous period. Suppose in turn that demand falls if the price is raised that period but that consumers soon get used to the new higher price level, so that it is only price rises rather than absolute price levels that hold back demand. It is also assumed that consumers will buy now (hoard) if they anticipate inflation. If P denotes the log of price, these two equations become:

$$D_t = D_0 - b_0(P_t - P_{t-1}) + b_1 dP^e_{t+1} \tag{1}$$

$$P_t = P_{t-1} + c(D_{t-1} - D_0) \tag{2}$$

In the absence of any inflationary expectations ($dP^e = 0$), the equilibrium rate of inflation is 0. If prices are held steady and there is no anticipated inflation, then there is no excess demand and so no tendency for the suppliers to raise prices.

If, however, consumers anticipate inflation at the rate $dP^e_{t+1} = i$, then there will be an upward pressure on prices, with the following path for prices:

$$P_{t+1} - P_t = - cb_0(P_t - P_{t-1}) + cb_1 i \tag{3}$$

Along a stable inflation path, $P_{t+1} - P_t = P_t - P_{t-1}$, and hence after rearrangement:

$$P_{t+1} - P_t = i.cb_1/(1 + cb_0) \tag{4}$$

This will only be a long-run equilibrium path if the expected rate of inflation is equal to the actual rate, and that requires either $cb_1 = (1 + cb_0)$, or $i = 0$. If the first condition holds, then inflationary expectations are self-fulfilling in the sense that whatever the level of i, the equilibrium rate of inflation will also be i.

If, however, $cb_1 < 1 + cb_0$, then the actual rate is less than the expected rate and ultimately that anticipated rate will fall. In this case, the only long-run equilibrium rate of inflation is zero, though it may take some time to achieve this if expectations are slow to adapt. If the condition is nearly satisfied, then expectations can be nearly self-fulfilling, in the sense that the actual rate of inflation will only lie a small way below that expected.

Can Moore's law be self-fulfilling?

As we saw in the last section, Moore's law states that the number of components per semiconductor chip could be expected to double every year. As noted above, this has been one of the most powerful trajectories in the semiconductor industry, if not in any industry. Moreover, twenty-five years or more after it was first advanced, it remains very accurate. But why should it hold as a 'law'?

First, it cannot be said to represent exogenous technological change, like the manna from heaven in some early macroeconomic analyses of technological change. Moore's law could only be achieved if the manufacturers of semiconductor fabrication equipment undertook a certain level of R&D expenditure, as well as other investment, and if chip manufacturers themselves invested in this technology and in the requisite skills and expertise to make working chips from such technology. But why should the investment programmes of these companies be at just the right level to ensure this rate of technology progress? How could it be known or guessed that they would invest just that much?

We want to explore the possibility that a trajectory of this sort could be self-fulfilling in the following sense. If firms had a vision of very rapid change then their investment levels would ensure that the vision was accurate; but if the vision had been of less rapid change, then they would have invested less, so that the rate of change in turn would have been slower.

In other words, could it be that if Moore's law had stated that the number of components per chip would double every two years, that would also have turned out to be true? Would the same apply if the law indicated a doubling of capacity every six months? To put it another way, how much flatter or steeper could the technological trajectory have been and still turn out to be true?

In asking this question, we do not mean in any way to diminish Moore's remarkable insight in formulating this principle. Indeed, for any prediction of a technological trajectory to remain accurate for at least twenty-five years is quite remarkable. And indeed, in the simple model we have developed to analyse this, the indications are that Moore's law is possibly self-fulfilling over a narrow range of trajectory slopes, but not over a wide range.

The model we use has three main components. First, the capital cost of chip production increases rapidly as the component density increases. Indeed, just as Moore's law states that the number of components per chip expands exponentially over time, so we assume that capital costs also increase exponentially over time, as technology advances.

Second, a group of n firms compete for a rapidly growing market. Total demand is assumed to follow a logistic curve and, in the early stages of the product life cycle at least, demand increases rapidly. This makes it possible for them to cover their exponentially increasing capital costs, at least for a time.

Third, market shares of the n firms depend on their relative technological positions. If a firm falls behind the others, it will rapidly lose market share to the others. This is certainly true in the semiconductor industry where one generation of memory chip (for example) would rapidly be made obsolescent by the next generation (which achieves higher component densities).

Rather than assuming Nash–Cournot conjectures with respect to the rate of technology advance, the model assumes that each firm predicts the others will follow the Moore's law vision, and then two decision scenarios are considered. In the first, the firm can decide to invest enough to keep up with the principal vision, or less – though that would be tantamount to a decision to exit – but will not consider investing more. In the second, the firm may also consider investing more than is required to keep up with the principal vision.

Finally, there may be net exit during the product life cycle, as the capital costs of production become unsupportable unless the firm is rewarded with a larger share of the market.

What follows is just a summary of the model. It consists of five equations:

37

$$C_{it} = T_{i,t+1}{}^b, \, b \ge 1 \tag{5}$$

$$\Theta_t = 2^{at}, \, a \, \varepsilon \, \{0.25,..,2\} \tag{6}$$

$$S_t = S_{max} / [\, 1 + \{(S_{max} - S_0)/S_0\}^{-(t-t^*)/t^*} \,],$$
$$\text{where } S_0 = 1, \, S_{max} \, \varepsilon \, \{2^6,..,2^{15}\}, \, t^* \, \varepsilon \, \{10,..,40\} \tag{7}$$

$$W_i = T_i^k / [\, T_i^k + (N{-}1)\Theta^k \,], \, k\varepsilon \, \{2,..,5\} \tag{8}$$

$$\pi_{i,t+1} = W_{it} S_{t+1} - C_{it} \tag{9}$$

The first is the cost equation, where C is capital cost and T_i is firm i's technology. The time subscripts indicate that to reach a level of technology T in period $t{+}1$, firms must invest T^b in the previous period (t). The second describes the vision of the technology (Θ) where a is the rate of advance (if $a = 1$, this would be Moore's law). The third equation describes a (truncated) logistic growth curve of total sales (value) of the technology. This is perhaps an unfamiliar way of writing a logistic curve but a very convenient one as the parameters are easily interpreted: S_{max} is the saturation level of demand, S_0 is the level of demand in period 0, and t^* is the point of inflexion (where demand reaches half the saturation level).[8]

W_{it} is the market share of firm i in period t, and depends on the technological performance of firm i relative to the $N{-}1$ other firms in the market (which are assumed to follow the technological vision Θ). This is not exactly a logit formulation but has similar properties.[9] Note that if there is net exit from the market, firm i's share will rise (*ceteris paribus*). Finally, $\pi_{i,t+1}$ *denotes the book value of profits for firm i* in period $t{+}1$: this is simply the excess of period $t{+}1$ sales over capital costs incurred in period t. While this is a very crude measure, the argument is that firms are investing ever more in capital equipment every period, and hence the investment in period t must be recouped by period $t{+}1$, or else the firm will decide to exit.

The model works as follows. Starting with n firms in period 1, we examine whether firms can invest enough to sustain the trajectory Θ and still make a profit in the next period. It turns out that the starting number does not have a significant effect on whether the vision is self-fulfilling because if market shares are too small to cover capital costs, exit takes place until a profit can be made by the remaining firms.[10] Firms continue to invest until there is no prospect of profit, and then again net exit takes place. When the number of firms reaches 1, investment will stop, as the single firm has no further incentive to invest. That incentive is that a profit can be made if the firm can secure its share of the market, but it will lose that share if its technology falls significantly behind that of the rivals (which are expected to follow the vision Θ). When there are no rivals, there is no incentive in this model, as total demand does not increase as the technology improves.[11]

As noted above, two scenarios are considered. In the first, the firm can decide to invest enough to keep up with the principal vision, or less – though that would be tantamount to a decision to exit – but will not consider investing more. In the second, the firm may also consider investing more than is required to keep up with the principal vision. The results in these two cases are not all that dissimilar, although in simulations where a low value of a is assumed (this is the vision of a shallow trajectory), there is a tendency under the second scenario towards overinvestment and overshooting. In that sense, shallow trajectories are not self-fulfilling when overinvestment is possible, while they would be if it were not.

Over 3,000 simulations were conducted with this model. For our present purposes, interest focuses on the question of whether the visions are self-fulfilling, and this can be summarised in three graphs and a table. Figure 3.3 shows that the most common outcome (mode) is that the technology race peters out within five periods, most frequently because the vision is unsustainable (and so not self-fulfilling). Nevertheless, there is a considerable number of simulations in which the race continues for fifteen or more periods, with the second mode at 50+ periods.

The frequency distribution describing the level of technology reached (Figure 3.4 is similar, though there is not a secondary mode at 45–50 or 50+. The reason for this difference is that the long-lasting technology races are often those with a vision of flatter trajectories, and so it is some time before investment costs become unsupportable.

Table 3.1 summarises the simulations for a variety of technology parameters. The first half of the table refers to scenario 1, where overinvestment (beyond that indicated by the vision) is not considered by firms; the second half refers to scenario 2, where it is considered. The tables would be the same whether the number of firms at the start were 5, 10 or 20 – the three values considered.

In both cases, the table shows the range of visions which are self-fulfilling in the sense that a technology race will last for at least ten periods. The choice of ten is arbitrary, but seems to be a natural dividing line between the self-fulfilling simulations and the rest Figure 3.3. In most cases there is always some vision that is self-fulfilling by this criterion. The only exceptions are for $K = 2$ (market share not especially sensitive to relative technological performance of different firms) and $t^* = 30$ or 40 (that is, a relatively late point of inflexion and hence a relatively slow initial growth of total sales).

For any value of k, the range of self-fulfilling visions tends to get wider as one moves towards the bottom left-hand corner of the table. This is for a higher saturation level of demand and an earlier point of inflexion (and so a more rapid initial growth). That is as expected. However, a saturation level of 10^{15} times the starting level of sales (that is, one million (US) billion) is pretty implausible. For a saturation level of one billion (10^9) times the starting level of sales, and $t^* \geq 20$, the steepest self-fulfilling vision is 1.25 – that is, where the capacity of the technology increases by a factor of $2^{1.25}$ (or 2.38) every period.

The second half of the table shows that with the possibility of overinvestment (generally this happens in the early part of the race when, in this model,

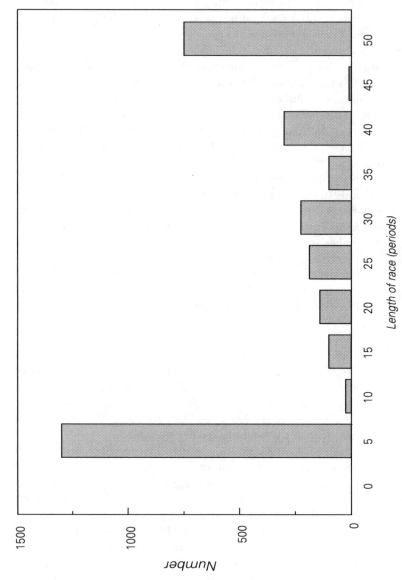

Figure 3.3 Length of technology race: frequency distribution

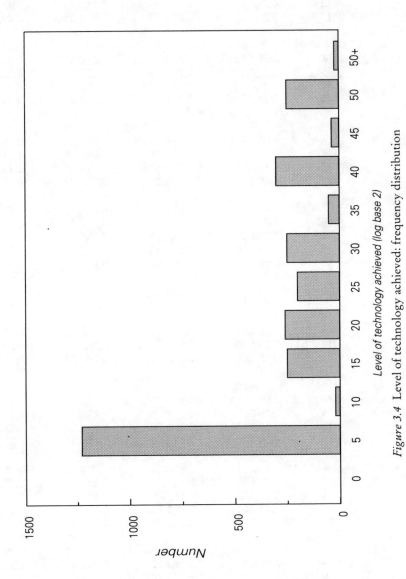

Figure 3.4 Level of technology achieved: frequency distribution

Table 3.1 Range of self-fulfilling visions

		Scenario 1		
K = 2	$t^* = 10$	$t^* = 20$	$t^* = 30$	$t^* = 40$
$S_{max} = 10\wedge6$	0.25,1.50	0.25,0.50	NONE	NONE
9	0.25,2.00	0.25,1.00	0.25,0.50	0.25,0.25
12	0.25,2.00	0.25,1.50	0.25,0.75	0.25,0.50
15	0.25,2.00	0.25,2.00	0.25,1.25	0.25,0.75
K = 3	$t^* = 10$	$t^* = 20$	$t^* = 30$	$t^* = 40$
$S_{max} = 10\wedge6$	0.25,1.50	0.25,0.75	0.25,0.50	0.25,0.25
9	0.25,2.00	0.25,1.25	0.25,0.75	0.25,0.50
12	0.25,2.00	0.25,1.50	0.25,1.00	0.25,0.75
15	0.25,2.00	0.25,2.00	0.25,1.25	0.25,1.00
K = 4	$t^* = 10$	$t^* = 20$	$t^* = 30$	$t^* = 40$
$S_{max} = 10\wedge6$	0.25,1.50	0.25,0.75	0.25,0.50	0.25,0.50
9	0.25,2.00	0.25,1.25	0.25,0.75	0.25,0.75
12	0.25,2.00	0.25,1.50	0.25,1.00	0.25,0.75
15	0.25,2.00	0.25,2.00	0.25,1.25	0.25,1.00
K = 5	$t^* = 10$	$t^* = 20$	$t^* = 30$	$t^* = 40$
$S_{max} = 10\wedge6$	0.25,1.50	0.25,0.75	0.25,0.50	0.25,0.50
9	0.25,2.00	0.25,1.25	0.25,0.75	0.25,0.75
12	0.25,2.00	0.25,2.50	0.25,1.00	0.25,0.75
15	0.25,2.00	0.25,2.00	0.25,1.25	0.25,1.00
		Scenario 2		
K = 2	$t^* = 10$	$t^* = 20$	$t^* = 30$	$t^* = 40$
$S_{max} = 10\wedge6$	0.25,1.50	0.25,0.50	NONE	NONE
9	0.25,2.00	0.25,1.00	0.25,0.50	0.25,0.25
12	0.25,2.00	0.25,1.50	0.25,0.75	0.25,0.50
15	0.25,2.00	0.25,2.00	0.25,1.25	0.25,0.75
K = 3	$t^* = 10$	$t^* = 20$	$t^* = 30$	$t^* = 40$
$Smax = 10\wedge6$	0.50,1.50	0.50,0.75	0.25,0.50	0.25,0.25
9	0.25,2.00	0.25,1.25	0.25,0.75	0.25,0.50
12	0.25,2.00	0.25,1.50	0.25,1.00	0.25,0.75
15	0.25,2.00	0.25,2.00	0.25,1.25	0.25,1.00
K = 4	$t^* = 10$	$t^* = 20$	$t^* = 30$	$t^* = 40$
$S_{max} = 10\wedge6$	0.75,1.75	0.50,0.75	0.25,0.50	0.25,0.50
9	0.25,2.00	0.25,1.25	0.25,0.75	0.25,0.75
12	0.25,2.00	0.25,1.75	0.25,1.00	0.25,0.75
15	0.25,2.00	0.25,2.00	0.25,1.25	0.25,1.00
K = 5	$t^* = 10$	$t^* = 20$	$t^* = 30$	$t^* = 40$
$S_{max} = 10\wedge6$	0.50,1.75	0.25,1.00	0.50,0.50	0.50,0.50
9	0.25,2.00	0.25,1.25	0.25,1.00	0.50,0.75
12	0.25,2.00	0.25,1.75	0.25,1.25	0.25,1.00
15	0.25,2.00	0.25,2.00	0.25,1.50	0.25,1.00

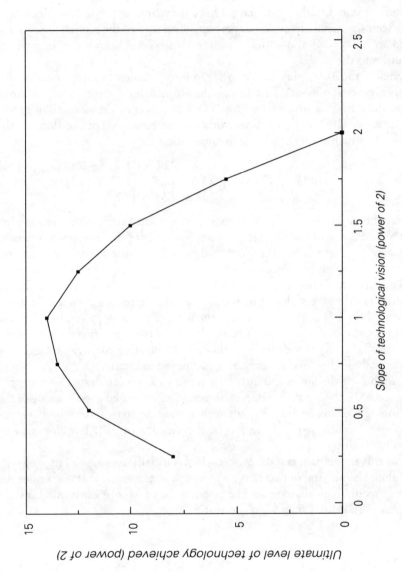

Figure 3.5 Technology advance and technology vision

technological advance is relatively cheap), the flatter visions are not self-fulfilling either. But broadly speaking, the upper limits of the ranges are about the same.

In short, we find here a range of self-supporting visions but not an unlimited one. On the evidence we have they form a contiguous block, and that seems plausible from the underlying structure of the model, though it is hard to be certain about that without a finer grid search (or an analytic solution to the model).

Finally, the 3,000-plus simulations can be conveniently summarised with a simple regression model. This models the ultimate level of technology reached (T at the date that investment stops) as a function of the simulation model parameters. The function is linear in all parameters, except the slope of the vision, a, which enters in a strongly quadratic way:

$$T_i = -2.7 + 2.5\,S_{max} - 0.65\,t^* + 1.0\,k + 22.0\,a - 11.9\,a^2 + 0.90\,D_{scen} \quad (10)$$
$$(0.1) \quad (0.03) \quad (0.3) \quad (2.9) \quad (1.3) \quad (0.73)$$
$$R^2 = 0.51 \quad n = 1024 \quad ESE = 11.7$$

where the variables are defined as above, except that $Smax$ is measured as a log to the base 2 ($\log_2$), and D_{scen} is a dummy variable for the investment scenario (see above) where $D = 1$ for scenario 1, and $D = 2$ for scenario 2. Standard errors are given in brackets.

The strongest effects are those of S_{max}, t^* and a (the vision). As k (the sensitivity of market shares to technological differences between firms) is increased there is a slight increase in the level of technology reached, but the effect is not especially strong. The results in the two scenarios do not show a statistically significant difference, though the positive coefficient suggests a fractionally higher level of technology achieved in scenario 2.

Combining the linear and quadratic terms in a, we can draw a relationship (Figure 3.5) between the final level of technology reached and the slope of the technology vision, Θ. Interestingly, this appears to have a maximum at $a = 1$ (Moore's law). It is relatively flat in the vicinity of $a=1$, but slopes away rapidly on either side.

For this model as it stands, Moore's law is usually amongst a range of self-fulfilling visions, and of that range it seems to be the vision that maximises the rate of technological advance. The importance of Moore's profound insight may be even greater than we realised at first.

4

THEORETICAL CONNECTIONS BETWEEN RAPID TECHNOLOGICAL CHANGE AND THE DEVELOPMENT OF MARKET STRUCTURE

4.1 INTRODUCTION

We saw in chapter 2 that there is a long tradition of studies which tend to emphasise one or other of the following observations. First, that R&D activity has an element of fixed cost to it, that these fixed costs are high, that there are economies of scale and that the incumbent monopolist has more to lose by failing to innovate than the prospective entrant has to gain, so that, all in all, technical change is concentrating.

The second, and opposed, group of observations is that radical technological change presents great difficulties for the organisation, it upsets existing structures and these structures give the large organisation an inertia that makes it difficult to change direction quickly. This argument then implies that rapid and radical change gives greatest opportunities to the small start-up firm.

Connected to these observations are two opposed though not incompatible hypotheses, A and B. Hypothesis A asserts that incumbents accelerate the speed of change in an attempt to shake off actual and potential competitors. This hypothesis rests on two assumptions: first, that the costs of technology development increase if that development is to be accomplished in a shortened time; second, that in the face of higher development costs (if he seriously intends to compete) and reduced product lifetimes, the laggard quits the race in that particular item of technology. With these two assumptions, accelerated change in a technology deters entry and is hence a concentrating influence.

Hypothesis B works in the other direction. Rapid technology change puts severe strain on an organisation which was set up to produce earlier versions of the technology. For that reason it is the small and perhaps new firm with organic structure that is better equipped to cope with the organisational pressures of rapid technology change. Under this hypothesis, rapid change creates an environment for which smaller, newer firms are better suited than the established incumbent, and hence accelerating technology change is deconcentrating.

As we argued in Chapter 2, while these two hypotheses are opposed they are not mutually inconsistent. One group of firms, the incumbents, may be responsible for accelerating change in a particular direction – where the entry-deterring effect of accelerating change is greater than the organisational stress. At the same time another group, the new entrants, is responsible for accelerating change in another direction where the relative importance of these two effects is reversed.

In particular, we conjectured that technology change along a simple and widely recognised technological trajectory is less disruptive to the organisation, so that the large incumbents have the edge in innovations of this type. On the other hand, technology change that departs from a recognised trajectory – for example, by radically redefining the product or proliferating extra product features – may be more disruptive, so that the smaller new entrant has the edge here. These two hypotheses need not be mutually incompatible.

The main objective of this chapter is to develop a simple model to illustrate the combined effects of these two hypotheses. In particular, the model will emphasise the role of 'visions of the future' for a particular technology. If the actual trajectory followed by a technology is consistent with a firm's vision of the future, that firm can enjoy economies of scale from rapid innovation. If it is not, the firm will face serious organisational difficulties unless it is small; or, to put it another way, it will encounter diseconomies of scale.

4.2 A MOTIVATING ANALOGY

Analogies are obviously dangerous, but this one (if read with due caution) summarises the problem in a very succinct way. The model we describe below is superficially like the analysis of ships and waterways. A big ship is best for crossing the ocean but not so good for navigating a winding waterway; a small ship can accelerate and slow down to navigate bends in the channel but in the open sea will soon be overtaken.

The analogy is worth pursuing as several of the special features of the following analysis are brought out here.

1 There are economies of scale. In the marine analogy, the attainable hull-speed (under normal frictional/turbulent conditions and so neglecting possibilities for planing) is roughly proportional to ship length. In the innovative environment, this would mean that the maximum rate of advance along a clearly defined trajectory is proportional to firm size, and so the large organisation has a clear advantage.

2 There is undue 'inertia' for large organisations. Strictly speaking, we are talking here about the kinetic energy of the ship. Kinetic energy is proportional to mass but engines (and braking systems) are not capable of

delivering power in proportion to the mass of the ship – far from it. Stopping distances (or turning circles) for large tankers are measured in miles, while the speedboat can turn 'on a sixpence'.

3 Channels are easier to navigate if you have a chart. This means that you can plan accelerations and deaccelerations to optimise passage through the channel. Without these, risk aversion will make the pilot slow down. Or, for non-nautical readers, winding roads are easier to navigate at speed if you know the road.

This translates in a straightforward way to the innovative environment. Most organisations do better when there is a clear vision of the future.[1] Large organisations seem to have a particular need for this to be articulated. Smaller organisations benefit from such a vision, but can adapt to unexpected circumstances more easily. But having said that, big ships find it hard to navigate corners, even if they have a chart.

4.3 FIVE MAIN FEATURES OF THE ANALYSIS

There are five main features of the model. These concern:

1 defining and measuring the speed and direction of change;
2 defining and measuring the anticipated trajectory;
3 economies of scale in R&D;
4 organisational adaptability to anticipated change; and
5 organisational adaptability to unanticipated change.

In the ship analogy described above, features 1 and 2 are pretty trivial: speed and velocity are measured in Euclidean terms, while anticipated trajectories are easy to define for the skilful map reader. In the analysis of product innovation, however, features 1 and 2 are by no means easy to handle. Defining and measuring the speed and direction of change is a difficult piece of empirical analysis. Identifying the anticipated trajectory is even harder.

In the basic model below, it is assumed that copying is impossible or very, expensive – or at least that is expected to be expensive after accounting for likely enfringement damages. We also explore what happens if copying is relatively easy – that is, after all, a feature of the markets under consideration in our study (microelectronic components). In a fairly straightforward manner it reduces the (barrier to entry) returns from rapid innovation. Indeed, we find evidence – particularly in the case of microelectronic memories – that once the rate of change in the technology starts to slow down it is easier for copiers to catch up with the leading edge, and hence the nature of competition in the market is very different from what it was when rapid innovation built up an entry barrier.

Defining and measuring the speed and direction of change

In the context of the organisation or the product, it is no easy matter to define and measure the rate and direction of change. For the most part, this analysis is intended to apply to rapid product change, rather than process change, but in principle it might apply to either.

To define and measure product change we shall look at many product dimensions or characteristics. Rapid change along a clear trajectory (see below for a discussion of issues around 'technological trajectories') is easy enough to identify: the progressive reduction in costs of DRAM memory, the reductions in access time (within a particular product group) and the increases in 'bits per chip' are clear advances along a well-defined and predictable path. Such change is easy to map: it involves movements (usually) outwards in a low dimensional characteristics space.

Defining and measuring the anticipated trajectory

Expectations are a notoriously difficult concept to measure. Economists seem to gravitate between four extremes:

- naïve expectations (no change);
- adaptive expectations (some form of extrapolation);
- rational expectations (as informed by the 'best' theory, whatever that may be); and
- perfect foresight (the actual outcome).

Here, the anticipated trajectory plays a key role in technology planning. The organisation is better adapted to cope with change if that fits in with its 'vision of the future' than if that does not. In the present context, it matters less how these visions of the future are formed or whether they are accurate, than the fact that firms form and articulate such vision, and act on them. In our empirical work we find frequent and well-publicised visions of the future, as interpreted by senior management of leading companies. These can be interpreted in a variety of ways, as we saw in the previous chapter.

Economies of scale in innovation

The presumption of economies of scale in innovation is deeply seated in certain parts of the economics literature. At the simplest level, there are fixed costs to R&D and hence economies of scale, both in terms of the number of innovations introduced and also in terms of the quantities sold of products embodying those innovations.

In addition to these fixed costs (which mean that a firm has to be of a certain size to achieve the benefits of R&D), there may be diminishing marginal costs in the process itself, though this is not undisputed. For a summary of evidence, see Baldwin and Scott (1987: 75–88).

Empirical studies cast doubt on whether R&D input increases with size, or whether R&D output increases with size. But neither of these on their own would refute the economies of scale argument. There may be economies of scale but reduced incentives for larger (monopolistic) firms. In particular, it is sometimes argued that there are incentives for small firms to innovate where there are none for the (unthreatened) monopolist, because the latter's innovations would simply be 'cannibalisation'. Conversely, the frequency of joint-venture activity in semiconductors is commonly accepted as *de facto* evidence of the importance of economies of scale.

Organisational adaptability to unanticipated change

The classic study by Burns and Stalker (1961) of rapid change in the electronics industry led to the familiar description of two extreme types of organisation: mechanistic and organismic (or more commonly, now, organic). Mechanistic organisations are best suited to stable (and predictable) conditions; when such mechanistic organisations attempt to cope with new forms of change and uncertainty, pathological systems result. Organic forms, on the other hand, are much better suited to changing conditions, especially where fresh problems and unforeseen requirements appear which cannot be broken down and distributed within an existing mechanistic structure.

Organisational adaptability to anticipated change

The final question we need to pose is whether (and how) the mechanistic organisation can cope with anticipated change. The answer would seem to be yes, as long as routines can be established, specialisation can continue, the definitions and rights of each functional role can survive, the hierarchical structure can still cope and vertical interaction is still the main mode of communication.

For certain types of incremental product innovation (within an existing feature space) these conditions will probably be satisfied. Old specialisations are altered incrementally, as are the definitions and rights of each functional role; the hierarchical structure survives because vertical interaction is still sufficient for most purposes. But for more radical innovations they will not: old specialisations become redundant and cross-divisional communication is required, so the hierarchy is under threat.

4.4 AN INTEGRATED SIMULATION MODEL

This section reproduces part of an earlier paper, Swann (1992)[2]. The discussion in Chapters 2, 3 and 4 suggests a variety of factors which will influence the relationship between rapid technology change, organisational structure, corporate visions and the evolution of market structure. This long section summarises a simple simulation model that was designed to explore the effects of *four* of these factors:

1 the variance (or unpredictability) of the technology trajectory;

2 the speed with which the organisation's 'technological vision' adjusts to ongoing technological developments;
3 the absorptive capacity of each division in the multi-divisional as regards to experience gained in other divisions; and
4 the extent to which competence-destroying innovations generate greater cost penalties for the division of a multi-divisional firm than for a comparable mono-divisional firm.

The model analyses the connection between technology change and market structure in three steps.

1 It is argued that the organisation's ability to respond to and manage rapid technology change depends on the extent to which that change is compatible with the organisation's 'vision of the future' of that technology.
2 The organisation's ability to cope with change that deviates from this trajectory depends in part on its corporate structure. In particular, the large divisionalised corporation may be best placed to enjoy economies of scale when change is consistent with vision, while the small (unstructured) firm is better at handling change that is inconsistent with vision.
3 By mapping out the comparative success of different organisations in the face of different technological trajectories, it is possible to map the development of market structure.

First we summarise the main features of the model, full details of which are given in Swann (1992). Then we summarise and interpret a number of simulations with the model.

The main features of the model

The model is described in four parts:

1 the technological trajectory;
2 the expectations formation mechanism, which embodies the firm's or division's 'vision of the future' of the technology;
3 the cost function, embodying static-scale economies, dynamic-scale economies and costs of innovating away from the expected path of the technology; and
4 the market demand equation, which is a simple logit market share model here.

For the sake of simplifying the programming involved to implement this model, the path of the technology is entirely demand driven: that is, users demand a particular trajectory and firms have to try to follow this at minimal cost. There are some obvious reservations about this assumption. First, it allows only a unique trajectory that *all* firms are following; but in many cases different firms may follow different paths through a given characteristics

50

space. Second, the exogeneity of the trajectory denies its undoubted role as an instrument of competitive (and technological) strategy, as illustrated above. But with Occam's principle in mind, it is a very useful assumption to make as it allows us to focus on the interaction between rapid (and unpredictable) technology change, 'visions', corporate structure and market structure, without having to introduce a large number of complicating factors. In the next section we see that the model could be adapted (under some reasonable assumptions) to explore the more realistic and less deterministic scenario of multiple visions.

Technology trajectory

The model analyses a technology with two main characteristics (X, Y). Over time, the technological trajectory demanded by users follows a path upwards and to the right through this $X-Y$ space. The model might informally be called a constrained random walk with drift and declining variance, where the angle followed by the trajectory from one period to the next is constrained to lie between 0 and 90 degrees. This ensures that there is no technical regress on either characteristic.

Formally the trajectory is given by the equations:

$$DX_t = \alpha_x \cdot \exp\{\beta_x t - \Gamma_x t^2 + \varepsilon_{xt}\} \tag{1}$$

$$DY_t = \alpha_y \cdot \exp\{\beta_y \cdot t - \Gamma_y t^2 + \varepsilon_{yt}\} \tag{2}$$

$$se\{\varepsilon_{xt}\} = \sigma_x \cdot \exp\{-\delta_x(t-1)\} \tag{3}$$

$$se\{\varepsilon_{yt}\} = \sigma_y \cdot \exp\{-\delta_y(t-1)\} \tag{4}$$

D is the first difference operator, α, β and Γ are parameters, t is the time period, ε is the random or stochastic elements to the trajectory, se denote standard error, σ is the standard error in period 1 and δ is a parameter.

In equations (1) and (2), the first terms give the drift in X and Y. The change in X or Y (neglecting the stochastic part) can be constant, steadily increasing or increasing then decreasing to zero. But it is constrained to be non-negative. The stochastic term (ε) has mean zero, but even if it is strongly negative the change in X or Y will not fall below zero. Equations (3) and (4) simply indicate that the stochastic term has constant or steadily declining variance.

It is useful also to define the *velocity* and *angle* of the trajectory implied at any time t. If the path is drawn on a conventional two-dimensional graph (X axis horizontal, Y axis vertical), then the angle is large (small) when DY/DX is large (small). The velocity is simply the Euclidean distance between (X_{t-1}, Y_{t-1}) and (X_t, Y_t).

$$\theta = \tan^{-1}(DY/DX) \tag{5}$$

$$V = \sqrt{(DX^2 + DY^2)} \tag{6}$$

These equations define a wide class of useful trajectories, quite wide enough for the purposes of addressing the questions posed in this book. In particular, it is interesting to compare a trajectory with moderate but declining variance with another with high and sustained variance.

Visions of the future

As the technological trajectory is determined by user demands, the firm's (or division's) problem is essentially to forecast an exogenous trajectory. This is more a case of reactive expectations formation than proactive declaration of a technological 'vision'. The shortcomings of this approach were noted above, but the advantage in computational tractability is considerable. The simulation model assumes that each firm (or division) tracks the path of the trajectory with a simple adaptive expectations model and is not sufficiently farsighted to follow a rational expectations approach using equations (1)–(4). The adaptive model is given by:

$$DX^e_t = \phi_x.DX_{t-1} + (1 - \phi_x).DX^e_{t-1} + AX_t \qquad (7)$$

$$DY^e_t = \phi_y.DY_{t-1} + (1 - \phi_y).DY^e_{t-1} + AY_t \qquad (8)$$

The ϕ are adaptive parameters and the superscript e denotes expectations. One working assumption to be explored is that small specialised firms have a comparatively large ϕ (they adapt quickly), while large firms have low values of ϕ (they are slow to adapt), for the reasons discussed in section 2.

The AX and AY variables are 'adjustment' factors: that is, they allow for cases where particular firms or divisions specialise their 'vision' in a particular direction away from the norm. Thus, for example, one firm may instruct different divisions to operate different adjustment factors; one may follow a middle line, while another specialises in anticipating a steeper trajectory and a third specialises in anticipating a shallower trajectory. This was particularly relevant in the semiconductor case, where large divisionalised firms could compensate for their inertia by such specialisation. Referring to the trajectories in microprocessors described in section 3, the components division (for example) would be responsible for innovations in one direction, while the electronic systems division (for example) would cover innovations in another direction.

Cost function

The heart of the model is the cost function of the firm. In particular, the capacity of the firm to respond to the evolving technology trajectory depends on how its costs are influenced by static and dynamic-scale economies; the velocity of technology change; the discrepancy between the actual position of the trajectory and what was envisaged or expected; and the difficulty of working with this (i.e. discrepancy costs).

The cost function used here distinguishes between scale economies accruing to the division and those to the firm, and likewise between discrepancy costs at a divisional and at a firm level. This distinction is important because on it will hinge the comparative success of specialised firms and multi-divisional firms. If scale economies apply at a firm level (because the firm has a large absorptive capacity and is good at transferring expertise across divisional boundaries), while discrepancy costs apply only at a divisional level (because this firm is sufficiently decentralised to allow individual divisions to adapt their operating 'visions'), that situation is most favourable to the large multi-divisional firm. If, on the other hand, the scale economies are confined to the relevant division, while discrepancy costs depend on the overall size of the firm, that is most favourable to the small specialised firm. For division i in period t, the cost function is:

$$C_{it} = c_0^{\{1 - a_1.M_{it} - a_2.\Sigma_j M_{jt} - a_3.IB_{it} - a_4.\Sigma_j IB_{jt}\}} + V_t.[b_0 + D_{it}^{\{b_1.M_{it} + b_2.\Sigma_j M_{jt}\}}] \qquad (9)$$

The variables are as follows: M is the 'mass' of a particular division. This is defined as:

$$M_{it} = S^T_{i,t-1} + S^O_{i,t-1} \qquad (10)$$

where the S^T term is the sales of technology T by division i in the previous period, while the S^O term is the sales of other related technologies by division i in the previous period. It is important that these should be *related* technologies: in short, they must be technologies which would contribute to static-scale economies in production of T.

$\Sigma_j M$ is the mass of the firm (summed across all divisions). IB is the 'installed base' or cumulative production experience within the division, defined as follows:

$$IB_{it} = \sum_{s=0}^{t-1} S^T_{is} \qquad (11)$$

$\Sigma_j IB$ is the installed base or cumulative production experience (with this technology) in *all* divisions of the firm. V is velocity defined above in equation (6). Finally D is the discrepency between the anticipated position of the technology and its actual position. Following the definition of V, it is defined as the Euclidean distance between the anticipated position and the actual:

$$D_{it} = \sqrt{[(X_t - X^e_{it})^2 + (Y_t - Y^e_{it})^2]} \qquad (12)$$

The parameter c_0 defines the base production cost for a small firm with no scale economies in the face of no technological change ($V = 0$); b_0 defines how these costs are increased as the rate of technology change increases, in the absence of any discrepancies between actual and anticipated trajectories. The parameter a_1 measures the static-scale economies at a divisional level; a_2 measures these at the firm level. The paramter a_3 measures dynamic-scale economies at a divisional level; a_4 measures these at the firm level. The parameter b_1 defines the extent to which discrepancies between 'vision' and actual cause readjustment costs that are exacerbated by divisional size; b_2 measures the same effect but for overall firm size.

In the simulations that follow, it is assumed that either a_1 or a_2 is zero. The static-scale economies (if there are any) apply either at the divisional level or at the firm level, but not both. The same assumption is made about the pair of parameters (a_3, a_4), and about (b_1, b_2). This assumption is made to simplify the comparisons between different simulations.

Logit market share model and sales

From the above cost functions for the divisions of different firms, the simulation model translates these relative costs into relative market shares in a simple way. The model uses a logit model defining market shares over relative costs. For mono-divisional firms, the cost enters the logit function in a straightforward way. For multi-divisional firms it is assumed that the board of the company selects the division best suited to make the innovation required, which is that division with the lowest costs in that period. This may be a crude way of modelling the operation of a multi-divisional firm, but it does capture the effect that the multi-divisional firm has multiple and diverse bases of expertise and experience on which it can call. Thus if C_{ft} is the production cost of firm f in period t, then for the multi-divisional firm:

$$C_{ft} = \min_i \{C_{it} \mid i \, \varepsilon \, f\} \qquad (13)$$

The market share model, then, can be defined for a set of firms F, as follows:

$$W_{ft} = \exp\{-k_1.C_{ft}\} / [k_0 + \sum_{j \varepsilon F} \exp\{-k_1.C_{jt}\}] \qquad (14)$$

where W defines the market share of a particular firm, k_1 is a parameter defining the sensitivity of market share to cost differences and k_0 is a parameter to cater for the 'don't buy' segment of the market. (In the simulations that follow in the present chapter, $k_0 = 0$ throughout so the market shares of the different firms in F always add up to 100 per cent.)

Miscellaneous assumptions

To close the model, a few other assumptions are required. Market shares are multiplied by total market demand for technology T to generate sales achieved by each firm. It is assumed that this total demand grows at a rate of g per cent per period from a base of S^T_0. Sales of related technologies by each division i are assumed to grow at the same rate h per cent per period, from a base of S^O_{i0}. Sales of technology T are assumed to be zero in period 0, and only to take off in period 1. These two assumptions together imply that $M_{i1} = S^O_{i0}$. (For

54

convenience it is assumed that $S^O{}_{i0}$ is the same for each i in the simulations below, so consequently the mass of each division at the start of the simulations is the same.)

The simulation results

First we describe a base set of parameters for the simulations and select two examples from the base set of simulations to illustrate the working of the model. Then we summarise the results of over 5,000 simulations run for a range of values for the model parameters and a range of trajectories.

Base simulation

For the base simulation the model is run for twenty periods with a population of four firms. Firms 1–3 are all mono-divisional firms, while firm 4 has three divisions, A, B and C. At the start, the mass of each firm 1–3 is set at 2 units, and so also is the mass of each division in firm 4. The only difference between firms 1–3 at the start is that they have different adjustment factors (AX and AY) in equations (7) and (8). For firm 1 the adjustment factors are zero; for firm 2, the adjustment factors mean that its vision is rotated towards the X characteristic and axis (flatter); for firm 3, the adjustment factors mean that its vision is rotated towards the Y characteristic and axis (steeper). Divisions A, B and C of firm 4 have the same adjustment factors as firms 1, 2 and 3 respectively. In a sense, therefore, each division, A, B and C, of firm 4 replicates firms 1, 2 and 3 (respectively) at the start. The critical distinction is that the divisions are part of a larger firm, while firms 1, 2 and 3 are not.

For this base simulation, the parameters are set at particular values as summarised in Tables 4.1 and 4.2:
For the two illustrative calculations, different values were chosen for the remaining parameters (a_1, a_2, a_3, a_4, b_1, b_2), as noted below.

It is worth dwelling on the assumptions about ϕ: these imply that the large divisionalised firm can adapt to the unfolding trajectory just as rapidly as the smaller firm. This is a generous assumption as far as the large firm is concerned, and section 5.2 examines what happens when different assumptions are made about ϕ.

Figure 4.1 illustrates the technology trajectory generated for this base simulation. The top part of the diagram shows the actual trajectory; the bottom part shows the velocity and angle of the trajectory in each period. The velocity is on average highest at the beginning and tails off later in the simulation. Also the variation in direction is greatest at the beginning, and the angle homes in on 45 degrees (the long-run solution when var(ε) tends to zero) at the end of the simulation. In short, this is quite a typical trajectory: uncertain with rapid change at the start, settling down to a smoother and slower path later on.

Table 4.1 Non firm-specific parameters

Trajectory parameters (equations 1–4)
$\alpha_x = \alpha_y = 4$
$\beta_x = \beta_y = 5\%$
$\Gamma_x = \Gamma_y = 0.5\%$
$\sigma_x = \sigma_y = 3$
$\delta_x = \delta_y = 10\%$
Cost function parameters (equation 9)
$b_0 = 1$
$c_0 = 100$
(other cost function parameters, see below)
Logit function parameters (equation 14)
$k_0 = 0$
$k_1 = 0.1$
Market growth parameters (section 3.5)
$g = 0\%$
$S^T_{.1} = 10$ (total demand for T in period 1)
$h = 0\%$
$S^O_{i0} = 2$ (other sales of division in period 0; same for all firms/divisions)

Source: Swann (1992)

Table 4.2 Firm-specific parameters

	Firm 1	Firm 2	Firm 3	Firm 4: Div A	Div B	Div C
				Expectations/vision parameters (equations 7, 8)		
$\phi_x = \phi_y$	0.8	0.8	0.8	0.8	0.8	0.8
$\dot{AX}$	0	1	−1	0	1	−1
$\dot{AY}$	0	−1	1	0	−1	1

Source: Swann (1992)

Figures 4.2 and 4.3 illustrate two runs of the simulation model and were chosen as they illustrate some of the main properties of the model. Figure 4.2 represents the case where $b_1 = 4\%$, $a_4 = 0.6\%$, $a_1 = a_2 = a_3 = b_2 = 0\%$. That is, where 'off-trajectory costs' depend on the size of the division rather than the size of the firm, but where dynamic-scale economies depend on the accumulated experience of the firm (and not just the division). Firm 4 benefits here because dynamic-scale economies spill over between different divisions. In periods 1, 2 and 8, firm 4's innovations come from division 3; in periods 3–5 they come from division 2; later the innovations come from division 1. The reason for this alternation is the different specialisations of different divisions: division C is best placed to handle the innovations when the angle of trajectory is steep (periods 1, 2, 8), division B is best adapted to innovate when the angle of the trajectory is flat (periods 3, 4, 5), and division A when the angle approaches 45 degrees. And this shuffling of production between divisions is viable because these dynamic-scale economies apply at the firm level.

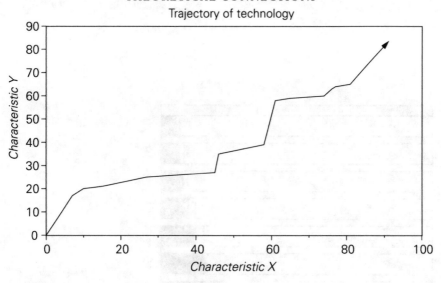

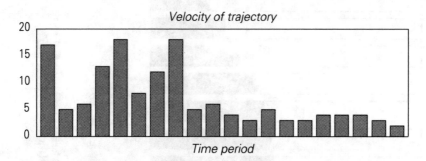

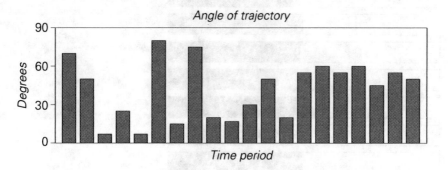

Figure 4.1 Base simulation: trajectory, velocity and angle
Source: Swann (1992)

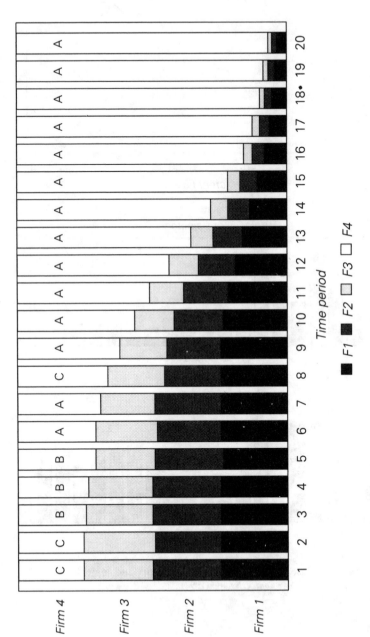

Figure 4.2 Market shares of firms 1 to 4
Base simulation: $b_1 = 4\%$ $a_4 = 0.6\%$
Source: Swann (1992)

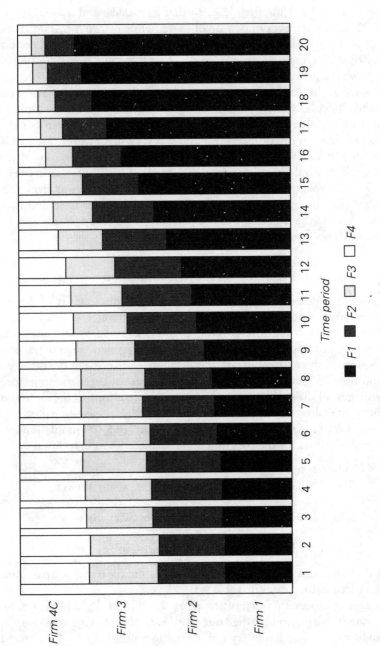

Figure 4.3 Market shares of firms 1 to 4
Base simulation: $b_1 = 4\%$ $a_3 = 0.6\%$
Source: Swann (1992)

That is clearly a critical assumption. If instead the dynamic-scale economies apply only at the division level, firm 4 fares much less well. Figure 4.3 illustrates the resulting sequence of market shares with the same parameter values as Figure 4.2, except that the dynamic-scale economy applies only at the division level and not the firm level so that $a_3 = 0.6\%$ and $a_4 = 0$. Now in period 20, firm 4 achieves only a small share, while before it had dominated the market. Firm 4 cannot shuffle production around as before and continue to enjoy the full dynamic-scale economies. As it turns out, firm 4 continues to locate production in division C which is the division best suited to the early (steep) part of the trajectory, but less well suited to the later (flatter) part. When the trajectory flattens out, firm 4 finds it better to continue exploiting what dynamic-scale economies there are in division C, rather than switching production between divisions. This may seem very myopic, for if firm 4 had foreseen the trajectory it would have located production in division A from the start, which would have been costly in the short run but better in the long run; it would expect to have achieved the same market share as firm 1. But remember that the trajectory has a random walk character to it, and firm 4 could not foresee the later shape of the trajectory in period 1. In the end, firm 4 (division C) does no better than firm 3.

Variations on the base simulation

A number of simulations were run to explore the implications of different parameter combinations. For the key cost function parameters $(a_1, a_2, a_3, a_4, b_1, b_2)$ a grid of twenty-seven different combinations was used. For the adjustment parameters (ϕ), two possibilities were explored. Two generic sorts of trajectory were explored (one with moderate and declining variance and the other with high and non-declining variance). For each of these two generic trajectories, the robustness of the simulations was explored by confronting the model with fifty different realisations of the trajectory. In all other respects the parameters are those of the base simulation. This makes a total of 5,400 simulations.

The grid of values for the cost function parameters was as follows:

$a_1 = 0\%$ or 4%
$a_2 = 0\%$ or 4% but with only one of them >0 at any time
$a_3 = 0\%$ or 0.6%
$a_4 = 0\%$ or 0.6% but with only one of them >0 at any time
$b_1 = 0\%$ or 4%
$b_2 = 0\%$ or 4% but with only one of them >0 at any time

The grid of values for the adjustment parameters and the trajectory parameters is summarised in four cases in Table 4.3.

An adaptive expectations parameter of $\phi = 0.5$ in cases II and IV represents a slower rate of adaptation by the large firm, 4, to the evolving trajectory and this can be expected to have very unfavourable results for firm 4. In cases III

Table 4.3 Grid of values for adjustment parameters and trajectory parameters

	Adjustment speed φ (x or y)				Trajectory	
Case	Firm 1	2	3	4 (divs A–C)	σ_x and σ_y	δ_x and δ_y
I (base)	0.8	0.8	0.8	0.8	3	10%
II	0.8	0.8	0.8	0.5	3	10%
III	0.8	0.8	0.8	0.8	5	0%
IV	0.8	0.8	0.8	0.5	5	0%

Source: Swann (1992)

and IV the trajectory has a greater variance than in cases I and II, and the variance does not decline ($\delta = 0\%$).

Tables 4.4 and 4.5 summarise the simulations in a way that sheds as much light as possible on the effects of the four factors of particular interest:

1 the variance (or unpredictability) of the technology trajectory (a comparison of case I with case III, and case II with case IV);
2 the speed with which the organisation's 'technological vision' adjusts to ongoing technological developments (a comparison of case I with II, and case III with IV);
3 the absorptive capacity of each division in the multi-divisional firm as regards gained in other divisions (a comparison of results where dynamic-

Table 4.4 Market share of firm 4: starting values and changes

Parameters	Case 1		Case II		Case III		Case IV	
	1	20–1	1	20–1	1	20–1	1	20–1
$a_2 = 0\ b_2 > 0\ a_3 > 0$ or $a_4 > 0$	10	−10	10	−10	7	−7	7	−7
	[0,25]	[−25,0]	[0,25]	[−25,0]	[0,25]	[−25,0]	[0,25]	[−25,0]
$a_2 = 0\ b_2 > 0\ a_3 = a_4 = 0$	10	14	10	14	7	4	7	2
	[0,25]	[−1,24]	[0,25]	[−1,24]	[0,25]	[−25,27]	[0,25]	[−25,25]
$a_2 = 0\ b_1 = b_2 = 0$	25	0	25	0	25	0	25	0
	[25,25]	[0,0]	[25,25]	[0,0]	[25,25]	[0,0]	[25,25]	[0,0]
$a_2 = 0\ b_1 > 0\ a_3 > 0$	25	−2	25	−17	25	2	25	−23
	[25,25]	[−22,20]	[25,25]	[−25,4]	[25,4]	[−22,22]	[25,25]	[−25,−14]
$a_2 = 0\ b_1 > 0\ a_3 = a_4 = 0$	25	0	25	0	25	2	25	−0
	[25,25]	[−0,1]	[25,25]	[−0,1]	[25,25]	[−0,5]	[25,25]	[−6,8]
$a_2 = 0\ b_1 > 0\ a_4 > 0$	25	40	25	−3	25	41	25	−21
	[25,25]	[11,68]	[25,25]	[−24,56]	[25,25]	[15,70]	[25,25]	[−25,26]
$a_2 > 0\ b_2 = 0\ a_3 = a_4 = 0$	93	0	93	0	93	0	93	−0
	[92,93]	[−0,0]	[92,93]	[−0,0]	[92,93]	[−0,2]	[92,93]	[−3,2]
$a_2 > 0\ b_2 = 0\ a_3 > 0$ or $a_4 > 0$	93	7	93	7	93	7	93	7
	[92,93]	[7,7]	[92,93]	[7,7]	[92,93]	[7,7]	[92,93]	[7,7]
$a_2 > 0\ b_2 > 0$	59	37	59	37	33	0	33	−5
	[0,93]	[0,99]	[0,93]	[0,99]	[0.92]	[−92,93]	[0,92]	[−92,92]

Source: Swann (1992).
Notes: Main entry is average over all simulations
　　　Figures in brackets are minimum and maximum values in simulations

Table 4.5 Market share of firm 4: effects of noisier trajectory and slower adjustment

Parameters	Case II – Case 1		Case III – Case I		Case IV – Case I	
	20	Avg 1–20	20	Avg 1–20	20	Avg 1–20
$a_2 = 0\ b_2>0\ a_3>0$ or $a_4>0$	0	0	0	−1	0	−1
	[−2,0]	[−3,0]	[−5,0]	[−8,0]	[−5,0]	[−8,0]
$a_2 = 0\ b_2>0\ a_3 = a_4 = 0$	−1	−1	−14	−10	−15	−12
	[−1,0]	[−2,0]	[−24,3]	[−14,−6]	[−24,0]	[−16,−7]
$a_2 = 0\ b_1 = b_2 = 0$	0	0	0	0	0	0
	[0,0]	[0,0]	[0,0]	[0,0]	[0,0]	[0,0]
$a_2 = 0\ b_1>0\ a_3>0$	−15	−8	4	2	−21	15
	[−39,−1]	[−21,−1]	[−30,28]	[−10,9]	[−44,−2]	[−28,−3]
$a_2 = 0\ b_1>0\ a_3 = a_4 = 0$	0	0	2	0	−0	−4
	[0,0]	[−1,0]	[0,5]	[0,1]	[−6,7]	[−7,−1]
$a_2 = 0\ b_1>0\ a_4>0$	−42	−17	1	−0	−61	−30
	[−89,−5]	[−39,−2]	[−14,16]	[−7,6]	[−93,−15]	[−49,−6]
$a_2>0\ b_2 = 0\ a_3 = a_4 = 0$	0	0	0	0	0	−1
	[0,0]	[0,0]	[0,1]	[0,0]	[−3,2]	[5,0]
$a_2>0\ b_2 = 0\ a_3>0$ or $a_4>0$	0	0	0	0	0	0
	[0,0]	[0,0]	[0,0]	[0,0]	[0,0]	[1,0]
$a_2>0\ b_2>0$	0	−2	−64	−52	−69	−57
	[−7,0]	[−11,0]	[−100,1]	[−89,−17]	[−100,0]	[−92,−20]

Source: Swann (1992).
Notes: Main entry is average over all simulations
Figures in brackets are minimum and maximum values in simulations

and static-scale economies apply at the *division* level ($a_3>0$ and $a_1>0$) with those where they apply at the *firm* level ($a_4>0$ and $a_2>0$); and
4 the extent to which competence-destroying innovations generate greater cost penalties for the division of a multi-divisional firm than for a comparable mono-divisional firm (a comparison of results where off-trajectory costs depend on *division* size ($b_1>0$ and $b_2 = 0$) with those where they depend on *firm* size ($b_2>0$ and $b_1 = 0$).

In Table 4.4, the grid of twenty-seven combinations of cost function parameters is simplified into nine groups. It was found that the typical results for each combination within a particular group were remarkably similar.

The first row refers to the case of no static-scale economies ($a_2 = 0$), off-trajectory costs that depend on the size of the firm ($b_2>0$) and some dynamic-scale economies (either at the firm or at the division level). In case I (moderate trajectory variance, and declining, and the same adjustment parameters for all firms), firm 4 starts with an average 10 per cent of the market (column headed 1), and sees its market share decline by an average of 10 per cent (column headed 20–1). The figures in brackets show the range of values (minimum, maximum) obtained over the simulations. In this case, there is some variability in the starting market shares for firm 4 and its decline, but in all cases the share is less than or equal to 25 per cent, and declines (or at least does not improve) by period 20. The results for cases II, III and IV are very similar.

The second row refers to the case of no static-scale economies, off-trajectory costs depending on the size of the firm, but no dynamic scale economies. Here, for case I, firm 4 starts badly (average share 10 per cent) but sees its market share improve by an average of 14 per cent. The reason for this is that firm 4 suffers in the early stages when the variance of the trajectory is high, and it pays especially high off-trajectory costs (because of its overall size). But by the end the variance of the trajectory has declined substantially and off-trajectory costs are small. Firm 4 is not penalised by its bad start because there are no dynamic-scale economies here. It should be noted, however, that when the variance of the trajectory does not decline (cases III and IV), firm 4's share only improves slightly (on average) by the end of period 20, and indeed for a range of simulations it does not improve but instead declines further.

Rows 3 to 6 all refer to the case of no static-scale economies and off-trajectory costs that depend on the size of the division (not the firm) or indeed are zero. Not surprisingly, these cases are more favourable to firm 4. In all cases the starting share is 25 per cent, as firm 4 is neither advantaged or disadvantaged relative to the others. When there are no off-trajectory costs, there is no change in market share thereafter. Otherwise, what happens thereafter depends on dynamic-scale economies, and differs for cases I–IV. With no dynamic scale economies (row 5, $a_3 = a_4 = 0$), there is little change in share, again because there is nothing much to give firm 4 an advantage or disadvantage (except in case IV, where firm 4 has a slower rate of adaptation to a trajectory whose variance does not decline and consequently incurs higher off-trajectory costs). With dynamic-scale economies at the firm level, firm 4 does have an advantage, and sees its market share expand considerably in cases I and III. In cases II and IV, however, firm 4 may again pay for its slower adaptation. With dynamic-scale economies at the division level only, the picture is less clear though on average firm 4's market share declines, especially if adaptation is slow (cases II and IV).

The last three rows refer to the case where there are firm-level static-scale economies. Clearly this is to the advantage of firm 4, and as long as off-trajectory costs do not depend on firm size ($b_2 = 0$), firm 4 starts to dominate the market in period 1 and continues to do so to period 20. Dynamic-scale economies offer a further advantage to firm 4 in this case. But as the last row shows, when off-trajectory costs depend on firm size the picture is more variable. On average, firm 4 expects to dominate the market in cases I and II. But in cases III and IV, when the variance of the trajectory does not decline, firm 4 expects an average of 33 per cent but cannot expect that to improve (on average). Indeed in some simulations firm 4's market share declines rapidly.

Table 4.5 presents the simulation results in a slightly different way, designed to emphasise the effects of slower adaptation in firm 4 and of a noisier trajectory. Cases II, III and IV are compared in turn to case I.

The first block of results, headed case II–case I, compares the finishing market shares for firm 4 (column headed 20) and the average market shares for firm 4 over periods 1–20 (column headed AVG 1–20) in cases II and I. If the entry in a particular column is negative, then firm 4 does worse in case II; if zero, then there is no difference; and if positive then firm 4 does better in case II. The second and third blocks, case III–case I and case IV–case I, are defined in an analogous way.

We can see that for three rows of parameter combinations, firm 4's average and final market share is unaffected by having a slower adaptation rate for firm 4 (case II–case I), a noisier trajectory (case III–case I), or both (case IV–case I). These are rows 3, 7 and 8, which refer to the following combinations: no firm-level static-scale economies coupled with no off-trajectory costs; and firm-level static-scale economies coupled with no firm-level off-trajectory costs, with or without dynamic-scale economies.

Moreover, in rows 1 and 5, the effects of a slower adaptation rate for firm 4 and a noisier trajectory on firm 4's performance are generally small. These rows refer to the following combinations: no firm-level static-scale economies coupled with firm-level off-trajectory costs and some dynamic-scale economies; no firm-level static-scale economies coupled with division level off-trajectory costs and no dynamic-scale economies. In the case of this first combination it may seem surprising that noisier trajectories and slower adaptation do not harm firm 4. The reason is essentially that firm 4 starts off very badly in this case and sees its market share decline to period 20; a noisier trajectory and slower adaptation make only a marginal difference to an already poor performance.

In the other rows, however, it is apparent that slower adaptation by firm 4 and/or a noisier trajectory can have a marked effect on firm 4's performance. In row 2, it is the noisier trajectory that damages firm 4's performance, while slower adaptation has little effect. In this combination, off-trajectory costs apply at the firm-level and for this reason a noisier trajectory will generate greater costs for firm 4 than the others.

In rows 4 and (especially) 6, slower adaptation by firm 4 can lead to very substantial reductions in firm 4's market share. These combinations refer to no static-scale economies, off-trajectory costs at the division level and dynamic-scale economies at the division and firm-level respectively. While firm 4 is not disadvantaged by firm-level off-trajectory costs, its slower adaptation will mean that it makes larger errors in predicting the trajectory and hence incurs higher costs.

Surprisingly, perhaps, in these two combinations a noisier trajectory can lead to an increase in firm 4's market share: the average score in period 20 is only just positive, but the range of simulations includes examples where firm 4's market share increases substantially. These improvements may appear unexpected, but they arise because when freed from firm-level off-trajectory costs, firm 4 need suffer off-trajectory costs no worse than the mono-divisional firms (1–3) as long as its adaptation rate is the same as firms 1–3. Indeed, when the trajectory is particularly noisy and one (or two) of firms 1–3 are suffering as a result, firm 4 can gain by reshuffling production to take advantage of the difficulties the other firms face, as we saw in the example above. But any such gains disappear as soon as adaptation becomes slower (case IV–case I) or when there are firm-level off-trajectory costs (see rows 1, 2 and 9).

Row 9 shows that with firm-level static-scale economies and firm-level off-trajectory costs, a noisy trajectory can lead to a very substantial decline in firm 4's market share. This is partly because firm 4 often did very well with the base trajectory, and because it suffers particularly from the firm-level off-trajectory costs.

Summary of the simulations

Table 4.6 offers a compact verbal summary of the simulation results. The diagram simply represents the contents of Tables 4.4 and 4.5 in a more compact way and does not really call for much further explanation. It shows for different combinations of static-scale economies, off-trajectory costs and dynamic-scale economies, the share of firm 4 in period 1, the direction of change by period 20, the effect of slow response or adaptation by firm 4 on its market share and the effects of a noisier trajectory on firm 4's performance. One further point should be noted: when the entry is in the form 'RISE/(FALL)', for example, this means that the average of the simulations shows a rise, but some may show a fall.

It is worth noting that no parameter combinations predict the following outcome: { <25%, same}. To see why this arises, consider the top branch of the tree in Table 4.6 (no firm-level static-scale economies, and firm-level off-trajectory costs). If there are no dynamic-scale economies, firm 4's market share rises when the trajectory becomes smoother later on (and when firm 4's off-trajectory costs start to fall). But if there are dynamic-scale economies of some sort, then firms 1–3 compound their head start, and firm 4's performance declines further. It appears unlikely that firm 4's performance will stay the same in this case.

Empirically speaking, it is difficult to say which are the most plausible simulations. One starting set of assumptions might be that static-scale economies are mainly at a divisional rather than a firm level; off-trajectory costs apply at a firm level; and there *are* dynamic-scale economies of some sort. These assumptions imply that firm 4 starts with a market share of < 25 per cent, and sees that share decline, a pessimistic outcome for the multi-divisional firm. Moreover, in such circumstances firm 4's performance will get slightly worse if the trajectory becomes noisier.

A more optimistic assumption would be that there are firm-level static-scale economies; combining this with the other two assumptions, the model

Table 4.6 Summary of simulations

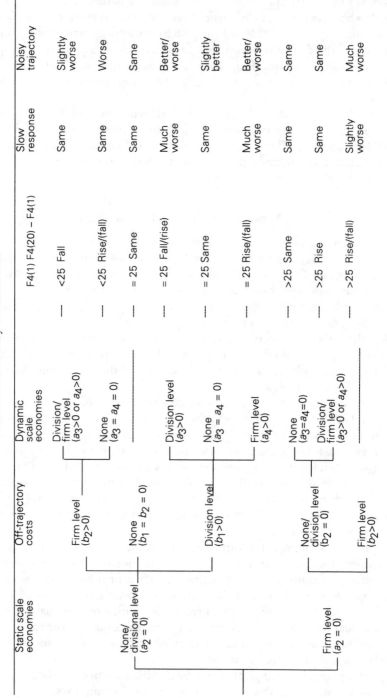

Static scale economies	Off-trajectory costs	Dynamic scale economies	F4(1)	F4(20) − F4(1)	Slow response	Noisy trajectory
None/divisional level ($a_2 = 0$)	Firm level ($b_2>0$)	Division/firm level ($a_3>0$ or $a_4>0$)	<25	Fall	Same	Slightly worse
		None ($a_3 = a_4 = 0$)	<25	Rise/(fall)	Same	Worse
	None ($b_1 = b_2 = 0$)		= 25	Same	Same	Same
	Division level ($b_1>0$)	Division level ($a_3>0$)	= 25	Fall/(rise)	Much worse	Better/worse
		None ($a_3 = a_4 = 0$)	= 25	Same	Same	Slightly better
		Firm level ($a_4>0$)	= 25	Rise/(fall)	Much worse	Better/worse
Firm level ($a_2 = 0$)	None/division level ($b_2 = 0$)	None ($a_3 = a_4 = 0$)	>25	Same	Same	Same
		Division/firm level ($a_3>0$ or $a_4>0$)	>25	Rise	Same	Same
	Firm level ($b_2>0$)		>25	Rise/(fall)	Slightly worse	Much worse

Source: Swann (1992)

predicts that firm 4 starts with > 25 per cent, and is likely to see its performance increase further – potentially, the exact opposite outcome! However, in this case, the outcome is much worse for firm 4 if the trajectory becomes noisier. This suggests that the presence and form of static-scale economies can be critical in these simulations, as well as the form of off-trajectory costs and dynamic-scale economies.

Conclusions

This simple simulation model was designed to explore the interaction between rapid and unpredictable technology change, firms' expectations or 'visions' for a technology, corporate organisation and market structure. Over 5,000 simulations were performed to predict market share over a sequence of twenty periods, for a range of parameter combinations and in the face of different technological trajectories. These simulations are summarised compactly in Table 4.6, above.

Our interest focused on four particular effects. First, we saw that an increased variance (or unpredictability) of the technology trajectory could adversely affect the market share of a multi-divisional firm. This was particularly relevant if the cost penalty incurred for a disjuncture between technological 'vision' and market trajectory (the off-trajectory cost) depended on the size of the *firm* more than the size of the *division*. It was noted, in our review of the literature, that large complex organisations find it especially costly to copy with such a disjuncture.

Second, we saw that if the large organisation took longer to adjust its 'technological vision' to ongoing technological developments, that could adversely affect its market share, even without a noisier trajectory. This was of particular relevance when off-trajectory costs depended on the size of the *division*, and there were dynamic-scale economies. As noted in the previous paragraph, the large firm is already disadvantaged when off-trajectory costs apply at the firm-level, and the combination of a slower rate of adaptation only leads to a small further deterioration.

Third, we saw that the absorptive capacity of each division in the multi-divisional firm as regards experience gained in other divisions played a vital role in the model. If static- and dynamic-scale economies depend on the size of the firm rather than just the size of the division, firm 4 enjoys a clear cost advantage, and the simulations confirm that this can have a substantial effect on its market share.

The other effect in which we were interested was the possibility that competence-destroying innovations generated greater cost penalties for the division of a multi-divisional firm than for a comparable mono-divisional firm. We modelled this by having off-trajectory costs depend on the size of the firm rather than the size of the division. We have seen above how, in combination with noisier trajectories, this effect can significantly influence the simulation results.

4.5 A LESS DETERMINISTIC VIEW

In the deterministic trajectory model described in the last section, it is as if a product that lies off the trajectory will not sell, so that firms have to try to produce the desired position on the trajectory, whatever their visions and whatever the cost penalties incurred if the vision is out of line with the trajectory. Moreover, the vision would be regularly adjusted to the evolving trajectory by a partial adjustment mechanism, but where the rate of adjustment is a *parameter* of the model. As we saw, this was computationally convenient, and even with it the simulation model was complicated enough.

But as we argued in the previous chapter, such an exogenous view of the trajectory is rather unsatisfactory. In this section, however, we note that a less deterministic model of multiple visions and no exogenously given trajectory could be reinterpreted within the existing simulation model, so that the results described above are of wider applicability.

The trajectory of that model could be reinterpreted as the centre of gravity of market demand. More precisely, the logit market share model would be redefined in the following way. Assume that product design in any period is constrained by the pre-existing vision (and related organisational routines), and hence cannot be changed at short notice. Then each firm will produce a product in line with its vision. Then using the same notation as before:

$$W_i = F(C_i, D_i | C_j, D_j; j = 1,..,n) \tag{15}$$

so that the market share of firm i depends on its costs (C_i) as before, and also on the technological distance (D_i) between its actual product and the design preferred by the greatest number of consumers (or the centre of gravity, as described above, which is how we now interpret the previously exogenous trajectory). Then a firm will do well if its vision is close to the centre of gravity, that is, if D_i is small, and also, of course, if its costs are small. And as with the original logit formulation, market share depends not only on the firm's absolute performance but also on its relative performance. If firm i does badly, but so do all the others (j), then firm i's market share will not suffer so much; but if firm i does badly and some other firms do well then firm i will suffer.

As before, firms would adjust their visions each period towards the evolving centre of gravity, as they learn more about that. This part of the model would be unchanged. The cost function would change, however, because there would be no cost penalty from having to produce along the trajectory – the firm no longer has to do this. Instead there could still be a cost of changing the vision from one period to the next (see below). At present that is treated not as a cost but dealt with by allowing a partial adjustment (which may be slower for large firms) and that is a reasonable and quite convenient simplification.[3]

There is one essential difference between the exogenous trajectory model described in the previous section and the modified version outlined here. In the original, the effect of distance between vision and trajectory appeared as an item in the cost function, while in the modified version it appears as a factor in the market share model. This would not matter if the disadvantages to the consumer of having a product that did not confirm to his/her ideal design could be converted to an equivalent cost penalty. In general, it requires quite strong assumptions to make such conversions which would apply equally to all consumers,[4] although ironically that is not necessarily true for a logit market share model.

There is, however, an additional problem. As the original model stands, the cost penalty incurred for producing along a trajectory that lies away from the firm's existing vision is an increasing function of firm size. But the equivalent cost penalty incurred by a consumer from using a product that lies away from his/her ideal design is not going to depend on the size of the producing firm.

On the matter of adjustment costs, an intermediate position would be to handle some of the vision adjustment as a cost (rather than an entitlement through the partial adjustment mechanism). This would be a function of the difference between the revised vision and what might be called the natural vision (i.e. that which flows from the accumulated technological competences, as described by Teece, 1988). This cost would be weighted by the size of the firm, while, as noted above, the consumer's cost penalty on buying a non-ideal design is not a function of the size of the producing firm.

This approach would have quite an interesting implication. The optimum strategy for large firms is not to change vision too fast but rather to produce at low cost, while the small firm changes vision more rapidly and is more expensive, but hits the centre of gravity with more accuracy. In practice, the products of large firms may not be sold at a lower price. Instead, they use their additional profitability from lower marginal cost to subsidise a larger network of supporting products and services, in which economies of scale apply. The consumer's choice is then to buy an ideal product from a small firm but with little support, or a compromise product from a large firm but with better support. Superficial inspection suggests that this is quite a common choice in some of the high technology markets to which our analysis is addressed.

4.6 APPLYING THE MODEL: MEASURING CONCENTRATION AND DISRUPTION

The last two sections in this chapter deal with two additional issues involved in relating the theoretical discussion of Chapters 2–4 to the case studies of Chapters 5–9. The first is the question of how to measure developments in market structure. The second is about what we could call the *macrodynamic* implications of the theory discussed above.

The purpose of this section is to explain how the above models may be made usable in the case studies that follow. The word 'testable' would be too strong, for while we seek to confront these hypotheses with data that will shed light on their relevance or irrelevance, we are some considerable distance away from a formal econometric test. This is partly a result of the shortages of data and the substantial effort required to collect and collate these. But equally it reflects conceptual difficulties: the theory as it stands is not readily applicable to available data and we need to draw out the implications of the theory in a way that will relate to available data. The present section concentrates on these conceptual issues.

A problem with the concentration ratio

Existing econometric studies of the relationship between the speed of change and the development of market structure tend to look at the correlation between the (say) four-firm concentration ratio and the level of expenditure on R&D, or the R&D intensity (i.e. the ratio of R&D to sales).

A problem with this is that the simple concentration ratio can (and in the industries we look at invariably does) hide much of the deconcentrating activity that actually takes place. This is because it is in the form of what we call market share disruption, or what Audretsch (1992) calls turbulence.

In our analysis we have found the following two measures very useful. One is the market share *disruption* defined as follows:

$$d(s,t) = \sum_{i=1}^{n} |w_{it} - w_{is}| \qquad (16)$$

that is, the sum (over firms $i = 1,...,n$) of absolute market share deviations between period s and period t. Most commonly we look at $d(t-1,t)$, the period-to-period disruption. Sometimes, however, it is useful to examine $d(1,T)$, the disruption from period 1 to period T – i.e. the first and last data points. These are, in effect, net disruption measures, where some period-to-period disruption may offset some other. It is useful also to compute *gross* disruption measures over a longer period, defined as follows:

$$gd(s,t) = \sum_{r=s+1}^{t} d(r-1,r) \qquad (17)$$

A comparison of $d(1,T)$ and $gd(1,T)$ can indicate whether the year-to-year disturbances are mutually offsetting, or whether there is a clear trend from beginning to end. The latter will tend to exceed the former, by a great deal if these disturbances are mutually offsetting, or by rather little if not.

The second, and rather simple, measure is to follow the market share of the 'top four' (say) of a particular period through the entire data sample. This is especially useful when looking at company rather than product shares. In the product case, we simply map the market share of that product from introduction onwards.

Actual market share data

One further useful application of these measures to actual market share data is to decompose changes in concentration ratios and disruption into two components: first, the change in the distribution of company market shares, ignoring any changes in ranking; second, the residual change in distribution attributable only to changes in ranking.

To separate these two measures, we compute the total disruption measures, as described above. We then sort market shares in each year into descending order (irrespective of the company) and compute the disruption to the 'pure' market share distribution, irrespective of company:

$$d^*(s,t) = \sum_{j=1}^{n} |w^*_{jt} - w^*_{js}| \qquad (18)$$

where w^*_{it} is the market share of the jth ranked firm in period t, and not firm 'j'. In short, the identity of firm j here could change from year to year.

Then the decomposition is made as follows:

$$d(s,t) = d^*(s,t) + dr(s,t) \qquad (19)$$

where $dr(s,t)$ is disruption due to reranking between periods s and t.

We shall also find it useful to compare disruption (and concentration) over all products with disruption (and concentration) over all firms. This, in short, refers to the different measures obtained in (16) and (18) according to whether the index (i) refers to product shares or company shares. Highly disruptive technology change would show up as a large measure for the product-level disruption. If the company-level disruption is low in comparison, it suggests that technology change is not as deconcentrating at the company level.

Two hypothetical models of entry, deconcentration and disruption

To see how concentration ratios can hide deconcentrating activity, consider the following two hypothetical sequences of market shares.

(a) In each period (starting from period 1) a new firm enters with a radically improved product. Over each product's life cycle we observe the following sequence of sales, where t is the introduction date for that product:

Period:	t	$t+1$	$t+2$	$t+3$	$t+4$	$t+5$	$t+6$	$t+7$
Sales:	1	2	3	4	3	2	1	0

The product life cycle is seven periods for each product.

(b) In each period $t = 1,...,T$, one firm enters, but none exits. Sales are the same as in model (a) for periods t to $t+3$ but thereafter they remain at 4 units per period. The product life cycle is unbounded; entry is certainly deconcentrating, but the worst that the incumbent feels is a gradual decline in its market share.

71

Figure 4.4 shows the path of concentration ratios in model (a) and model (b), while Figures 4.5 and 4.6 to 4.9 show the paths of the two additional measures (disruption and firm 'n' shares, for $n = 1, 3, 6, 12$) in the case of each model. Figure 4.4 shows how the concentration ratio in model (a) falls at first, settles at 75 per cent and then rises back to 1 when entry stops. For model (b), on the other hand, the concentration ratio steadily declines to 25 per cent (where entry has stopped). On the face of this measure alone, model (b) offers a more deconcentrating path than model (a).

However, as Figure 4.5 shows, the disruption measures give a very different picture. The disruption in model (b) falls steadily from 67 per cent to 33 per cent and on downwards; all that is happening here is that all incumbents lose an (ever-declining) market share to the next new entrant. In the case of model (a), however, disruption falls in periods 3 and 4, only to rise thereafter and settle at 50 per cent by period 8.

While model (b) seems to be most deconcentrating in terms of movements in the concentration ratio, model (a) is most deconcentrating in terms of the disruption measure. This comes about because of the finite (seven-period) life cycle of each product in model (a), while the product life cycle for (b) is effectively unbounded.

Figures 4.6 to 4.9 indicate the deconcentrating character of model (a). Figure 4.6 shows how the market share of firm 1 declines in both models. In model (a), the share declines to zero in period 8, while in model (b) the share continues to decline but never reaches zero. Figure 4.7 shows the equivalent picture for firm 3. Here the peak market share achieved under model (a) is somewhat higher but again, that share plummets much more rapidly in model (a) whereas in model (b) the share declines very gracefully. Figures 4.8 and 4.9 are more exaggerated versions of this, with model (a) offering the best short-term scope for the new entrant but model (b) offering the longer life cycle. In that sense model (a) is clearly more deconcentrating; it offers the best (short-term) scope to new entrants.

4.7 THE MACRODYNAMICS OF INNOVATION AND CONCENTRATION

In Chapter 2, we suggested that the dual causal relationships between market structure and innovation and (the reverse) from innovation to market structure could lead to some quite interesting closed system dynamic behaviour. We argued that if concentration has a positive effect on innovation, and if innovation reinforces concentration, then in response to an exogenous increase in innovative activity we find a *virtuous circle* of continuing positive feedback, with increased concentration and increased innovation. Conversely, if concentration has a negative effect on innovation and innovation has a negative effect on concentration, then in response to an exogenous increase in innovation we find a spiral of reduced concentration and increased innovation.

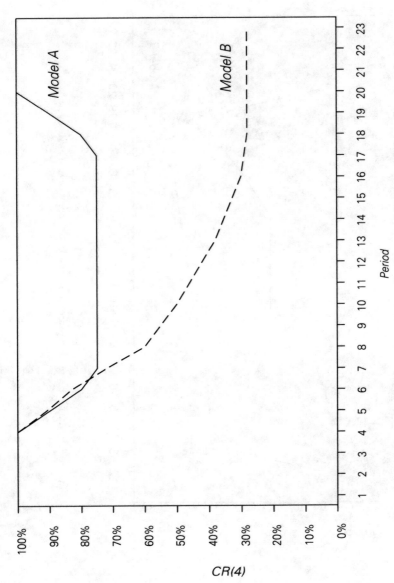

Figure 4.4 Four firm concentration ratios: two models of entry/life cycle

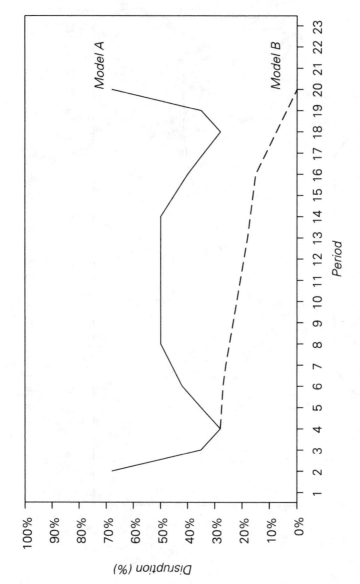

Figure 4.5 Market share disruption measures: two models of entry/life cycle

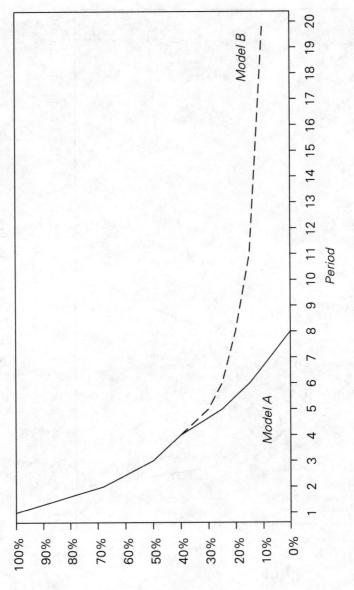

Figure 4.6 Market share, firm 1

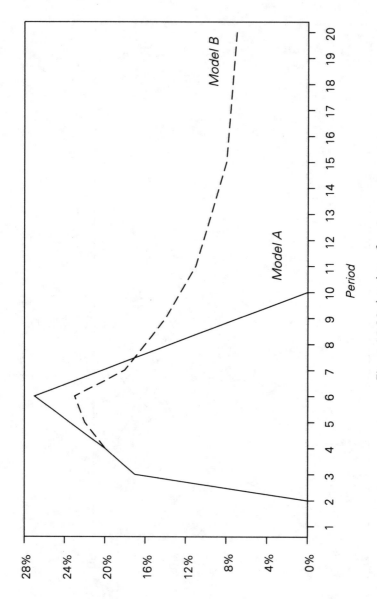

Figure 4.7 Market share, firm 3

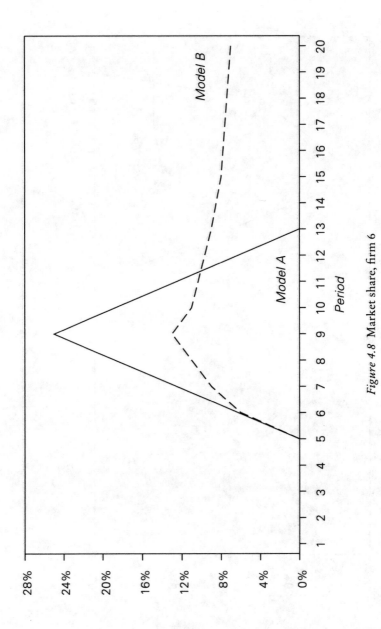

Figure 4.8 Market share, firm 6

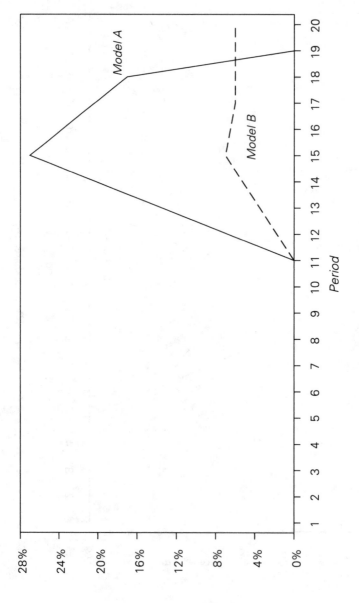

Figure 4.9 Market share, firm 12

This final section of Chapter 4 sets out a simple dynamic model to demonstrate these results. Let I define innovation and C define concentration, and assume that each causal effect operates with a lag of one period, so that:

$$I_t = I_0 + aC_{t-1} \tag{20}$$

$$C_t = C_0 + bI_{t-1} \tag{21}$$

The long-run solution for this (where $I_t = I_{t-1}$ and $C_t = C_{t-1}$) is as follows:

$$I = (I_0 + aC_0)/(1-ab) \tag{22}$$

$$C = (C_0 + bI_0)/(1-ab) \tag{23}$$

From which it is easy to derive the following derivatives with respect to exogenous shifts in innovative activity (I_0) and concentration (C_0):

$$dI/dI_0 = dC/dC_0 = 1/(1-ab) \tag{24}$$

$$dI/dC_0 = a/(1-ab) \tag{25}$$

$$dC/dI_0 = b/(1-ab) \tag{26}$$

An exogenous increase in innovative activity will have a positive log-run *multiplier* effect on further innovation of $1/(1-ab)$, as long as $0<ab<1$, and this will hold *regardless* of the sign of a and b. This exogenous increase in innovation will have a positive long run effect on concentration if $b>0$ and negative if $b<0$. An exogenous increase in concentration will lead to a similar positive long-run *multiplier* effect on concentration, regardless of the signs of a and b; the long-run effect on innovation will be positive if $a>0$, and negative if $a<0$.

The paths followed by innovation and concentration in response to any of these exogenous shocks are quite interesting. Figures 4.10–4.12 show the response to an exogenous increase in innovative activity in three different cases: Figure 4.10, a and b both positive ($a = 0.7$, $b = 0.7$); Figure 4.11, a and b both negative ($a = -0.7$; $b = -0.7$); and Figure 4.12, a positive and b negative ($a = 0.7$, $b = -0.7$).

The lags in this simple model mean that the path is a zig-zag to the new long-run solution. Alternatively, if one relationship is negative and the other positive, we find that innovation and concentration follow a jointly cyclical pattern (rather like the hog cycle of agricultural economics).

Composite exogenous changes in I_0 and C_0 can generate even more interesting patterns. An exogenous increase in both the rate of innovation and the degree of concentration will, with a positive and b negative ($a = x$, $b = -x$), give a convergent spiral where, in turn, innovation and concentration increase, then innovation increases further but concentration decreases, then both decrease, then concentration increases while innovation decreases! But the long-run solution is one of much increased innovation and slightly increased concentration.

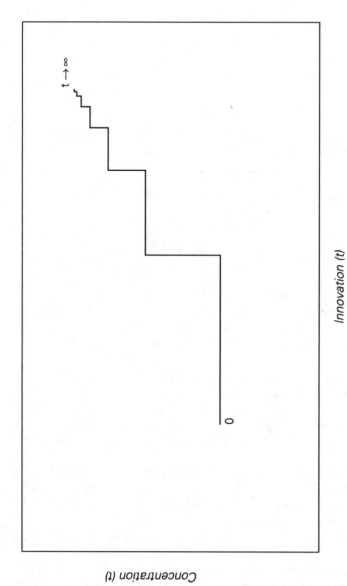

Figure 4.10 Effects of exogenous increase on concentration (*a* and *b* both positive)
Note: $a = b = 0.7$

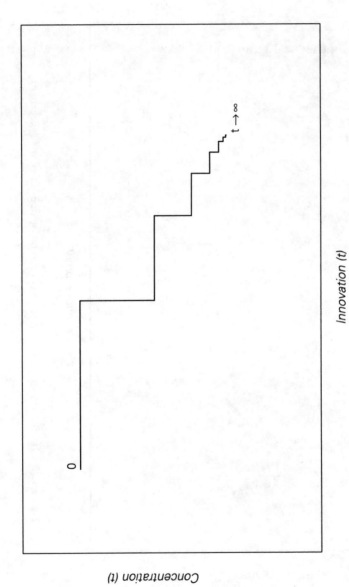

Figure 4.11 Effects of exogenous increase on concentration (*a* and *b* both negative)
Note: a = b = –0.7

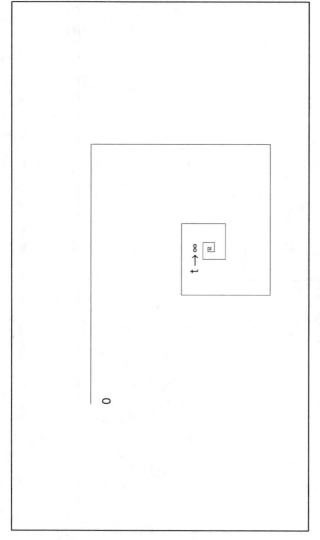

Figure 4.12 Effects of exogenous increase on concentration (*a* positive and *b* negative)
Note: a = –b = 0.7

5

CASE STUDY: MICROPROCESSORS

5.1 INTRODUCTION

The five case studies that follow explore the central hypotheses outlined in Chapter 4. We ask whether the experience of the market in question supports the argument that radical change incompatible with prevalent corporate visions is deconcentrating, while incremental (albeit very rapid) change compatible with such visions is concentrating. Are these useful hypotheses to interpret the evolution of the market in question? As the concept of vision is hard to pin down in quantitative terms, and as some key data here were not available to us, what follows in these cases is not detailed econometric analysis. Rather, it is a preliminary attempt to see whether the history of these markets is broadly supportive of the arguments advanced above.

Wherever feasible, we have tried to describe technology visions at an early stage of these market histories, basing our descriptions on accounts in the trade press of the time and other (mostly) secondary sources. In addition, we have tried to plot actual technology trajectories in these markets, to see how these compare with early visions. With the help of some market research data from Dataquest Europe (in Chapters 5, 6 and 7) and other sources in Chapters 8 and 9, we have tried to map the deconcentrating and concentrating trends in these market histories. But it must again be emphasised that this is inevitably some way short of a comprehensive and integrated econometric analysis.

As the first three case studies all come from the semiconductor industry, we start this chapter with a background sketch of that industry. This will be useful in understanding Chapters 6 and 7 on memory components and standard logic chips. Section 5.3 describes the particular background to the microprocessor itself. It represented a very rapid and truly radical product innovation for the semiconductor industry, with important implications for the development of market structure. Section 5.4 examines a key component of our analysis: 'visions of the future' of microelectronics before and after the introduction of the microprocessor. We see that some companies' visions of the future closely matched the ultimate development of the technology, and that gave them a continuing competitive edge in the industry; conversely, others' visions were substantially at variance with what actually happened. Section 5.5 charts the initially deconcentrating effect of radical technological change in the introduction of the microprocessor, while section 5.6 charts the subsequently reconcentrating effects of steady incremental innovation in the form of new generations of microprocessor device. Section 5.7 uses one other approach to summarise the turbulence in the market. Section 5.8 concludes that this case illustrates both theoretical traditions, but at different times. Early product innovation is radical and deconcentrating while later product innovation is incremental and reconcentrating.

5.2 BACKGROUND TO THE SEMICONDUCTOR CASES[1]

The semiconductor industry was chosen as a striking example of the theoretical effects outlined above, although different categories of semiconductor have rather different histories as Chapters 6 and 7 will show.

Figure 5.1 shows the relationship between the various product categories that we shall mention in this chapter (and others), concentrating especially on integrated circuits (many components integrated into a single chip). These different categories are (not surprisingly) at different stages in their life cycles. Standard logic is in a maturity and/or decline phase. Microprocessors, peripheral chips and RAM memory still seem to be in their growth phases, though the growth curves have not been smooth. Finally, single chip microcomputers and ROM memory seem to have entered their maturity phase by the mid-1980s.

The growth and decline of different semiconductor products might have been expected to lead to a substantial change in market structure. And yet, by the conventional criterion of concentration ratios (for example, the four-firm concentration ratio), there appears to have been little change in concentration. Using data in Webbink (1977), Braun and Macdonald (1978), Malerba (1985), and elsewhere, we calculate that the four-firm concentration ratio in the world semiconductor market as a whole remained more or less unchanged over the period 1972–86. This shows just how much the concentration ratio can hide, as there was undoubtedly substantial disruption to that market with frequent changes to the 'league table' of company shares. New entrants quickly capture significant market shares and incumbents find their market shares are soon eroded as new classes of semiconductor appear. In short, while the share accounted for by the top N firms may not change very much, the identity of those N firms does change rather a lot.

To summarise this disruption or turbulence in market shares we use the measures described in Chapter 4. Briefly, if $w_{i,t}$ is the share of company i in period t, the disruption measures are defined as follows:

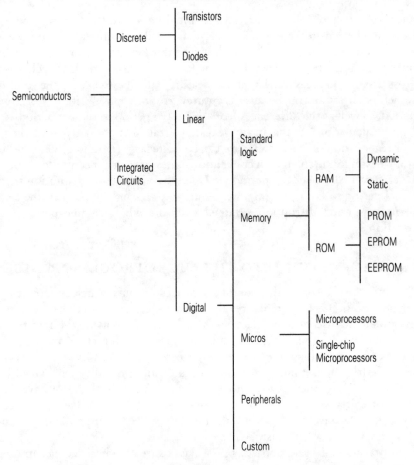

Figure 5.1 Semiconductors: product classification

$$w_{.t} = \sum_{i=1}^{N} |w_{i,t} - w_{i,t-1}| \tag{1}$$

$$w_{.*} = \sum_{i=1}^{N} |w_{i,T} - w_{i,0}| \tag{2}$$

$$w_{..} = \sum_{t=1}^{T} w_{.t} \tag{3}$$

The first shows the absolute extent of disruption to market shares between one period and the next. That is, it measures the sum of absolute changes to market shares across the group of N firms. The second shows an equivalent measure, but here calculated from the initial period to the last, rather than from one period to the next. As such it shows the net disruption to market shares from the initial period to the last. The third measure is simply obtained by summing the first measure from the first to the last period; as such it is a gross disruption measure. The third measure will tend to exceed the second, sometimes by quite a bit, because it captures gross disruption within the sample period, as well as the differences from the initial period to the last period.

Our calculation find that in any year the overall disruption to market shares – or reallocation of market shares – can be quite large (around 14 per cent) in comparison to the changes in conventional measures of concentration (about 1 per cent). And over the period (1972–86) as a whole the disruption from initial period to last (ignoring intervening years) is only about half the total period-to-period disruption summed over the whole sample period (i.e. equation 3).

5.3 BACKGROUND TO THE MICROPROCESSOR CASE

The microprocessor is the computer processor on a single silicon chip, introduced in 1971, that has revolutionised electronic circuit design, and promoted the use of microelectronics in areas well outside the traditional domain of application. This case study illustrates the initial deconcentrating effect of the introduction of the microprocessor, followed by the reconcentrating effect of continuing incremental innovation in eight- and sixteen-bit devices. Latterly, there is evidence that developments in the most advanced areas of thirty-two-bit microprocessors, and RISC chips, has again been somewhat deconcentrating, but unfortunately we lacked the data to examine this part of the market's history in such detail.

At first sight, the microprocessor is a classic case of radical deconcentrating technology change. The microprocessor was a radical innovation in the sense that it led to a radical revision in circuit and computer design. Before that, circuit design had used the building blocks of standard logic (conventional gates and elements of Boolean algebra), and circuit designs were 'hard wired'. After the introduction of the microprocessor in 1971, circuit design became a matter of software rather than hardware design. The replacement of hardware design skills by software design skills as the scarce resource posed a radical challenge for those companies that would compete in the new market. We see below that the microprocessor represented a mode of thinking that did not appear in prevalent 'visions of the future' in the late 1960s and early 1970s.

The earliest history of the microprocessor shows that it was the relatively new entrants (in particular, new start-up companies) which were responsible for the rapid developments in the technology. In particular, Intel, one of the early 'Fairchildren' – start-ups formed by former staff of the well-established semiconductor manufacturer, Fairchild – took the technology in a direction that incumbents seemed unlikely to. But later, when the sixteen-bit microprocessor had been developed, Intel – by then the market leader in microprocessors – forced the pace of change with enhanced components and networks of supporting products in a way that severely discouraged entry except in the production of second-source components.

Some established firms were slow to participate in the microprocessor market. It is instructive to compare market shares in the total integrated circuit market in the late 1960s with those in the microprocessor market in 1975. Apart from Motorola (and perhaps Texas Instruments), the leaders in the first market do not have a significant presence in the second and vice versa. The introduction of the microprocessor posed such a challenge that none of the established firms could react in a way that gave them a significant share of the microprocessor market even by 1975, four years after introduction (Golding, 1971: 152; *Economist*, 1976: 53).

Regrettably, the data we have do not allow a thorough analysis of market shares over the entire period from 1967 to the present; we have only been able to analyse data on the period 1975–86. And while that period emphasises the deconcentrating trends in that particular market, there is also evidence of a concentrating phenomenon. The early pioneers in the microprocessor market eventually win overall.

Section 5.5 examines the deconcentrating phase, while section 5.6 examines the reconcentrating phase. First, however, we look at visions of the future and technology trajectories.

5.4 'VISIONS OF THE FUTURE' AND TECHNOLOGY TRAJECTORIES

Pre-announcements of new products – that is, where a manufacturer announces the intention to introduce a new product some time in advance of the actual date of introduction – are widespread in the semiconductor industry. In another paper (Swann, 1990b), we have examined the use of product pre-announcements in microprocessors, paying particular attention to their use as short-term tactics to discourage consumers from buying a rival's product; the consumer who hears that a better product is soon to be introduced may be persuaded to wait for its arrival rather than buy one of the models currently available.

In this book, however, we are primarily concerned with the longer-term strategic use of pre-announcements or publicised visions of the future. These go beyond the announcement of a discrete product to map out an anticipated trajectory for future developments in the technology. The vision is instrumental in allowing the large concern to exploit the potential economies of scale in rapid technological change.

In section 3.6, we discussed Moore's law, the main guiding vision for the development of semiconductor technology, and saw that it presented a dilemma for technology development in the late 1960s. One popular vision of how this issue could be resolved was the idea of widespread customisation of chip design. (To those unfamiliar with the technology, it is rather like the colour-matching schemes of the major paint manufacturers. The demand for ever more finely differentiated colours and shades of paint can be met better by local paint mixing facilities than by ever wider ranges of 'off-the-shelf' pots.) This vision of local customisation turned out to be wrong as a forecast of future developments (whatever its intrinsic merits); and yet this vision was vital as it appears to have underpinned the product strategies of some of the main large concerns at the start of the 1970s.

That explains (at least in part) why they had such difficulty in adapting to the radically different trajectory offered by the microprocessor. The micro-processor was a completely different approach to the problem of how to ensure that high functionality chips were still sufficiently general purpose to allow large-scale production. The key idea was to make the logic chip into a small-scale von Neumann computer (or at least the processor, if not the memory); then what the chip would do depended on what instructions were stored in the program memory. The same piece of hardware could perform quite different functions by altering the software. And if (as was widely believed at the time, even if it subsequently turned out to be false) economies of scope in software were almost as generous as economies of scale, this trajectory offered a clear solution to the difficulties of the standard logic trajectory.

Nevertheless, this latter vision was clearly very difficult for the large incumbents to assimilate. As noted before, Intel, the originator of the microprocessor, was one of the many new 'Fairchildren'; these companies made a mark in areas of radical product innovation, the inference being that such new product areas were too challenging for the Fairchild organisation to assimilate, so that these technologies would only see the light of day through spin-off companies. The genealogy of 'Fairchildren' is shown in Rothwell and Zegveld (1982: 30–1).

Certainly the early period after the introduction of the microprocessor was deconcentrating, as indicated in the previous section. And yet the potential economies of scale and scope implicit in the microprocessor trajectory did ultimately have a concentrating side to it. And when the microprocessor market started to grow, the Intel vision of the future became accepted as something close to a consensus view of where microprocessor technology was going. That, in turn, led to a consolidation of Intel's market position.

Figures 5.2 to 5.7 map out the character of trajectories in this technology for the six leading producers of 'own-design' microprocessors over the period. To do this we draw on the three main technology parameters defined in Swann (1986): bit size, generation (processor power) and features (processor only, RAM, ROM, I/O, single chip computer and a/d features). The vertical axis in these graphs ranks products according to bit size and within each bit size by 'generation' (or power). The horizontal axis ranks products by the

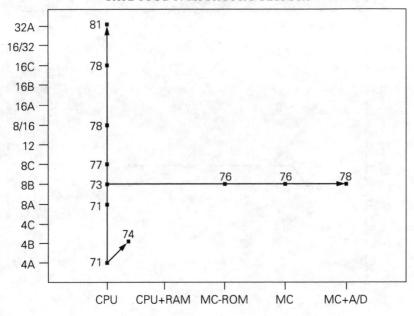

Figure 5.2 Microprocessor trajectories (Intel)
Source: Based on Swann (1985: 45–6)

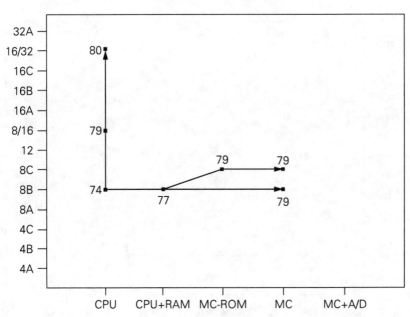

Figure 5.3 Microprocessor trajectories (Motorola)
Source: Based on Swann (1985: 45–6)

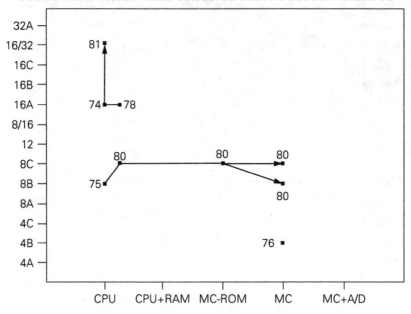

Figure 5.4 Microprocessor trajectories (National Semiconductor)
Source: Based on Swann (1985: 45–6)

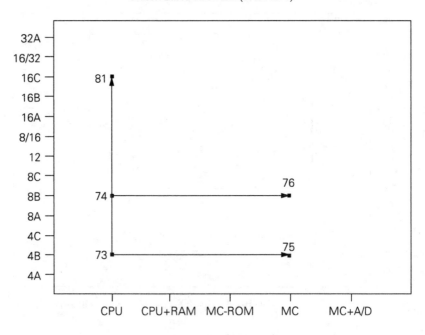

Figure 5.5 Microprocessor trajectories (Rockwell)
Source: Based on Swann (1985: 45–6)

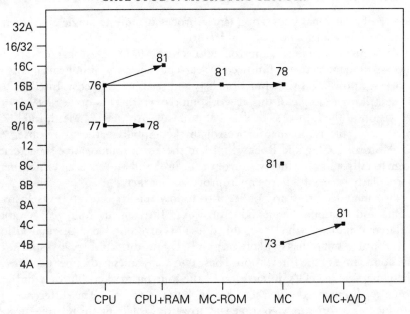

Figure 5.6 Microprocessor trajectories (Texas Instruments)
Source: Based on Swann (1985: 45–6)

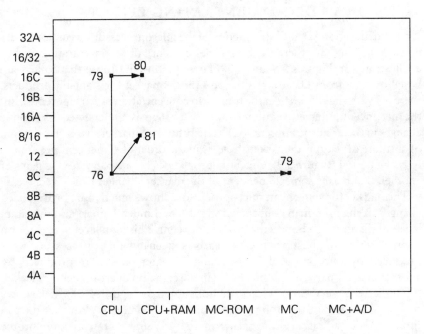

Figure 5.7 Microprocessor trajectories (Zilog)
Source: Based on Swann (1985: 45–6)

degree of functional integration (from processor only to single chip micro-computer with analogue to digital features).

The sequences of product introductions from 1971 suggest that most of the successful manufacturers followed a clear-cut trajectory of improvements in processor power, bit size, functionality, and reductions in cost. Intel's is the most striking example of this at work; moreover, this fits quite closely with its 'vision of the future' as declared at quite an early stage. Indeed, Intel was very successful in the microprocessor market. Similar patterns are observed for Motorola, Zilog and Rockwell; again these firms' innovative trajectories seem to tally with the 'Intel vision of the future', and Motorola and Zilog were particularly successful in the microprocessor market.

Two manufacturers do not seem to follow this trajectory: Texas Instruments and National Semiconductor. Texas Instruments followed a rather different trajectory, which probably does not correspond to its original 'vision of the future' but reflects a likely reappraisal of product strategy in response to the dominance of the Intel vision. These two companies had some successes in these markets (e.g TI's domination of the four-bit market) but they did not come to dominate the market like Intel and Motorola. The differences in product trajectories may go some way towards explaining the relative success of companies in this market.

5.5 DECONCENTRATING EFFECTS

As noted in section 5.3, the introduction of the microprocessor was undoubtedly deconcentrating. But there has been other evidence of deconcentrating effects, as illustrated in Figures 5.8 and 5.9. (These graphs and those that follow are based on data from Dataquest Europe.) In the market for eight-bit products, there is a very slight decline in the four-firm concentration ratio (Figure 5.8), but the deconcentrating effect of technology change is understated by simple changes in this concentration ratio. The disruption in market shares (i.e. the sum of absolute deviations in market share) is in the order of 40 per cent per annum over the period (Figure 5.9). Given that the losses of one party are the gains of another, that means some 20 per cent of the market 'changes hands' each year.

The market for sixteen-bit microprocessors shows much more pronounced changes in the four-firm concentration ratio and much higher (and unstable) levels of disruption – between 20 and 80 per cent. This high level of disruption is attributable to the fact that the early sixteen-bit microprocessors were produced by one group of firms, while the later ones were produced by another group – particularly successful in the eight-bit microprocessor market.

This latter observation is clearly demonstrated by Figure 5.10, which shows the market shares of the 'top three' of different years. It is clear that the top three of 1976 had rather little market share by 1986, which tends to reinforce the picture of deconcentration, though the trend among the top four of 1978 is much less pronounced.

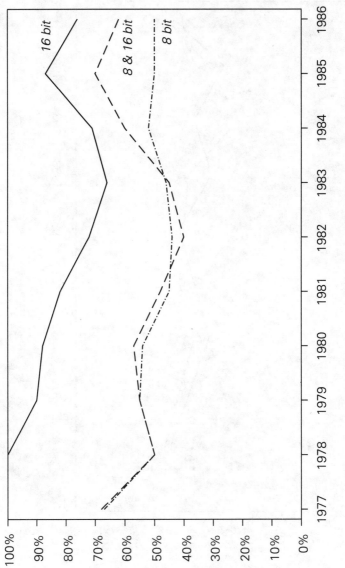

Figure 5.8 Four firm concentration ratio: microprocessors, world market
Source: Calculated with data from Dataquest Europe, Denham UK

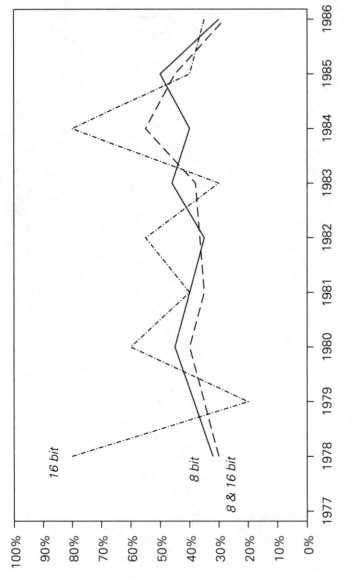

Figure 5.9 Disruption measure: microprocessors, world market
Source: Calculated with data from Dataquest Europe, Denham UK

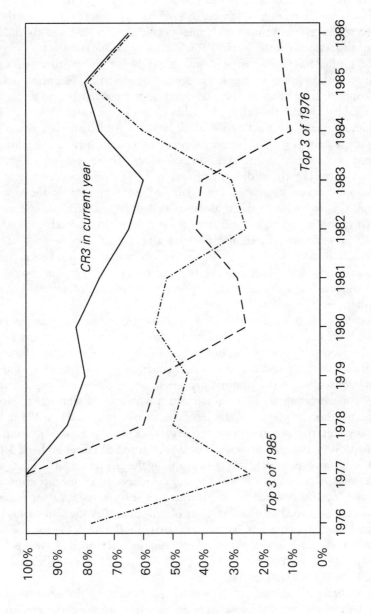

Figure 5.10 Three firm concentration ratio and shares of top three in 1976 and 1985. Sixteen-bit microprocessors, world market
Source: Calculated with data from Dataquest Europe, Denham UK

5.6 RECONCENTRATING EFFECTS

But as Figure 5.10 shows, the simple concentration ratio in the sixteen-bit market also illustrates a reconcentrating effect. The group of three which would ultimately emerge as leaders in 1985 had a respectable market share in 1976, and the group of four which emerge as leaders in 1985 had about 50 per cent of the sixteen-bit market in 1978.

The ultimately greater success of the eight-bit microprocessor manufacturers in this sixteen-bit market suggests that ultimately technology change was concentrating. But in the early stages, the sixteen-bit products were produced by some of the originally rather strong IC manufacturers (e.g. Texas Instruments and National Semiconductor) and gained market share from some of the strongest eight-bit microprocessor manufacturers. The joint effect of eight and sixteen-bit markets can be assessed by reference to Figure 5.9 above. Ultimately, the addition of the sixteen-bit device was concentrating, as the four-firm concentration ratio (labelled '8+16') increased above what it was in the eight-bit market alone (labelled '8'). Until 1983, however, concentration in the eight- and sixteen-bit markets combined was approximately the same as in the eight-bit market alone.

It is also instructive to note that disruption in the two markets combined tends to be less than disruption in either individually (Figure 5.9 above). This again suggests that some of the disruption in one market offsets disruption in the other.

Of course, quite a bit of the deconcentrating trend in the microprocessor market is the occurrence of 'second sourcing'. This is the trend where a group of firms produces copies of an original design by a pioneering producer. The appearance of this trend may suggest a reduction in concentration, since the second source is not the original producer. But such trends are, in another sense, concentrating as the originator of a particular design has a stronger market position as a result of the second source activity (Swann, 1987).

To abstract from second source activity, we examine the concentration ratio and disruption measures among original producers in Figures 5.11 and 5.12. In the eight- and sixteen-bit markets individually the position is fairly neutral, but when these markets are combined there is evidence of a concentrating effect. The concentration of production in the eight-bit microprocessor market is ultimately reinforced by concentration of production by the same firms in the sixteen-bit microprocessor market. At first, in Figure 5.11, the four-firm concentration ratio in the two markets combined (labelled '8+16') is below that in eight- and sixteen-bit markets separately, but eventually it lies above that in the eight-bit market (labelled '8').

Thus there is evidence of concentrating effects in the microprocessor market even though early trends were towards deconcentration, and the market structure in the eight-bit market is substantially different from that in the sixteen-bit market.

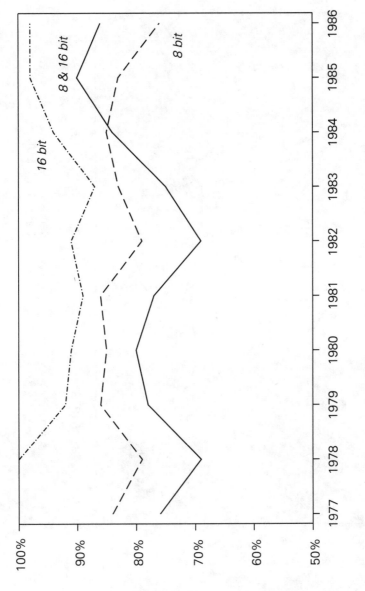

Figure 5.11 Four firm concentration ratio: microprocessors, own design products only, world market

Source: Calculated with data from Dataquest Europe, Denham UK

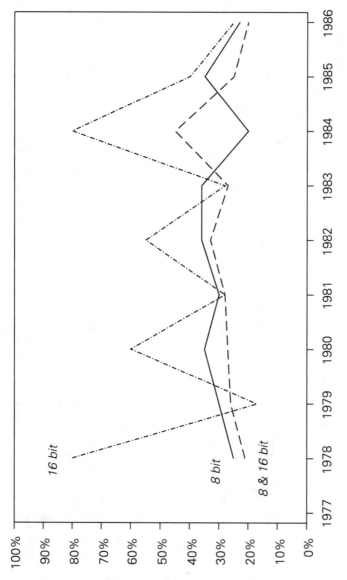

Figure 5.12 Disruption measure: microprocessors, own design products only, world market
Source: Calculated with data from Dataquest Europe, Denham UK

5.7 AN OVERALL VIEW OF CONCENTRATING AND DECONCENTRATING EFFECTS

One further way of looking at the concentrating and deconcentrating trends in this market is given in Figure 5.13. This summarises in a simple way whether at a particular time the trend is concentrating or deconcentrating, and also the degree of turbulence at any time.

It is constructed as follows. First, the market share of each company in year t is regressed on its market share in year $t-1$, for each year in the sample. This yields one regression coefficient, b_{1t}, for each year (except the first, as then data on $t-1$ is unavailable). Second, the market shares in any year are sorted into order – call these the market share ranks. Then the market share corresponding to each rank is regressed on the corresponding market share in the previous year. (Thus, the largest market share in year t is regressed on the largest in year $t-1$ and the smallest in year t on the smallest in year $t-1$.) This yields a second regression coefficient b_{2t}. The graph actually plots $b_{it}-1$ against $b_{2t}-1$; these latter coefficients are what would be obtained if the change in market share between $t-1$ and t were regressed on $t-1$.

The second coefficient, $b_{2t}-1$, is a simple measure of change in concentration. If it is positive, it means that the biggest market shares are tending to rise while the smallest market shares are tending to fall. That is an indication of an increase in concentration. The coefficient $b_{1t}-1$ represents a combination of two effects: the change in concentration and any turbulence or disruption in market leadership. It is easy to show that $b_{1t} <\,= b_{2t}$. If there is no disruption or turbulence, so that the ranking of companies in period t is the same as the ranking in period $t-1$, we simply find that $b_{1t} = b_{2t}$. But if there is turbulence, the coefficient b_{1t} is strictly less than b_{2t}, as some reversals in ranking have taken place.

Figure 5.13 plots a time series for $b_{1t}-1$, $b_{2t}-1$ and the difference between them (shown as a bar chart). When $b_{1t} - b_{2t} = 0$, this corresponds to the case of no turbulence or disruption. The pattern is quite an interesting one. We observe a considerable amount of movement over the period. With the exception of 1978–9, the trend from 1977–82 is deconcentrating, while the trend over the period 1982–5 is reconcentrating. And then again, the movement over 1985–6 is sharply deconcentrating.

Turbulence is highest in 1983–4, also the period in which the reconcentrating trend is strongest. Turbulence is lowest in the period 1985–6, also the time of greatest deconcentration. Otherwise, the level of turbulence is fairly stable. With only two exceptions, the two coefficients b_{1t} and b_{2t} have the same sign, meaning that turbulence is never so strong as to turn a concentrating trend in terms of ranks into a loss of market share for all leading firms in the previous year. The exceptions are 1978–9 and 1982–3, when the regression on ranks indicates a modest increase in concentration, but for individual firms this is outweighed by the level of turbulence.

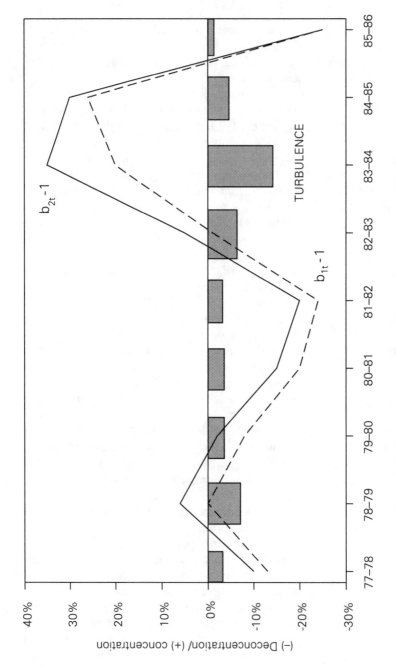

Figure 5.13 Concentration and turbulence: microprocessors, 1977–86
Source: Calculated with data from Dataquest Europe, Denham UK

5.8 CONCLUSIONS

The microprocessor gives an outstanding illustration of the deconcentrating and (subsequently) concentrating effects of technological change. Early microprocessors were a radical innovation, incompatible with the main visions of the future, and were products with which the new start-up firms were best adapted to cope. In that sense, the introduction of the micro-processor was essentially deconcentrating. Later developments, particularly along the lines used by Intel, were to set out a clear vision of the future and accelerate the rate of change along that trajectory. These developments were, by contrast, essentially concentrating, with Intel and Motorola coming to dominate this particular market. Both episodes marry quite neatly with the theory set out in Chapter 4.

6

CASE STUDY: MEMORY CHIPS

6.1 INTRODUCTION

This chapter examines the effects of rapid rates of innovation on market structure within solid-state memory chips. The principal focus is on two types of device, dynamic random access memory (DRAMs) and static random access memory (SRAMs).

The direction of developments in solid-state memory chips has been far less prone to uncertainty than many others in semiconductor technology. For example, even by the mid-1970s it was fairly clear that each new generation of memory chip would have four times the storage capacity of the previous generation (and get faster over time). Thus, on this basis, the effects of rapid technical change would be expected to favour the larger firms and lead to market concentration.

This chapter is organised into eight further sections. Section 6.2 describes the background to the semiconductor industry. Section 6.3 introduces the empirical analysis of the memory market, while section 6.4 outlines the conceptual framework for the analysis. Section 6.5 examines the experience of six generations of dynamic RAM memory (DRAM), while section 6.6 looks at market concentration across generations. Sections 6.7 and 6.8 examine the corresponding developments for NMOS Static RAM and CMOS Static RAM. Section 6.9 concludes.

6.2 THE SEMICONDUCTOR INDUSTRY

The following characteristics of the semiconductor industry are particularly important here. First, there are two extremes in terms of the types of firm in the market. At one end are the 'captive producers' for whom semiconductors are manufactured entirely to meet internal needs. The most notable examples are the US companies IBM and AT&T.[1] At the other end are firms which produce and sell their entire output on the open market (referred to as 'merchant producers') to other manufacturers (e.g. computer firms, consumer electronics companies and so on). Most US semiconductor companies fall into the latter category, though from around the mid-1970s many started to decrease their overall dependence on commodity chip production.[2]

In between these two extremes are firms which manufacture for internal consumption as well as sell on the open market. This typifies the large diversified companies. In the 1980s these were principally Japanese, a few European firms (e.g. Philips, Siemens and SGS–Thomson) and some Korean firms (e.g. Samsung, Lucky-Goldstar and Hyundai). In general, Japanese producers have a substantially lower dependence on the semiconductor market for their total sales: in 1979, semiconductors' share of total sales for Japanese electronics firms was typically well under 10 per cent, compared with more than 70 per cent and for US companies (Chase Econometrics, 1980: 1.5–1.6).

Second, the semiconductor market has been subject to extremely sharp fluctuations between slump and boom. Three principal depressions occurred over 1974–5 (after the oil price rise), 1980–2 and 1985–6. In the 1974–5 depression, semiconductor companies (particularly in the USA) cut back on capital expenditure and reduced their workforce. Subsequently, when demand recovered many US producers were unable to meet demand (especially in the solid-state memory market). This supply gap was filled by the large diversified Japanese producers giving them a foothold in the US memory chip market. Consequently, US suppliers were much more reluctant to reduce capital spending despite the recession in the early 1980s; however, their profitability was adversely affected which restricted their capability to invest in new capacity. The diversified structure of the Japanese producers served to insulate them against the worst effects of the semiconductor recession and these firms were able to continue large-scale capital investment, thereby gaining a technological competitive edge.

Third, the prices of new semiconductor products generally fall very rapidly after their introduction on to the market. Prices are initially high (primarily due to low yields) and the market at this stage is largely in the hands of the most innovative firms. Over time, price reductions occur due to producers moving down the 'learning curve' and yields increase. Thus delayed entry can have a substantial impact on revenues and profitability.

Fourth, the industry is characterised by a high rate of both radical and incremental innovations. Thus, for example, new types of chip have been introduced (e.g. the microprocessor, SRAMs, flash-EPROMS, ASICs and so on). New generations of chip have also been introduced within any product category (for example, memory chips with greater storage capacity, more powerful microprocessors and so on). Moreover, there have been improvements within any single generation of product; for example, memory chips of any given capacity have become faster and consumed less power.

Solid-state memory chips

Solid-state memory chips were around in the 1960s but their strategic importance emerged principally after Intel's introduction of the 1K dynamic random access memory (DRAM) in late 1970 and the rapid growth of computer markets. This device was followed by a 4K version in 1974 while a 1K static random access memory (SRAM) was introduced a year or so earlier. DRAMs are easier to manufacture (as they have fewer components per memory cell) but their requirement for 'refreshing' means that they are slightly less easy to design with.

Solid-state memory chips have a simple and repetitious structure. Thus, memory chips show a higher level of integration (i.e. density of components on a chip) than other types of integrated circuits such as microprocessors which have a more complex structure. Within memory chips, DRAMs have the simplest (and hence highest density) structure. High volume production of this device, in combination with the simplicity of the basic cell, has meant that the DRAM can be used for experimentation, to push technology into higher levels of component density and result in the accumulation of valuable production experience which can feed into other devices. Thus, DRAMs are often referred to as the technology drivers of the semiconductor industry. In effect, these devices have been considered of strategic importance in the industry and the conventional wisdom has been that firms forced to exit DRAM production would have to surrender technological leadership in other semiconductor devices.

6.3 EMPIRICAL ANALYSIS OF MEMORY MARKET

The memory chip market is dominated by DRAMs (which in the 1980s accounted for around 75 per cent of the memory chip market), followed by SRAMs and EPROMs (which largely make up the remainder). Due to its large share of the total market, competition has been most intense in the DRAM segment. The main focus here is on DRAMs, with a briefer treatment of fast MOS SRAMs.[3]

Data collection

For each memory chip, data were collected (wherever possible) on the date of its introduction, the size of the device, the model number, its (typical) access time, power dissipation (on standby and active operation) and the fabrication technology (e.g. TTL, NMOS, CMOS and so on). This was obtained primarily from the journals *Electronics* and *Integrated Circuits International*. Data on power dissipation were not always given for the products and thus the information on this parameter could not be used to examine time trends systematically.

Generally, the leading edge memory devices have been initially fabricated in MOS (metal oxide semiconductor) and later in bipolar technology. This pattern can be observed for SRAMs. However, development of DRAMs has been so rapid and the product lifetime of each generation so short that generally these have not moved into the bipolar phase. Market share data could only be obtained for MOS devices, thus changes in technical performance of bipolar memory chips were not used in the final analysis.

Technical data were used to generate time series graphs of changes in access time for the different sizes of DRAMs and SRAMs. The interpretation of such graphs needs to take the nature and aims of the data collection into account. In this respect, the focus of this work was to examine the leading edge of memory chip technology and was thus, for example, concerned with identifying the memory chips with the fastest typical access time. Semiconductor firms often introduced a memory chip which was available in a range of speeds. In these cases, the device with the fastest access time was selected. Thus, the data presented are biased towards the fastest devices produced by any firm. Thus, the plots of access time for each size of memory chip can be used to determine the leading edge (i.e. fastest devices). However, they cannot be used to determine the slowest chips as these were deliberately excluded from the data.

Data on annual worldwide sales (by volume) of MOS memory ICs were obtained from Dataquest Europe. This data also included information on the average prices of the various devices, allowing both total revenue from sales as well as changes in the cost per bit over time to be plotted.[4]

Market share data were used to derive measures of both market concentration and changes (or 'disruption') in the market over time. Market 'disruption' in each year was calculated by summing the absolute change in market share for firms between that and the previous year. The four-firm concentration (CR4) (i.e. the market share of the top four firms in any particular year) was used as a leading indicator of concentration in the market. However, the CR4 can stay the same while the identity of the leading firms changes. Thus, the CR4 was also calculated for *firms* which had dominated the early (and similarly for those that dominated a later) period of the market. With these three measures of concentration it was possible to determine whether certain firms characteristically dominated the market during the specific stages of the life of the product.

6.4 CONCEPTUAL FRAMEWORK OF ANALYSIS

Changes in market shares and rates of technical change were examined in the framework of the product life cycle. In this respect, the life cycle of each memory device was divided into six main categories based on the sales (i.e. number of memory chips sold) curve of the product (Table 6.1). These are product introduction, early growth, late growth, maturity (i.e. saturation), decline and stagnation. The exact point at which these stages start and end is somewhat arbitrary but is usually based on the level of sales and their inflexion points, and this is the convention adopted here.

Table 6.1 Characteristics of different stages in the product life cycle

Stage I: Introduction
Introduction of innovation (and domination of the market) by a producer (or small number of other firms). Small level (though possibly with a high growth rate) of sales
Stage II: Early growth
Growth rate of sales high and reaches a maximum. Rapid growth in number of firms supplying the product
Stage III: Late growth
Sales continue to rise though growth rate beginning to decline and reaches zero
Stage IV: Maturity
Sales reach a plateau (i.e. maximum sales with slight variation in value) and growth rate approximately zero. Entry rate rises rapidly, reaching a peak and approximately stabilising
Stage V: Decline
Sales decline rapidly and the growth rate is increasingly negative. Rate of entry of new firms falls rapidly, reaches zero and then starts to become negative (i.e. firms exiting industry is greater than number entering)
Stage VI: Stagnation
Sales plateau to relatively low level, perhaps simply meeting replacement demand. Negative (but constant) entry rate

Source: Adapted from Gort and Klepper (1982)

The broad characteristics taken to define each phase are as follows.

- Stage I ('introduction') arises with the introduction of the innovation, generally by a single producer.
- In stage II ('early growth'), the rate of growth is high and reaches a maximum. (This stage also corresponds to a rapid increase in the number of suppliers and net entry rates of firms are positive.)
- Stage III ('late growth') is characterised by a declining growth rate which falls to zero (at which point sales are at a maximum).
- In stage IV, the growth rate is approximately zero and sales have more or less reached a plateau.
- In stage V ('decline') the growth rate begins to decline again and becomes increasingly negative (with sales starting to fall.) (The number of firms entering the market falls to below the number exiting, thus the total number of suppliers starts to fall).
- Finally, in stage VI ('stagnation'), the market may stabilise (with sales remaining approximately constant) and then eventually decline to zero due to product obsolescence or the introduction of a new product, for which the whole process is repeated.

Other approaches have also been used in the literature. For example, Gort and Klepper (1982) divide the product life cycle into five main stages, based on the number of firms supplying the market and the types of innovation characterising the different stages. Perez and Soete (1988) are concerned with the barriers to entry and windows of opportunity in the different stages of the life cycle of technology. Golding (1971) presents a three-stage model of the life cycle of semiconductor technology based on industry interviews in which he examined changes in sales revenue, semiconductor yield and production costs over time.

In the early stages, the market is likely to be dominated by firms which are the technological leaders (i.e. companies which are either the first into the market or very fast followers). Such firms may drive the technology forward in the early stages (a time when prices are also falling).

These early stages are characterised by growing technological and economic barriers to entry which would make it difficult for less technologically dynamic firms to keep up with, or successfully displace, the market leaders.

The strengths of firms which dominate these early stages vary. For example, some companies may be particularly adept at rapid product innovation but have little capacity (or desire) to continue into the later stages of the life cycle which are characterised by low prices and high volume production. Langlois *et al.* (1988) consider that such characteristics typify many of the US merchant producers. Such firms may thus deliberately adopt a price skimming policy in order to derive maximum benefit during the early period of high prices, exit from the market when the product starts to mature, shift production into the next generation of device and repeat this overall process. These strategies have sometimes been attributed to firms such as Intel and Fujitsu (OTA, 1983). Other technological leaders may, however, choose to remain in the market (and continue on to the further stages) and compete with other entrants by relying on a combination of production experience to move down the learning curve and capacity for low-cost high-volume production. In the literature such 'learning' appears virtually taken for granted. However, this process is neither automatic nor costless but requires the firm to take an active role in a stream of activities to push up yields, iron out bugs, decrease costs and so on.[5] In these early stages in the life cycle (characterised by a rapidly growing market) the number of producers would increase over time.

After stage IV (i.e. maturity), technological change may have stopped. Thus, after this stage, less technologically dynamic firms would find it easier to challenge the dominance of the market leaders. By stage V, market conditions would involve a combination of low prices and a rapid decline in total sales leading to intense price competition. Low-cost producers would be at an advantage and force other firms out of the market (thus leading to a fall in the total number of producers). During the final stage (stagnation), there is intense competition in a static market and the number of producers falls further.

6.5 SIX GENERATIONS OF DRAM

The size (i.e. storage capacity) of memory chips has increased very rapidly over time. However, DRAMs have played the pioneering technological role and been the first to move to the next generation (i.e. bit size) of device. DRAMs have been closely followed by EPROMs and SRAMs (Figure 6.1).

DRAMs have a very small product lifetime which, in combination with the high capital costs, has meant that incremental innovation tends to take the form of a move to a device which has four times the storage capacity of the previous generation; it is not economical to move in jumps of a factor of two. Thus, the 1K was followed by the 4K, 16K and so on (Table 6.2). The rapid life cycle of DRAMs meant that towards the end of the 1980s only those devices larger than 256K had not reached the period of rapid decline. The following analysis examines technical change and market structure for six generations of DRAMs (from the 4K to 1Mb device).

Table 6.2 Classification of stages in the DRAM life cycle

Stage		4K	16K*	16K†	64K	256K	1Mb
I	Introduction	1974–5	1976–7	1979–80	1979–80	1982–3	1985–6
II	Early Growth	1975–7	1977–80	1980–3	1980–4	1983–6	1986+
III	Late Growth	1977–8	1980–2	–	–	1986+	
IV	Maturity	1978–9	1982–3	1983	1984		
V	Rapid Decline	1979–83	1983+	1983+	1984+		
VI	Stagnation	1983+					

Source: Calculated using data from Dataquest Europe, Denham UK
Notes:
* 16K refers to the triple power supply version
† The single voltage version of this size of DRAM

4K DRAMs [6]

Development work on the 4K DRAM started in the early 1970s with samples sent out towards the end of 1973. The next year, when this chip was moving to volume production, coincided with a recession in the semiconductor industry, when US firms cut back on capital production and reduced their workforces.

Examining market and technological developments for the 4K DRAM shows a number of features. First, the number of producers initially increased rapidly, peaked in 1978 and declined. Second, the market (as measured by the CR4) initially became less concentrated over time, reaching a minimum of about 60 per cent in 1979, started to reconcentrate and returned to 100 per cent by 1984 (Figure 6.2). Third, the share of the initial market leaders followed a similar path. Fourth, the market share of the four firms that turn out to be the market leaders in 1985 starts off at less than 5 per cent but steadily and consistently increased over time. Fifth, three peaks are observed in market disruption in which around

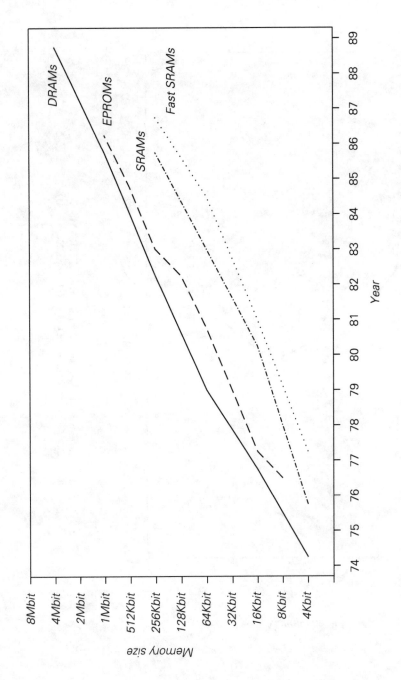

Figure 6.1 Introduction of memory chips
Source: Based on data from Dataquest Europe, Denham UK

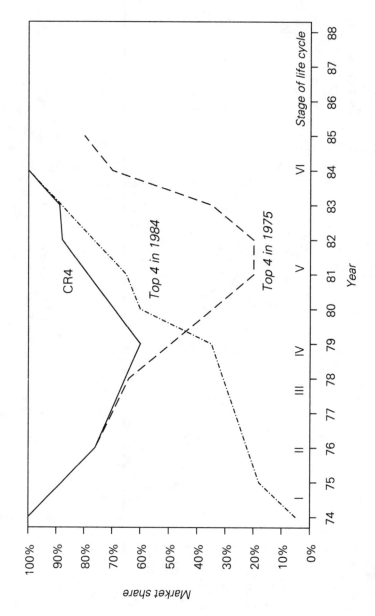

Figure 6.2 Market concentration for 4K DRAM
Source: Calculated with data from Dataquest Europe, Denham UK

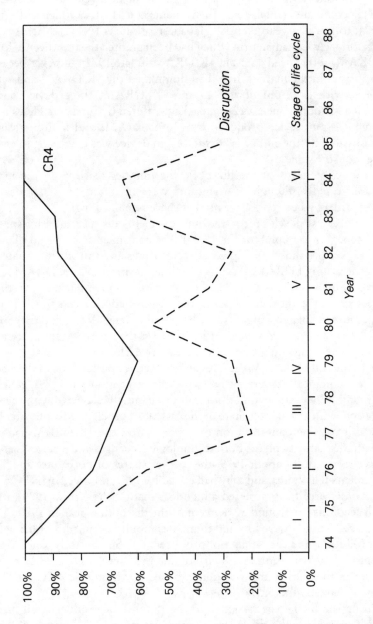

Figure 6.3 Concentration and disruption for 4K DRAMs
Source: Calculated with data from Dataquest Europe, Denham UK

25 to 40 per cent shares change hands (Figure 6.3). Disruption tends to be high at the beginning and end of a product life cycle (see Chapter 4).

The top four positions in the early stages of the life cycle were occupied by three US companies (Intel, Texas Instruments and Mostek) which had entered in 1974, followed a year later by a Japanese producer (NEC). Microsystems International (a Canadian firm which had been granted the Intel licence for the 1K DRAM) introduced a 22-pin 4K DRAM in late 1972 but never became a major player in the market. Intel had dominated the 1K DRAM and set the standard with a 22-pin device. In the 4K DRAM, three device designs competed for dominance: a 22-pin package offered by Intel and TI, a slightly different 22-pin device produced by Motorola/AMI and a 16-pin version from Mostek. By the end of 1976, the 16-pin device was beginning to emerge as the industry standard.

In the early stages of the life cycle the number of firms in the market increased rapidly, though new entrants were unable to displace the early market leaders whose collective market share remained high.

Technological development and improvements (as measured by speedier access time, for example) for the 4K DRAM continued to occur up till about 1979. Figure 6.4 shows the range of access times and introduction dates for each generation of DRAM. At the same time, the price of a 4K DRAM fell by a factor of ten from 1974 to 1978 where it stabilised in nominal terms (Figure 6.5). Significantly, the dates at which reductions in both access time and price stopped approximately coincided with the end of stage IV (i.e. maturity) of the 4K DRAM life cycle. Moreover, it is after 1978 that there is a steep decline in market share of the initial four leaders (Figure 6.2).

Up to the end of stage IV, the CR4 and collective market share of the leading four technological leaders were (with the exception of 1979) generally congruent. However, beyond this point these initially deviated with the CR4 increasing while the market share of the early leaders fell rapidly but later both showed increasing concentration occurring. After the 4K DRAM had gone through the maturity phase, both technological changes and price falls appear to have stopped. By about 1979, the market shares of both Intel and Texas Instruments fell rapidly and they had exited by 1981, followed by NEC a year later. These three firms suffered a high loss market share from 1979 to 1980 which accounts for around 80 per cent of the disruption peak in 1980.

In stage V, prices were low and total sales rapidly declined, favouring low-cost producers, and the number of producers fell. Significantly, only Mostek (a firm with a reputation as a high-volume producer) continued as a major supplier in the market and was joined by AMD, Motorola, STC (ITT) and National Semiconductor.

During the final stage (stagnation) the number of producers fell further. Mostek emerged as the single largest producer from 1983 onwards, followed by STC and SGS–ATES (both relatively less technologically sophisticated European companies).

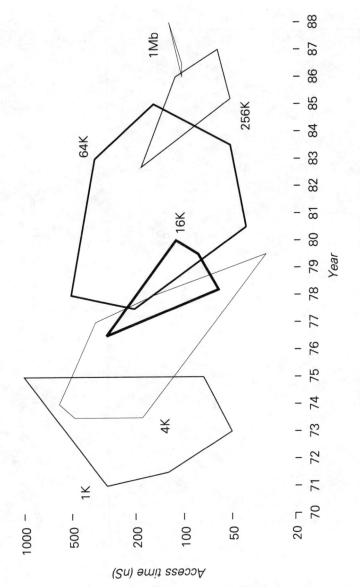

Figure 6.4 Access time of DRAMs by size of device

Source: Calculated with data collected from various issues of *Electronics and Integrated Circuits International*

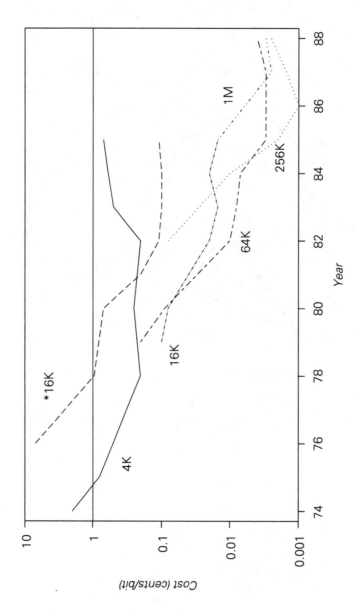

Figure 6.5 Historical cost curves for DRAMs
Source: Based on data from Dataquest Europe, Denham UK

16K DRAM (three power supply)

Two versions of the 16K DRAM were produced. The first was a multiple voltage supply device followed a few years later by a single supply version. The (three-voltage supply) 16K MOS DRAM (hereafter referred to as 16K* in the graphs and text) was introduced in 1975 (very soon after the 4K DRAM).

In 1975, three US merchant producers, Mostek, Intel and Texas Instruments, announced the 16K DRAM with limited production taking place the next year. Fujitsu, the Japanese computer manufacturer, entered the market in 1977 along with three other US firms, Motorola, National Semiconductor and Fairchild. Texas Instruments was initially unable to move down the learning curve as quickly as the other entrants, as its first 16K DRAM did not use 'double polysilicon' (adopted by both Mostek and Intel). Hence, there was a delay while it reintroduced a 16K device based on this technology (UN, 1986: 169). Consequently, Texas Instruments lost market share in the first year or so with the result that the top four producers in 1977 were Mostek, Intel, National Semiconductor and Fujitsu.[7]

All three initial US entrants experienced production problems (considered to be one factor which allowed a number of Japanese suppliers to gain market share) and hence market deconcentration for the 16K* device was much faster than for the 4K DRAM. Thus, the CR4 and market share of the initial top four (in 1977) producers fell dramatically from 1977 to 1978 (the collective share of the latter dropped from around 95 per cent to about 45 per cent). Market disruption in 1978 was extremely high (just over 95 per cent).[8] This disruption was principally a result of major losses by the early market leaders and the gains by both a new entrant, NEC which had captured nearly a 20 per cent share, and the re-entry of Texas Instruments.[9]

Japanese suppliers had entered the market about two years behind the leading US players. However, they began to make major inroads into the market, largely at the expense of US suppliers, after shortages arose in 1978. These shortages arose mainly for two reasons (OTA, 1983: 189). First, as a result of the 1974–5 recession, US producers had reduced their workforces and cut back on investment in both new capacity and R&D expenditure. They were thus unable to meet the sudden rapid increase in demand when the market recovered, which was connected with the cost per bit for the 16K DRAM falling below that of the 4K device in 1978. Second, in the late 1970s, IBM could not supply its own needs for 16K parts from captive production and began to purchase these devices on the open market.[10]

In terms of the world market, however, there was remarkably little change in the share of the initial (and final) top four producers from 1978 until about 1982 (though market disruption varied between about 20 and 30 per cent).[11] This represented the period up to the end of stage III (i.e. up to where the market continued to grow). This stability cannot be explained in terms of technological development (i.e. faster access time)[12] which had stopped after about 1978. Another explanation is that rapid market growth favoured early market leaders as they were further down the learning curve than later entrants. Moreover, another incentive for the early leaders to remain in the market was the slowdown in price falls of 16K* DRAMs over the period from 1978 to 1981. After 1981 when the technological frontier, in terms of increasingly speedier access time, had stopped advancing the collective share of the initial four firms declined rapidly while that of the final four market leaders began a steep climb.[13]

These latter leaders comprised Siemens, STC (ITT), SGS–Ates and NEC, all low-cost, high-volume producers. Thus, as for the 4K device, the firms that came to dominate the market towards the end of the product cycle were substantially different from the early entrants.[14]

The early technological leaders (characterised principally by innovative capacity rather than volume production) for the 16K* DRAM again appear to have deliberately exited or decreased output after the first few stages of the product life cycle to shift production to the next (and higher priced) generation of DRAM. Thus, while Intel's share over the first two stages of the 16K* DRAM life cycle (i.e. 1976 to 1980) fell from over one-third of the market to 2 per cent or so, by 1979 Intel had moved on to the next generation of DRAM and introduced the single-voltage 16K DRAM.[15] By 1985 both Intel and Mostek had exited while the combined share of the other two, National Semiconductor and Fujitsu, was around 8 per cent.[16] Disruption increased (peaking in 1983), largely due to the fall in market share of the early leaders. A later peak in 1986 was due to a combination of the loss of share by the early leaders and the rapid rise of firms such as Siemens, STC and SGS–Ates in the latter parts of the life cycle.

16K DRAM (single power supply)

The second generation 16K DRAM (using a single voltage) was introduced in 1979 by Intel. This technology was based on technological innovations used for the single-voltage 64K DRAM (ICE, 1979: 2–12). In the first few years, the market share of the initial top four firms, Intel, Hitachi, Fujitsu and Motorola, fell only slightly, then declined rapidly to around 70 per cent by 1983 (i.e. by the end of stage II), subsequently recovered and the market then reconcentrated.[17] Over this time, there was a rapid increase in the share of the top four firms that dominated the market in stage V.[18] However, three firms, Motorola, Hitachi and Fujitsu, continued to be in the top four throughout the life cycle of the 16K DRAM (Table 6.3). Texas Instruments appears not to have been able to enter the market successfully and achieved a market share of a few per cent at best.

Rapid technical change (in terms of faster access time) and falling prices continued until about 1982 (Figures 6.4 and 6.5). Disruption was generally high, for example, between 60 per cent and 70 per cent from 1981 to 1983.[19] In the first few years such disruption principally represented loss of market share

Table 6.3 The changing patterns of market leadership in DRAMs

Memory introduction dates and the initial leading four firms in each market segment:

Date	1974	1976	1979	1979	1982	1985
Leading firms	Intel	Mostek	Intel	Motorola	Hitachi	Toshiba
	TI	Intel	Hitachi	Fujitsu	Fujitsu	Hitachi
	Mostek	NEC	Fujitsu	Hitachi	NEC	AT&T
	NEC	Fujitsu	Motorola	TI	AT&T	NEC

Number of major suppliers in world market three years after introduction of DRAM:

Date	1974	1976	1979	1979	1982	1985
DRAM size	4K	16K*	16K	64K	256K	1Mb
Japanese	1	4	2	6	6	7
US	8	8	5	3	5	4
European	1	2	0	0	0	1
Korean	0	0	0	0	0	1

Source: Based on data from Dataquest Europe, Denham UK
Note: One of the four US producers of the 1Mb DRAM within three years of its introduction was the previously captive producer AT&T

by the predominant leader, Intel. Subsequent disruption was high because of losses and gains between the top four firms with Motorola emerging as the leading supplier with more than 50 per cent of the market by 1985.[20]

64K DRAM

US producers were concerned at Japanese firms' successful entry into the US market for 16K parts. By the late 1970s, competition in the DRAM market between US merchant firms and large diversified Japanese companies was becoming increasingly intense, with both groups positioning themselves for market leadership of the next generation of DRAM. Thus, in 1979–80 it was estimated that expenditure on semiconductor plant and equipment by the ten largest Japanese firms was more than $1.2 billion while that for the ten largest US producers was around $2.1 billion (Borrus *et al.*, 1983: 234–5). Moreover, Siemens (a European firm) and AMI had announced that they would be leapfrogging the industry by using VMOS technology (Altman, 1978: 80).

Industry consensus was that the 64K DRAM would be a single-voltage device (Capece, 1979: 125). Thus, moving from the 16K to 64K DRAM was a bigger jump than previous technological leaps in DRAMs due to having to increase memory capacity by a factor of four and operate on a single voltage. As an intermediate step, a number of firms had produced the single-voltage 16K DRAM. As the following will show, in practice the technological difficulties were greater than had been envisaged, leading to delayed entry by a number of producers.

Unlike previous generations of the DRAM, it was a Japanese firm, Fujitsu, which was first with a 64K sample, followed by Motorola, Texas Instruments and then Hitachi. Fujitsu initially offered a twin-voltage supply device (as did Hitachi) followed by Texas Instruments which announced a single-voltage version using scaled NMOS technology (ICE, 1979: 2–12). By 1980, there were another three Japanese suppliers, Mitsubishi, Toshiba and NEC, but only one more US entrant (Intel, which had less than a 1 per cent share) in the market. Intel had previously taken a leading position in the market for earlier generations of DRAM (and had invented the 1K DRAM in 1970) but appears to have been slower off the mark than its competitors. Its weak market position was further undermined when in August 1981 it had to withdraw its 64K DRAM due to soft error problems and had to resample the next year.[21]

By 1981, five Japanese firms (Fujitsu, Hitachi, Mitsubishi, NEC and Oki) had attained volume production of 64K DRAMs but only two US producers (Texas Instruments and Motorola). All were large diversified companies.

Japanese suppliers had generally taken leading positions in the market, largely through extrapolating the design for their 64K DRAMs on the earlier 16K DRAM (Borrus et al., 1983: 235). Thus they were able to use the substantial experience and knowledge accumulated from the design and manufacture of the earlier generation of DRAM, first to produce the 64K DRAM quickly and second to move down the learning curve.

On the other hand, US manufacturers ran into three main problems. First, many US firms had opted to move to innovative production processes and designs, some of which ran into problems. Most US firms had decided on a new design for the 64K DRAM which would result in a smaller chip. Unfortunately, these smaller designs (as Intel, for example, found to its cost) were prone to soft errors (from alpha particle radiation emitted from the packaging) and had to be withdrawn from the market. Japanese designs were larger and did not suffer from this problem. In effect, attempts by other US firms to lose the competition through innovation turned out to be a risky strategy. Thus, National Semiconductor was:

> gambling millions on the most sophisticated design in the industry for the . . . 64K RAM. (. . .) If it can master production of this design, it will have a head start on making the ultra-high-capacity 256K chips of the late 1980s.
>
> (Uttal, 1981: 96)

Unfortunately, National Semiconductor had problems achieving sufficiently high yields using its 'triple poly' process. Texas Instruments had used a technologically more complex design which took longer to complete and so was unable to meet planned shipment dates (Bylinsky, 1981: 55).

Motorola was more fortunate in having followed a similar design to the Japanese and was thus able to achieve early market entry. Yet even Motorola

118

had to recall some 2 million 64K DRAMs in early 1983 which had higher than 'normal' failure rates[22] though these problems were resolved quickly with production moving to full capacity by May (ICE 1984: 34–5).

Second, design of the 64K DRAM required 'continuity in teamwork' and long-term development (Bylinsky, 1981: 55). High staff turnover in the US semiconductor industry generally ran counter to these requirements, apart from Texas Instruments and Motorola which had located away from Silicon Valley.

Third, delayed entry (and thus low yields) meant higher production costs due to being at an earlier stage of the learning curve. Thus, price competition would be more difficult to sustain. Unfortunately, the industry moved into a recession over 1980–2 and semiconductor prices fell, with extremely adverse effects on profit levels. Thus, industry analysts estimated that while sales in 1981 were only 10 per cent down on the previous year, profits on average declined by 65 per cent.[23]

The rate and severity of these price falls were unforeseen. While the exact prices quoted vary with different sources, all suggest that actual prices were much lower than expected. Thus, for example, in early 1980 industry estimates for the price of 64K DRAMs were around $50. However, by 1981–2 actual prices had fallen to $10, then stabilised at around $5–7 before falling to $3–5 by the end of the year (OECD, 1985: 35). Similarly:

> industry analysts had not expected 64K RAM prices to fall below $10 per chip until 1982, Japanese firms had begun to quote a $4 price by late 1981 in an effort to pre-empt American market competition.
>
> (Borrus et al., 1983: 236)

The price falls had a knock-on effect for other DRAMs and thus, for example, depressed the prices of the 16K parts. At the same time, a number of firms seeking to enter the market were having production problems. In effect, given the rapidity of the price falls, delayed entry by firms would be very costly.

Intense price competition in memory chips caused major difficulties for US merchant firms, particularly those most reliant on sales of these devices, such as Mostek (ICE, 1982: 68). Similarly, National Semiconductor (a firm with a reputation as an aggressive low-cost producer) was forced by short-term profitability pressures to sacrifice strategic product planning and cut back on expenditure on new capital investment in memory production for which it was a commodity supplier.[24] In effect, such problems not only threatened the capacity of US merchant firms to compete successfully in the current generation of DRAMs but, more significantly, to participate in future generations:

> these low prices have deprived US manufacturers of the early profits they had expected to make on the 64K – profits they need to finance new products. Stragglers into the 64K market will have trouble making money on the chip.
>
> (Bylinsky, 1981: 57)

Concern over DRAM prices and the loss of share by US companies in their domestic market led the US Justice Department to investigate allegations of price fixing from late 1981 to early 1982 by six Japanese firms, Hitachi, Mitsubishi, NEC, Toshiba, Fujitsu and Oki.[25]

Overall, there were a number of growing technological and economic barriers to entry into the fast moving 64K DRAM market. For instance, both access time and prices decreased rapidly from 1978 to about 1981 (Figure 6.4) while the latter continued to fall until 1986 (Figure 6.5). Yet, despite these difficulties market deconcentration was very rapid over the first few years. Thus, by 1981 both the CR4 and the collective share of the top four firms in 1980 (Fujitsu, Motorola, Hitachi and Texas Instruments) had fallen from 90 per cent to around 70 per cent.[26] Over this time, the share of the top four firms in 1988 (Samsung, NEC, Matshushita and Texas Instruments) had built up rapidly. (In 1981, the share of this group refers to NEC and Texas Instruments as Matsushita did not initiate production until 1983 and Samsung a year later.)

This suggests that rapid technical change combined with falling prices was not enough to stop the early leaders from rapidly losing market share. (Market deconcentration, however, was considerably less for the largest five producers.) One explanation is that while, by the early 1980s accelerated innovation both within and between generations of DRAM was leading to a shake-out, the firms left in the market were generally fairly evenly matched in terms of economic resources and technological strengths. Thus, these losses were to firms of similar size and structure.

The firms having the greatest difficulties were US merchant producers (e.g. Intel, National Semiconductor and Mostek) for which semiconductors represented a very high proportion of total sales. On the other hand, firms which were either able to continue in the market or make significant gains tended to be the biggest (generally diversified) manufacturers such as the Japanese electronics companies and larger US producers such as Texas Instruments and Motorola. Such a situation led one industry commentator to state that:

> the signs are unmistakable that it's no longer the Silicon Valley companies but the bigger corporations that have the experience and resources to handle complex development and manufacturing programs such as the 64K and its successors require.
>
> (Bylinsky, 1981: 57, my emphasis)

Consequently, some US merchant producers had to look to Japanese suppliers for technology in order to enter the market (a stark reversal of historical technology transfer deals between US and Japanese companies). For example, in 1982, National Semiconductor went to Oki Semiconductor for 64K DRAM technology[27] and the following year signed a long-term agreement for the development of future generations of this device.[28]

Overall though, while market deconcentration was rapid, losses in share by the leaders might have been much greater without these technological and economic changes. For example, while the firms that dominated the latter part of the life cycle initially made rapid gains (at the expense of the initial leaders), their share was remarkably stable up to about the point where prices had stabilised. In this respect, the disruption curve took the form of a trough between 1982 and 1985.[29]

After 1981, the rate of deconcentration started to slow down and by 1984 – corresponding to the end of stage II of the 64K DRAM life cycle – the CR4 had fallen to about 50 per cent but then started to rise. The collective market share of the top four firms in 1980 fell slightly faster and reached a plateau over 1984 and 1985. Over this period, the share of the top four firms in 1988 stabilised at around 25 per cent.[30]

After 1982, economic recovery led to boom conditions, halting the price fall of 64K DRAMs, for example. US producers found it difficult to meet the surge in demand and began investment in new facilities (OECD, 1985: 25)[31]. Unsurprisingly, a number of other firms also entered the market. Significantly, though, these were all new start-ups, such as the US-based Micron Technology and the European firm Inmos (which had attempted to leapfrog into 64K DRAMs). Four Korean manufacturers, all large diversified companies, were also seeking to enter the market, of which the first successful entrant was Samsung (an electronics company), entering production under licence from Micron Technology.[32]

The rate of loss of share by the initial leaders (and gain by the subsequent leaders) was much higher after about 1986. An economic downturn in 1985 led to the 64K DRAM falling in price, when the initial market leaders started to reduce production and shift to the higher priced 256K part.

The decline in prices also put pressure on US producers. Intel, which had played a pioneering role in the early history of DRAMs, decided to exit completely from DRAMs and Texas Instruments pondered whether to follow suit, leaving only Mostek (acquired by United Technologies in 1979) and Micron Technology as volume 64K DRAM producers.[33] However, Mostek was also experiencing problems in the 64K DRAM market due to price degradation with estimated losses of $328 million in 1985.[34] Mostek was sold for $70 million to the European firm, Thomson, in the mid-1980s to form Thomson Components–Mostek Corporation (TCMC) in a deal which provided United Technologies with technical assistance and access to Mostek's technology.[35] Over the next year, Mostek's workforce was cut drastically, from 10,000 to 800, and Thomson withdrew the company from the commodity DRAM business, instead shifting it to gate arrays, telecom chips and standard cells. It retained memory production only in fast SRAMs and military DRAMs.[36]

Market disruption increased dramatically in 1988 (around 70 per cent compared with 40 per cent the previous year), with the Korean firm Samsung taking the leading position with a share of slightly more than 25 per cent.[37]

121

256K DRAM

By the early 1980s the large diversified Japanese electronics companies had come to dominate the 64K DRAM market, at the expense of US merchant firms, and were perhaps poised to achieve this in the next generation of DRAM. Given US sensitivity to such an outcome, Japanese suppliers began to increase investment in US-based facilities.

Hitachi was the first to enter the 256K DRAM market, in 1982. By the next year another five Japanese but only two US companies (AT&T and the merchant firm, Mostek) had started production.[38] This entry of new producers resulted in a high initial value of disruption. However, other US firms were also aiming to supply the market. For example, National Semiconductor was planning to introduce a triple poly device for the first quarter of 1984.[39] Motorola was also planning entry but had delayed its sample, scheduled for early 1983, to improve the design of its DRAM.[40]

Access time of leading edge 256K DRAMs fell from 1983 to 1985. However, this did not stop rapid market deconcentration. Thus, by 1985 the CR4 had decreased to just over 75 per cent, though the share of the initial top four leaders fell even faster. Both Mostek (which never achieved a market greater than 0.5 per cent) and AT&T had exited from the market by about 1986. Mostek withdrew because of major losses incurred through price degradation in the market. AT&T had been much more successful but internal demand for 256K DRAMs rose so rapidly that (except to initial customers) it stopped supplying on the open market (ICE, 1985: 136). New entrants which had made significant gains were other Japanese firms and Texas Instruments. Overall market disruption from 1983–6 was approximately stable at around 35 per cent.

By 1985, demand in the USA was down by 30 per cent from the previous year and the industry faced a recession.[41] Competition intensified, with 256K DRAM prices reaching around $5–7 in March 1985 compared with $25–50 the previous year.[42] As with earlier generations of memory chips, however, continuous and rapid price falls had taken place from the introduction of first samples (in 1982) through to 1985 (Figure 6.5). However, US merchant producers were particularly badly affected, especially as most had not entered the market as quickly as many Japanese suppliers and were thus still in the early (and thus low-yield high-production cost) stages of the learning curve. For example, Texas Instruments did not start volume production until 1985, while in the same year National Semiconductor announced that it was stopping sampling until the market recovered and instead shifted production to customised chips.[43] According to Charles Sporck of National Semiconductor this was a much more widespread problem in which 'all domestic manufacturers, with the exception of Texas Instruments, have more or less decided it is impossible to continue competing in the dynamic random access memory market'.[44] Thus, despite the strategic importance attributed to

DRAM technology, US producers were faced with major losses (estimated at around $1 billion) and were forced to cut back staff and capital investment.[45]

Inmos had just entered the market in 1985 and the recession contributed to its decision to phase out direct manufacture of DRAMs and instead license its designs to Inter Alia and NMB Semiconductor while shifting its focus on memory products to SRAMs.[46]

Korean firms also had problems. In 1985, price degradation led Hyundai to close its US wafer fabrication plant (opened the previous year at a cost of $40 million), which lost $21 million in that year,[47] and sell it to Siemens. Lucky–Goldstar had planned to enter the 256K DRAM market but instead had to go for 64K (CMOS) SRAMs.[48]

Japanese manufacturers were also affected by the price falls. For example, Hitachi's first half-year profits were down for the first time in nearly a decade while Fujitsu's profits were down by about a third compared with the previous year.[49] However, on the whole, Japanese firms shifted production from the 64K DRAMs to the (relatively higher priced) 256K devices. Moreover, their diversified structure and large size allowed them to continue capital investment despite the economic downturn; Japanese firms were estimated to have spent $3 billion on capital investment, with NEC, Toshiba and Hitachi each accounting for $500 million.[50]

By early 1986, both Intel and Mostek (which in the early history of memory chips had been the acknowledged technological leaders in the DRAM business) had exited from DRAMs, leaving only two large US firms (AT&T and Texas Instruments) and a new merchant producer (Micron Technology) for which this device continued to play a major development role.[51] Motorola and AMD relegated DRAMs to a much more limited development role, while others shifted to using SRAMs and EPROMs as technological process drivers.

US memory firms were coming under sustained technological and economic pressure from the Japanese suppliers and started to retaliate. Thus, in 1986, Texas Instruments filed a DRAM patent lawsuit against Japanese firms (initially Hitachi, Oki, Fujitsu and Toshiba but later extended to include Matshushita, NEC, Mitsubishi and Sharp). A Korean firm, Samsung, was also named in the infringement action. NEC, however, filed a counter infringement against Texas Instruments the next month.[52] Micron Technology alleged that Japanese firms were dumping 256K DRAMs on the US market and in 1986 the US International Trade Commission initiated an inquiry into alleged dumping, resulting in the US–Japan Trade Agreement which essentially established floor prices for DRAMs (and EPROMs).

The market shares of the leading Japanese firms started to decline after about 1986. However, this deconcentration was not primarily due to a lack of advances in the technological frontier nor to price stability in the market but to US concern about its trade deficit in semiconductors with Japan which led to the US–Japan Trade Agreement. This had a number of effects. First, minimum (referred to as floor minimum values, FMVs) prices were established, below which Japanese suppliers could not sell. FMVs were calculated for each producer on the basis of confidential cost data sent to the ITC which then added a 12 per cent profit allowance. Flouting FMVs meant that dumping duties of between 20 and 110 per cent would be imposed on Japanese-made 256K DRAMs.[53] In response to FMVs and falling demand, Hitachi reduced chip production by about one-fifth, including a virtual shutdown of all production of DRAMs, while shifting production in the USA from memory to logic ICs.[54]

Second, MITI asked the leading Japanese producers to cut production in order to reduce trade friction with the USA[55] and thus lessen the possibility of trade sanctions being applied.

Third, Japanese firms began to place large orders for chips from US firms in a bid to address the market access issue.[56] The rise in orders was not supported by actual demand, but the Japanese companies were keen to demonstrate that they were responding to MITI demands to buy foreign chips.

Fourth, Japanese firms deliberately reduced investment in new plant to lower their potential manufacturing capability. Thus, while Japanese producers had increased volume production until 1986, in the following years Hitachi and Toshiba continued to lower output, while other major Japanese firms (e.g. NEC, Fujitsu and Mitsubishi) stabilised production. Consequently, the productive capacity of the major (Japanese) players was deliberately constrained while at the same time many US suppliers had exited from the market. The subsequent market recovery in 1987 resulted in a shortage of DRAMs and prices rose (Figure 6.5). Higher prices potentially encouraged the re-entry of US merchant firms into DRAMs, though by 1988 only Intel and Vitelic were producing these devices. However, the principal beneficiaries were the large diversified companies in both Korea (principally Samsung and Lucky–Goldstar)[57] and Europe (Siemens), with the former group attempting to enter memory chip production by leapfrogging to the 256K DRAM level.

Market disruption jumped to around 50 per cent in 1987 due to a fall in the market shares of Japanese firms and an increase by other suppliers (principally Texas Instruments and the Korean firm Samsung).[58] Some of the larger US merchant firms were beginning to re-enter the market, primarily through technological deals with Japanese companies. Thus, Motorola had set up a joint venture in Japan with Toshiba.[59] (This latter venture ran into problems as 256K DRAMs made by Motorola using Toshiba dice in Japan and assembled in Malaysia were also subject to FMVs.[60])

By 1988, the leading established Japanese producers were further reducing output in order to move on to the 1Mb DRAM, though both NEC and Fujitsu were still among the top four suppliers. Texas Instruments had captured the leading position while Samsung (the most advanced Korean firm) was fourth.[61] High demand led other producers (such as the new Japanese start-up firm, NMB) to continue to produce the 256K part and was considered to slow down the shift to the 1Mb device. Intel was considering re-entering the DRAM market (initially through buying parts from Samsung).[62]

1Mb DRAM

By the mid-1980s, the large Japanese electronics companies had decisively overtaken the highly innovative US merchant semiconductor firms and emerged as the undisputed technological winners in the DRAM market. Overall, though, this market was becoming increasingly dominated by large (US, Japanese, Korean or even European) diversified firms which had the economic and technological resources to plough into ever more costly capital investment and weather adverse market conditions.

NTT was one of the first companies to signal entry to the next generation of DRAM by announcing a 280K DRAM (using an 0.8μm design rule) as a small intermediate step to the 1Mb part.[63] At the end of 1984, Toshiba announced the development of a 1Mb DRAM,[64] followed by Fujitsu in June 1985.[65]

At the same time, a number of other firms (in Europe, the USA and Korea) signalled their intention to enter the race for 1Mb DRAMs. Thus, in 1984, Siemens[66] (a European company not considered to be at or near the leading edge of solid-state memory technology) was planning to manufacture 1Mb and 4Mb DRAMs by the end of the 1980s through the development of sub-micron process technology. Siemens planned to manufacture 1Mb DRAMs in 1986.[67] In 1985, Siemens made further progress through a technological agreement with Toshiba on the design, testing and wafer fabrication of 1Mb CMOS DRAMs.[68]

In early 1985, AT&T (which before its sales of 256K DRAMs on the open market had been a captive producer for memory chips) announced that it would be developing a 1Mb DRAM with volume production to be achieved within a year.[69]

Korean firms – aided by the government – were also seeking (through a strategy of leapfrogging) to close the gap with the leading Japanese producers despite only having entered advanced semiconductor technology in the early 1980s. Thus, in 1985, the Korean government set up a programme to develop VLSI technology to aid the entry of four domestic firms (Samsung, Lucky–Goldstar, Daewoo and Hyundai) into advanced DRAM technology, with production of 1Mb DRAMs scheduled for 1989.[70] Only Samsung and Lucky–Goldstar were already DRAM manufacturers while the others were seeking to enter semiconductor production. Total investment in plant and equipment was estimated to be around $1 billion over the next five years.[71] Market entry was to be achieved through licensing agreements on state-of-the-art technology. (At the same time, an R&D alliance of Korean firms was established to develop 4Mb DRAMs over a three-year period.)

Accelerated development in the DRAM market meant that only the largest firms were able to stay in the race. A few new US memory start-ups (e.g. Micron Technology and Vitelic) had entered the DRAM market with the 256K device but price falls during the 1985–6 recession adversely affected their ability to finance continued technological development. Thus, by the time that the industry had moved to the 1Mb DRAM, the market had become highly concentrated with large firms playing the leading role.[72] Two relatively new firms, Vitelic and Micron Technology, also entered the 1Mb market but two years after the leading players. As expected, Japanese firms were the first to enter the market. Toshiba (which had been a late entrant in 64K DRAMs but had become a major producer of the 256K part) was the most advanced and in October 1985 had already reached volume production ahead of its nearest rivals, Hitachi and AT&T. By the next year, another four Japanese firms (NEC, Mitsubishi, Fujitsu and Oki) but only one US firm (Texas Instruments) had entered the market.[73]

With the exception of Toshiba, many firms experienced yield problems[74] which delayed the move to volume production.[75] For example, sampling was not carried out until 1987 by Siemens, Samsung (the only Korean supplier to have entered the market by 1988) and Micron Technology, with volume production the following year. Vitelic started production earlier but ran into problems and filed for bankruptcy. NMB (the 1984 Japanese start-up) began volume production in 1988 (through a technology licence from Vitelic in 1986).[76] Unsurprisingly, there appears to have been no reduction in access time of the 1Mb DRAM between 1986 and 1988 (Figure 6.4).

Despite these factors, market deconcentration for the 1Mb DRAM was very rapid (and the CR4 declined slightly faster than for the 256K DRAM).[77] The market share of the initial leading four firms fell dramatically, principally due to losses by the market leader, Toshiba, and to AT&T exiting in 1987 (perhaps to divert production for in-house needs). However, the market was still highly concentrated, with the top six producers in 1988 accounting for about 80 per cent of the market.[78]

Increases in demand and the slow move to volume production led to shortages of the device. In mid-1988, it was estimated that supply could only meet 60 per cent of demand.[79] Thus, Texas Instruments' production of 1Mb DRAMs had already been sold to users (and it had thus turned to NMB for additional supplies), both Hitachi and Mitsubishi were quoting delivery times of six months or more and Toshiba was not taking orders from new customers.[80] The memory chip shortage and rising prices were leading a number of US merchant producers (such as National Semiconductor) to consider re-entering the market.[81] Motorola had already re-entered the DRAM market (through a joint venture with Toshiba).

On the surface it would appear that capacities for technological development were becoming less effective for deterring market entry. However, this is misleading. Many firms (typically the US merchant suppliers) had been shaken out of the DRAM market. Those that remained were the large diversified companies which were generally evenly matched economically and technologically. Thus, by the late 1980s, the DRAM market had become more concentrated and the locus of innovation in the DRAM market had shifted from small to the large firms.

6.6 MARKET CONCENTRATION ACROSS GENERATIONS OF DRAM

Earlier it was found that the market share of some of the initial market leaders in particular DRAM segments rapidly declined after a few years. This could occur for a variety of reasons. Generally, however, it was considered that some of the early market leaders deliberately exited to move from a generation of device which had become substantially cheaper to the next (higher priced) generation of chip. Such behaviour would suggest that market structure would be much more stable if considered across all the various DRAM markets. Market concentration over all sizes of DRAM decreased over time, with the CR4 falling from 100 per cent in 1974 to 60 per cent by 1978, and then stabilising at around 55 per cent until 1987.[82] Overall, market disruption was much less over time across all DRAM markets than within each generation of DRAM.[83]

DRAM market development

In one sense, the market for DRAMs has become increasingly concentrated over time. Thus while in the early 1970s the dominant role was played by small new start-ups (Intel and Mostek), by the late 1980s, technological leadership had shifted to the large producers, typically Japanese companies, though diversified European and Korean producers had also entered the market (Table 6.3).

This result is not unduly surprising. First, large firms would be most effective in losing the competition in markets where there was a relatively clear vision of the future. Low uncertainty in the direction of change is a characteristic feature of solid-state memories. Thus, to quote the US Office of Technology Assessment:

> One of the attractions of the memory market – in addition to the vast market – is the relative orderly and predictable progress of the tech-nology; circuit design is vital – along with excellent process capability – but more straightforward than logic or microprocessors. Everyone in the industry knows that generations of dynamic RAMs will be 256K chips, followed by 1 megabit. . . . Progress in static RAMs and in the various types of ROMs is likewise rather easy to predict.
>
> (OTA, 1983: 190, my emphasis)

Second, the steady increase in the capital costs of entry into the industry was another factor militating against small firms.[84]

6.7 NMOS STATIC MEMORY CHIPS (SRAMs)

Data on technical change and market structure for SRAMs are given separately for NMOS and CMOS devices. Early generations of MOS SRAMs were initially fabricated in NMOS, but later these were made in CMOS. Over time, however, sales of CMOS SRAMs overtook those of NMOS and the latter technology appears not to have been used for devices beyond about 64K.

The 4K fast NMOS SRAM was introduced in 1977, followed by the 16K device three years later and a 64K part in 1984 (Table 6.4). Market data are given for three generations (4K, 16K and 64K) of fast NMOS SRAMs. Market concentration for the 4K and 16K device appears to follow a similar pattern of initial deconcentration and then reconcentration. The 64K SRAM, however, appears to have maintained a highly concentrated market with the CR4 remaining at 100 per cent from 1985 to 1988.[85] Thus, only market share data for the first two devices are analysed below.

Table 6.4 Classification of stages in the NMOS life cycle

Stage		4K	16K	64K
I	Introduction	1977	1980–1	1984
II	Early growth	1977–82	1981–4	1984–5
III	Late growth	1982–4	1984–5	1985–7
IV	Maturity	1984	1985	1987
V	Rapid decline	1984–8	1985–8	–
VI	Stagnation	–	–	–

Source: Based on data from Dataquest Europe, Denham UK

4K NMOS SRAM

Intel was the first firm to introduce a fast 4K SRAM (the 2147) and monopolised the market for about two years before other firms entered (ICE, 1979: 2–11). Intel was later joined by NEC, National Semiconductor and Motorola. The decline of these four early leaders appears to go through three phases (Figure 6.6). In the first phase (from 1978 to 1983), there is a very rapid decline in their market share. The early part of this phase is characterised by very high levels of disruption (largely through the loss of market share by Intel). Surprisingly, though, this phase corresponds to the period over which the access time (Figure 6.7) and the price of the 4K NMOS SRAM (Figure 6.8) continued to decrease. However, the most rapid decrease in access time took place between 1975 and 1978 and the rate of decrease was much slower from 1978 to 1983. Significantly, the market leader (Intel) accounted for virtually 100 per cent of the market in 1977 and 1978. Intel's share rapidly declined over

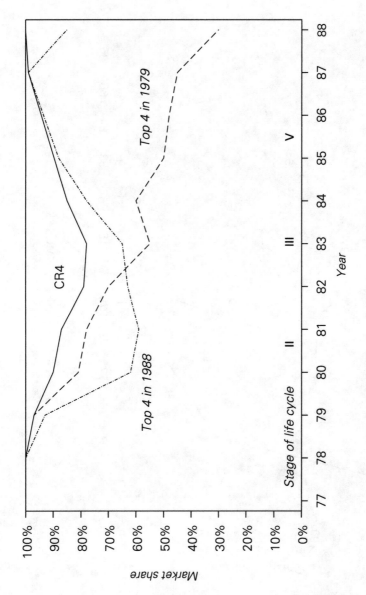

Figure 6.6 Market concentration: 4K NMOS SRAMs
Source: Calculated with data from Dataquest Europe, Denham UK

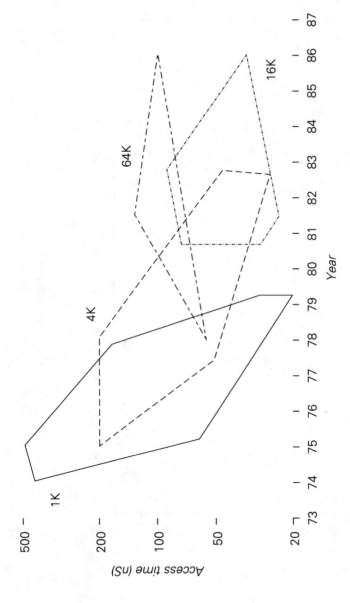

Figure 6.7 Access time of NMOS SRAMs

Source: Calculated with data collected from various issues of *Electronics* and *Integrated Circuits International*

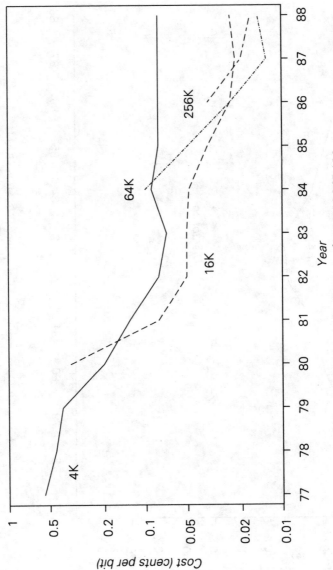

Figure 6.8 Historical cost curves: fast NMOS SRAMs
Source: Based on data from Dataquest Europe, Denham UK

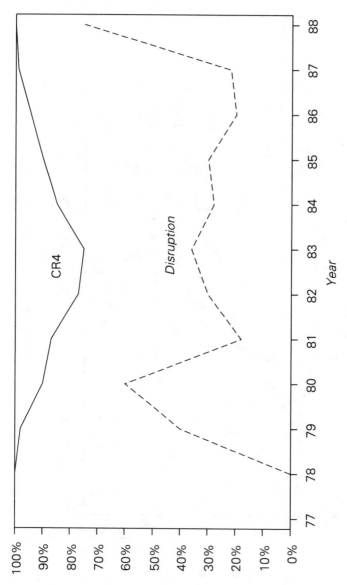

Figure 6.9 Concentration and disruption: 4K NMOS SRAMs
Source: Calculated with data from Dataquest Europe, Denham UK

the period of slower technical development. Moreover, one of the firms, AMD, that emerged as the market leader in the latter part of the life cycle of the 4K NMOS SRAM appears to have made substantial gains in share from 1983 onwards. (Motorola – which only obtained a very small share of this market – exited in 1983.)

In the second phase (covering 1983 to 1987) the decline in market concentration of the early leaders slowed down considerably and disruption was much lower as well as being roughly constant. During this phase the collective share of the final market leaders (AMD, Intel, NEC and TCMC) increased rapidly. Market leadership fluctuated between Intel and AMD though TCMC (Mostek) slowly started to increase its share. Finally, the share of early (and final) leaders fell sharply from 1987 to 1988 and disruption rose to 75 per cent (Figure 6.9).

16K NMOS SRAM

Intel was the first firm to introduce the 16K NMOS SRAM and had the entire market in 1980. By the next year, two Japanese producers, Fujitsu and NEC, and a new UK memory firm, Inmos, had entered the market in a significant way and Intel's share fell to about 5 per cent, resulting in the level of disruption rising to above 150 per cent.[86] Disruption from 1982 through to 1985 was around 30 per cent, before climbing to 80 per cent in 1988.[87] Despite a rapid rise in the number of firms in the market these early leaders (apart from Intel, which never recovered) only suffered a small loss in collective share between 1981 and 1983 – that is towards the end of stage II (early growth) of the product life cycle. Their decline became increasingly rapid over the next five years (covering 'late growth' and 'decline'). The market concentration of these four firms, largely accounted for by Fujitsu and Inmos, fell from about 90 per cent in 1983 to just over 20 per cent by 1987.[88]

Technological entry barriers appear to have been much more difficult to sustain and access time declined only for about 12 months (mid-1980 to mid-1981). Moreover, prices of 16K MOS SRAMs fell from 1979 to 1982 and remained stable until about 1984 (subsequently they fell slightly over the next two years and then stabilised).[89]

Both Inmos and Fujitsu remained in the top four for the entire period though they were eventually overtaken, initially by Toshiba and then AMD. These two latter firms had begun to emerge from stage III of the product life cycle onwards – a period at which the number of firms had started to decrease. High disruption from 1986 onwards largely represented loss of market share by Inmos and Fujitsu to Toshiba and AMD.[90]

Market concentration across generations of fast NMOS SRAMs

Smaller firms appear to have done better in the fast NMOS markets than in the higher volume DRAM markets. However, all but two firms (both large diversified Japanese companies) had continued on to the 64K level (Table 6.5), the others having shifted to CMOS technology. This result may be indicative of the inertia of large firms, suggesting the difficulties they may have in changing direction quickly.

Table 6.5 The changing pattern of technological leadership in NMOS fast SRAMs

Date	1977	1980	1984
Size	4K	16K	64K
Leading firms	Intel NEC National Semiconductor Fujitsu	Intel Inmos Fujitsu NEC	Fijitsu Toshiba

Source: Based on data from Dataquest Europe, Denham UK

6.8 CMOS STATIC MEMORY CHIPS (SRAMs)

Fast CMOS SRAMs were introduced in the early 1980s (Table 6.6). However, entry into this market did not occur on a significant scale until the mid-1980s. For example, there were only three firms producing these devices in 1983. Thus firms which had entered CMOS technology early on were at a distinct advantage, as were new firms set up to exploit the shift within MOS technology. Consequently, market concentration was extremely high in the early period of CMOS SRAMs.

Table 6.6 Classification of stages in the CMOS SRAM life cycle

Stage		4K	16K	64K	256K
I	Introduction	1981–2	1982–3	1984–5	1986–7
II	Early growth	1982–3	1983–6	1985 +	–
III	Late growth	1983–4	1986 +	–	–
IV	Maturity	1984–7	–	–	–
V	Rapid decline	1987 +	–	–	–
VI	Stagnation	–	–	–	–

Source: Based on data from Dataquest Europe, Denham UK

4K CMOS SRAMs

The market for 4K CMOS SRAMs was substantially smaller than for its NMOS counterpart; unit sales of these devices peaked in 1984 at approximately 3 million and 22 million respectively.[91] Thus relatively few firms produced for the 4K CMOS market and Motorola was the only producer until 1984. Established semiconductor firms (apart from Matra–Harris, the European subsidiary of Harris Semiconductor) did not enter this market.

Motorola's dominance was challenged only by Cypress (a new US start-up) which started production in 1984 but which by 1988 (when Motorola exited) accounted for about 60 per cent of the market.[92] Other new US merchant firms (and Matra–Harris) did not begin production until 1986. Significantly, Matra–Harris appears to have entered this market through the transfer of technology and masks from Cypress with an agreement signed in 1985.[93] Market concentration was high since Motorola and Cypress were the only producers up till 1985. Not surprisingly, though, Motorola virtually monopolised the market and in 1987 (a year before it exited) still had around a 50 per cent share.

The technological frontier of this device in terms of access time advanced from 1979 (60nS) to mid-1981 (20nS) while the price of 4K MOS SRAMs continued to fall from 1977 to around 1982. However, the lack of competitors to Motorola in the first three years meant zero market disruption. The successful entry (initially) of Cypress and later other new firms (principally UMC, Inmos and Saratoga) caused increasing disruption.[94]

16K CMOS SRAMs

Unlike the 4K CMOS SRAM, the situation for the 16K version was much more competitive and Motorola's presence was weak. Market concentration fell from early on in the product life cycle and the number of firms increased rapidly.[95] Hitachi and IDT were the first firms into the market, followed by a European firm (Matra–Harris) and a Japanese producer (Sharp). (In 1982, Matra–Harris and Harris Semiconductor set up a joint venture to produce 16K CMOS SRAMs.[96]) Hitachi dominated the market, accounting for more than 80 per cent, for the first three years. Disruption initially peaked in 1985, reflecting a major drop in Hitachi's share which went to new entrants.[97] Despite this, Hitachi remained the market leader until 1987 when its share was nearly halved, to 18 per cent, and it was just overtaken by Cypress which was reflected in high disruption. The three other early leaders were unable to make major inroads into the market and all generally had much less than a 10 per cent share.[98] Significantly, technological advance (in terms of faster access time) continued until around 1987 (falling from 50nS to 15nS), during which time the price of 16K MOS SRAMs was also decreasing (Figure 6.8). None the less, both technological advance and rapidly falling prices were unable to stop market deconcentration.

64K CMOS SRAMs

Market concentration in the 64K CMOS SRAM – introduced in 1984 – fell even faster than for the previous generation. Of the initial four leaders, two were Japanese (NEC and Hitachi), one the new UK start-up Inmos and one was the US-based firm IDT. NEC retained market leadership in the first two years but was subsequently displaced by Hitachi which itself was overtaken by another Japanese firm, Fujitsu, a year later. Another large Japanese company, Toshiba, had entered in 1985. By 1988 there were no US firms in the top four.[99] In that year, the first three were Japanese and the fourth European (Inmos).[100]

Technological development appears to have been much more difficult for subsequent generations of fast SRAMs and there appears to have been no improvement in access time for the 64K device. Thus the lack of technical development removed a key barrier to the entry of other firms into the market, leading to high levels of deconcentration. Prices did, however, fall very rapidly from 1984 to 1987 (Figure 6.8). Unsurprisingly, market disruption was higher than in the previous generations of devices, particularly in 1986 when both the early leaders, Hitachi and NEC, suffered a major loss in share, primarily to Fujitsu but also to Toshiba.

256K CMOS SRAMs

Japanese firms were the first to announce the development of the 256K SRAM, sample and shift to mass production. US firms entered the market later. Thus, while RCA was the first US firm to sample these devices at the end of 1986[101] this was about a year later than either Toshiba and NEC, by which time Japanese firms were starting mass production.

By the late 1980s, the 256K CMOS SRAM was still in its early development. However, there was no change in access time for this device over time which would suggest that market concentration would decrease very rapidly. This cannot be verified with the data available.

Some potential entrants to the 256K SRAM ran into problems. For example, in December 1987 Inmos closed its US (Colorado) plant which had been developing this (and the next generation) device. Consequently, production of the 256K device was planned to shift to its UK (Wales) plant.[102] However, in the second quarter of 1988 Inmos announced that it would exit from 256K SRAM production and instead license the technology to other firms.[103] This was considered a result of the unwillingness of Thorn–EMI (then the owner of Inmos) to commit the additional resources required to upgrade Inmos' UK facilities to enable these devices to be produced.

Towards the end of 1980, 1Mb SRAMs were being sampled, principally by the large Japanese firms but also by the large diversified European company Philips.

Market concentration across generations of fast CMOS SRAMs

Changes in the nature of the leading firms in CMOS SRAMs is not as clear cut as for DRAMs. For instance, some new start-ups (e.g. Cypress, IDT, Inmos) were among the initial leaders in the early 1980s (Table 6.7). However, over time the large diversified Japanese firms became more dominant.

Table 6.7 The changing patterns of technological leadership in CMOS fast SRAMs

Date	1981	1982	1984	1986
Size	4K	16K	64K	25K
Leading	Motorola	Hitachi	Hitachi	Fijitsu
Firms	Cypress	Matra–	Inmos	Mitsubishi
	Inmos	Harris	NEC	AMD
	Matra–	Fujitsu	IDT	Hitachi
	Harris			

Source: Based on data from Dataquest Europe, Denham UK
Note: The table shows memory introduction dates and the initial leading four firms in each market segment

6.9 CONCLUSIONS

The solid-state memory market is a key sector in semiconductors. Over time, new types of memory chip have been introduced – with EPROMs and SRAMs closely following on from each generation of DRAM. DRAMs dominate the memory chip market (though SRAMs, EPROMs and EEPROMs are also important sub-markets). For DRAMS, the time period between the introduction of subsequent generations of memory chip has been more or less constant at about three years. However, moving from one generation to the next has become a bigger, costlier and more difficult step.

DRAMs have historically been considered to be strategically important in the semiconductors industry through their role as a process technology driver. By the late 1980s, this view has been undermined as a number of previously leading US merchant producers were forced to exit from DRAMs and adopted other types of memory chip, such as the EPROM, as a test vehicle for technological improvements.

In the early and mid-1970s, the DRAM market was dominated by a few small firms (principally Intel and Mostek) who played a highly innovative role both in introducing new generations of DRAMs and subsequently improving the performance of each memory chip. These highly innovative and dynamic firms appear to have tended to dominate the early stages of the product life cycle which have been characterised by high prices and rapid technological development. Such firms have then exited and moved on to the next generation of device. Later stages have tended to be dominated by larger, less technologically dynamic firms engaged in high-volume production.

A critical feature of memory chips generally has been that by the end of the 1970s the nature and direction of change was becoming increasingly predictable. Thus, the vision of the future with regard to these devices was becoming much clearer (e.g. standardised pinout, fourfold increases in memory capacity between one generation of DRAM and the next). Consequently, the market become increasingly dominated by the large diversified firms.

This process was accelerated in the early 1980s, as most US DRAM firms –

in their attempts to outrun Japanese firms – ran into problems shifting to new technological processes for 64K devices. Thus, many of these 64K parts suffered from soft errors which delayed production and allowed the mass entry of the large diversified Japanese producers. Moreover, delayed entry for these US producers meant that prices (and thus profits) were low. As a result many of the early technological leaders (such as Intel and Mostek) exited from DRAMs.

Around the mid-1980s, many US firms were able to increase their market share. However, this was not due to technological factors but primarily a result of US government pressure which lead to Japanese firms restricting output and purchasing US memory chips.

In the late 1980s, rapid technological developments meant that even the large US merchant semiconductor firms were forced to exit DRAMs and shifted to using EPROMs as technology drivers. Market leadership has since been captured by the large diversified Japanese firms and a Korean producer (Samsung). However, these markets are still undergoing rapid shifts in leadership, suggesting that the firms remaining in the market are fairly evenly matched technologically and economically.

One major implication of these findings is that policies encouraging small firms into market which are characterised by rapid rates of technical change and a relatively clear 'vision of the future' are likely to be ineffective. A more appropriate action would be to encourage joint programmes (e.g. R&D) by large firms.

In the early 1990s, Japanese firms at the forefront of memory chip technology are likely to face problems of a different nature than those they suffered when trying to catch up with the US leaders. In this respect, Japanese firms appear to be in the process of changing their organisational structures (e.g. spinning-off their R&D divisions) and repositioning themselves to be better placed to deal with increased technological uncertainty.

At the same time, the situation is still very much in a state of flux, with competition re-emerging from both the US and Korea. Thus, US firms have regrouped under SEMATECH in a renewed attempt to re-enter and capture markets for 4Mb, 16Mb and 64Mb, while Korean firms such as Samsung (which successfully entered DRAM production) have now closed the gap with Japanese producers. Such issues are examined in more detail in Chapter 10.

7

CASE STUDY: STANDARD LOGIC

7.1 INTRODUCTION

Earlier chapters have examined the worldwide microprocessor and MOS memory markets. This chapter focuses on standard logic integrated circuits. Standard logic chips are of particular importance in microelectronics for two main reasons. First, these were the first type of integrated circuits (ICs) and represented a radical shift from the previous generation of semiconductors (viz. transistors). Second, the early technological history was highly turbulent and had a major impact on market structure.

Prior to the commercial introduction of the transistor, the electronics industry had been dominated by large diversified valve producers. These firms manufactured electronic components principally for incorporation into finished goods. The radical shift from valves to transistors in the 1950s had allowed the introduction of 'merchant semiconductor producers' (i.e. firms which manufactured semiconductors for sale on the open market). This radical jump in technology undermined the pre-eminence of the valve-producing firms which were only able to achieve a minority share in semiconductor markets.

This situation changed dramatically with the shift to integrated circuits – the next generation of semiconductor technology. Integrated circuits were based on a radical innovation, the planar process. One result of this innovation (applicable to both ICs and discrete devices) was an unexpectedly rapid fall in semiconductor production costs. As a result, firms which delayed entry into integrated circuit technology (principally the large diversified valve-producing companies) were at a significant experience and cost disadvantage *vis-à-vis* earlier entrants.

The initial products based on integrated circuit technology were logic circuits (i.e. 'standard logic'). Logic circuits are most commonly used in computers, related peripheral equipment and industrial equipment for carrying out arithmetical operations or control purposes. In some ways, the first logic ICs drew on designers' experience of circuits built using discrete devices. The rest of this chapter is in two main parts. The first examines the early

139

history (from the 1960s through to the beginning of the 1970s) of standard logic chips in the US, European and Japanese markets. This part draws largely on Golding (1971), Malerba (1985) and Wilson *et al.* (1980), and will show that in the 1960s a series of rapid and unforeseen technological developments in semiconductors was triggered by the commercial introduction of the IC. In effect, this period was characterised by an *unclear vision of the future*, an environment which favoured small or new firms (less committed to previous generations of technology) which were able to respond quickly to rapid shifts in markets and technology. The magnitude and speed of both technology and market changes during this period were so great that they were highly disruptive even for the leading merchant firms.

The effects on the large diversified valve-producing firms was even more profound. By the end of the 1960s, these large firms in both the USA and Europe had effectively lost technological leadership to the highly dynamic merchant semiconductor firms and been forced to exit from leading edge semiconductors. Only the large established Japanese electronic firms were able to make a successful transition into integrated circuit technology and meet the challenge from the US-based merchant producers.

The second part is much more quantitative and examines the relationship between rates of technology change and market structure. In this respect, changes in the technology are given from the early 1960s through to the late 1980s while market share data for standard logic are examined for the period from 1979 to 1988.

7.2 THE US EXPERIENCE

The following will show that the early history of integrated circuits in the USA was characterised by rapid and unforeseen changes resulting in high levels of market disruption. During this period, the large US-based diversified valve-producing firms lost technological leadership to the merchant semi-conductor firms in the strategically important integrated circuit technology, due to either delayed entry or an inability to cope with the sudden and rapid shifts to different technologies.

The first types of standard logic ICs

The monolithic integrated circuit was first commercially produced by Fairchild, rapidly followed by Texas Instruments. ICs were first used to replace circuits for standard logic. Early designs of standard logic chips used either Texas Instruments' 'Series 51' resistor coupled transistor logic (RCTL) or Fairchild's 'Micrologic series' direct coupled transistor logic (DCTL) (Table 7.1).

According to Golding (1971: 161), Fairchild's Micrologic family was better placed for commercial markets than Texas Instruments (which had entered the semiconductor market in the early 1950s and primarily served the military

Table 7.1 Commercial introduction of standard logic ICs in the USA

Logic type	Firm	Date[1]	Property name
DCTL	Fairchild	1961	Micrologic
RCTL	TI	1961	Series 51
DTL	Signetics	1962	Utilogic
	Westinghouse	1963	200 series
	Fairchild	1964	930 series
	TI	1964	Series 53
TTL	Sylvania	1964	SUHL[2]
	Transitron	1964	SUHL
	TI	1965	54/74 series
	TI	1968	Low power TTL
	Fairchild	1967	9000 series
	TI	1970	Schottky TTL
	TI	1973	Low power Schottky
ECL (CML)	Pacific (TRW)	1962	
	Motorola	1963	MECL[3]
MOS	General Microelectronic	1965	
	General Instrument	1965	
	Fairchild	1965	

Sources: Golding (1971: 81); Wilson *et al.* (1980: 41)
Notes:
1 There is uncertainty about the exact date of certain innovations as well as the identity of the first firm to introduce some innovations
2 Sylvania ultra high level logic
3 Motorola emitter coupled logic

market) with its Series 51 range of ICs (which, for example, were used in the Minuteman Missile (Wilson *et al.*, 1980: 84)). Micrologic came to dominate the computer logic market which, although small, was expanding rapidly (Golding, 1971: 161; Kraus, 1973: 95).

Over the period from 1961 to 1965, Fairchild sold more ICs than TI, though in value terms, TI (with its greater emphasis on the military market) had the larger share (Golding, 1971: 161). Fairchild consolidated its market position by substantially reducing the prices of some Micrologic chips in May 1964 (Golding, 1971: 161).

Both RCTL and DCTL had problems of noise immunity (i.e. the logic gates could be triggered by voltage changes in different parts of the integrated circuit) and were superseded by diode transistor logic (DTL).

DTL and the rise of Fairchild

DTL was faster (Figure 7.1) and more reliable. ICs based on this type of logic were first offered commercially by Signetics in 1962.[1] These relied on a 'triple diffused' process and sold under the name Utilogic (Table 7.1). Two years

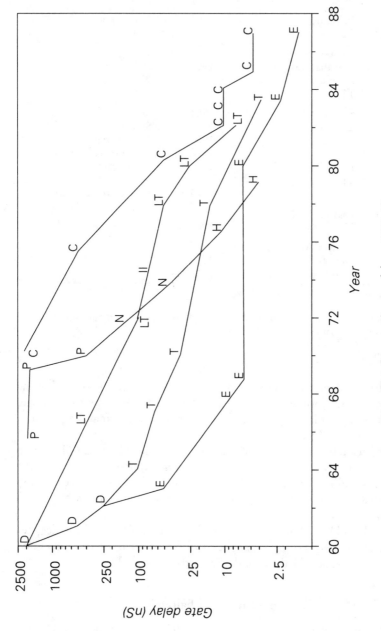

Figure 7.1 Progress in gate delays, 1960–88
Source: Based on Swann (1986: 71) updated with data from various issues of *Electronics*

later proprietary versions of DTL were being offered by both Texas Instruments (Series 53, which also used a 'triple diffused' process) and Fairchild (930 series, based on an epitaxial process). Westinghouse (a large diversified valve-producing firm) had been engaged in work on microcircuits on a US military contract in the 1950s and was thus able to enter IC production rapidly with its proprietary version of DTL, the 200 series (Tilton, 1971). Fairchild emerged as the market leader in DTL and by August 1967 the 930 series was being second sourced by ten firms including Texas Instruments, Motorola, Raytheon and Westinghouse (Golding, 1971: 162).

Fairchild made major market gains in this early period of the development and commercialisation of integrated circuits. In the US semiconductor market, Fairchild had moved from tenth position with a 5 per cent share in 1960 to third place with 9 per cent by 1963 and then to second position with 13 per cent by 1966. Fairchild's rise in integrated circuits – the leading edge of semiconductor technology – was even more pronounced, resulting in the previous market leader, Texas Instruments, being relegated to second place. Fairchild had a 24 per cent market share in ICs by 1967, up from 18 per cent in 1964, while Texas Instruments' share had been almost halved, from 32 per cent in 1964 to 18 per cent by 1967 (Tilton, 1971: 69).

Fairchild's dominance was short lived. In the next few years falling demand for and oversupply of DTL, coupled with an explosive growth of demand for a rival type of logic circuit with better performance characteristics (transistor-transistor logic, TTL), led to a rapid fall in Fairchild's market share and the re-emergence of Texas Instruments as the market leader.

The sudden switch to TTL and market destabilisation

TTL was faster (which was its main advantage), consumed less power and had better noise immunity than DTL. In 1967, users started to switch from DTL to TTL in increasing numbers and demand for TTL chips increased very rapidly (*Electronics*, 1967: 179).[2] Thus, while TTL accounted for 12 per cent of IC production in 1966, by the next year its share had doubled (*Electronics*, 1967: 179) and by 1974 it accounted for nearly one-third of the total IC sales of $1.3 billion (Cole, 1975: 45). Falling demand for DTL was exacerbated by oversupply due to faster than expected increases in yields and the large number of suppliers which had entered the market due to its popularity.

Fairchild had been too slow in recognising the market opportunities of TTL which, ironically, it had invented in 1964 (Wilson *et al.*, 1980: 84). This institutional inertia has been attributed to Fairchild's organisational structure whereby individual units each had separate profit and loss accounts. This may have led to production units being reluctant to shift from older successful products to other, initially less profitable but ultimately more successful, devices. Thus, TTL had been commercially introduced in 1964 by Sylvania, under the name SUHL (Sylvania ultra high level logic). Texas Instruments had rapidly followed Sylvania and produced its own proprietary version of TTL (Series 54/74) within a year.[3] Fairchild brought out its own version of TTL (Series 9000) in 1967 (Wilson *et al.*, 1980) but was at a severe disadvantage due to its late entry.

Competition in TTL markets

Sylvania's proprietary TTL was the major source of competition to Texas Instruments' 54/74 series. Sylvania had introduced a faster series of TTL circuits termed SUHL-2 which had a 5nS propagation delay (Figure 7.1). Sylvania also produced a SUHL-1 family which was considerably slower (11nS delay). According to *Electronics* (1970: 46), Sylvania was the market leader in TTL in the early 1960s, and even Texas Instruments conceded that the SUHL family of logic chips was more popular than its 54/74 series (*Electronics*, 1967: 179) which had an average propagation delay of 10nS (TI, nd). However, problems arose in the shift to the faster SUHL family, which Sylvania was rumoured to be unable to produce (*Electronics*, 1967: 179).

Sylvania's problems had led a number of firms to bring out logic chips very similar to SUHL. By the end of 1967 these included Motorola, Raytheon, Westinghouse and Philco–Ford (*Electronics*, 1967: 179). Texas Instruments pressed ahead through a series of rapid innovations in TTL, with low-power TTL (average power dissipation of 1mW/gate compared with 10mW/gate with the standard 54/74 devices) introduced in 1968, a faster version (Schottky TTL, with an average propagation delay of 6nS) in 1970 and then low power Schottky in 1973. Thus, Texas Instruments was able to gain a technological competitive edge over Sylvania through a series of rapid product improvements in its TTL family. At the same time, Texas Instruments was aided by the aggressive pricing of National Semiconductor which was second sourcing the 54/74 series.

Towards the end of the 1960s, Sylvania was estimated to have suffered annual losses of between $3 million and $6 million (*Electronics*, 1970: 46). Sylvania stated that this was due to a decline in the military sector and intense price competition in the computer market (*Electronics*, 1970: 46.) Sylvania (unlike Texas Instruments) seemed to have been unable to shift its heavy reliance on the rapidly declining military (accounting for about 97 per cent of total IC demand in 1962 and falling to 37 per cent by 1968) to commercial and industrial markets which had been expanding very quickly. These developments were largely attributed to losses incurred because of the decline in the military/aerospace markets on which Sylvania was heavily dependent (Kraus, 1973: 62). Sylvania closed down its IC facility in Woburn in late 1970 and by January 1971 had effectively withdrawn from semiconductors production (Kraus, 1973: 62; *Electronics*, 1970: 46).

Other firms offering proprietary versions of TTL in the USA were Fairchild, Signetics, Sprague Electric, Transistron, Westinghouse and Motorola.

However, none of them was able to offer effective competition to Texas Instruments' TTL family. Fairchild was at a considerable disadvantage as it was entering TTL some three years after the market leaders and at a time when the technology was being driven forward very quickly (Figure 7.1). Signetics' proprietary TTL (termed 'designers' choice logic', DCL) had a propagation delay comparable to the SUHL–1 family and was thus too slow to compete with TI's 54/74 series (*Electronics*, 1967: 179). Sprague was producing Signetics DCL under licence as well as its 8800 series (containing twelve TTL circuits) which had a propagation delay of 12nS (*Electronics*, 1967: 180). Transitron may have been expected to offer a greater challenge given that it had been able to market a TTL IC within a few months of its introduction by Sylvania. However, this had been a result of poaching the inventor of Sylvania's TTL (Golding, 1971: 250). Overall, Transitron's R&D capability was weak owing to a historical lack of investment in such activities (Golding, 1971: 169).

The large diversified valve producer, Westinghouse, was unable to keep up with the pace and unpredictability of change in IC technology and had seen its market share decline over time. In 1964, Westinghouse had been the fourth largest producer of ICs with 12 per cent of the US market but three years later its share had fallen to less than 5 per cent (Tilton, 1971: 69). In December 1968 it withdrew from the commercial IC market (Kraus, 1973: 56).

In 1970, TI had a 41 per cent market share in TTL integrated circuits worldwide and by the early 1970s had emerged as the clear winner in the bipolar logic war. By 1980, TI had about a 25 per cent share worldwide in TTL logic ICs and a 12 per cent share in semiconductor sales (Dosi, 1984: 172).

Overall, then, the large diversified valve-producing firms in the USA lost technological leadership in the early and highly turbulent period of the commercialisation and rapid development of integrated circuit technology to the merchant semiconductor firms. Texas Instruments emerged as the clear leader in stanation logic markets, but was subsequently challenged by other merchant producers. As the following will show, these US-based merchant producers similarly emerged as the technological winners in the European market.

7.3 THE EUROPEAN EXPERIENCE

Entry barriers to the European semiconductor industry (unlike the US) were high and there was no significant entry of new European-based merchant firms. During the 1950s, the industry continued to be dominated by the large diversified European valve-producing firms. Thus, the main source of competition to the established electronics companies came from the subsidiaries of the US-based semiconductor merchant producers.

The following will show that both the large and small European-based firms were unable to compete with the US-based merchant producers and were forced to exit from volume IC markets. Large firms experienced problems due to delayed entry into IC process technology which undermined their competitiveness *vis-à-vis* the European subsidiaries of the US-based merchant producers. Subsequent attempts to close the technological gap with the US firms were thwarted by a combination of the unexpected shift to TTL and the onset of a major worldwide semiconductor recession. Smaller European-based firms had adopted the key IC process technology (the 'planar process') much earlier but were adversely affected by delays in entering TTL ICs.

Delayed entry into ICs by the large European firms

US merchant semiconductor firms had initiated commercial production of silicon (digital) integrated circuits based on a radical innovation – the planar process – in the early 1960s. This production process substantially reduced the costs of both discrete and integrated circuits. The major European-based firms delayed adoption of the planar process into IC technology until the mid or late 1960s (Table 7.2).

Table 7.2 First commercial production of digital ICs by firms in the UK

Logic	Firm	Date	Proprietary name
DCTL	TI (UK)	1962	
RTL	Plessey	1965	Clansman
DTL	Ferranti	1964	Micronor I
	Ferranti	1965	Micronor II
	Mullard	1966	200 series
	Elliott–Automation	1966	930 series
	TI (UK)	1967	53 series
	SGS	1967	930 series
	AEI	1967	Utilogic
	STC	1968	930 series
	Plessey	1968	53 series
TTL	Mullard	1967	54/74 series
	Ferranti	1967	54/74 series
	STC	1968	9000 series
	TI (UK)	1968	54/74 series
	SGS	1968	9000 series
ECL	Ferranti	1967	Micronor 3
	Marconi	1968	ECCSL
	Plessey	1968	MECL
MOS	Ferranti	1967	
	Plessey	1967	MOSFET

Source: Golding (1971: 81)
Note: The 54/74 series ICs were imported by TI for about three years before full production began at its UK subsidiary in 1967–8

European firms thus largely produced discrete components (rather than ICs) using the mesa process (rather than the planar process) based on germanium (rather than silicon) (Tilton, 1971: 116). There were two main reasons for this. First, European firms were much less dependent on military procurement and therefore put more emphasis on lower cost germanium-based semiconductors for commercial and consumer markets. Second, demand for valves and discrete semiconductor components was large and remained buoyant while the market for ICs in Europe was much smaller than in the USA in both absolute and relative terms. For example, in 1967 ICs accounted for around 30 per cent of total semiconductor consumption in the USA compared with only 5 per cent in Europe (Carrell, 1968).

Siemens and Philips, the two largest European firms, waited for the market in ICs to develop before committing major resources to production facilities. Siemens delayed entry into IC technology, first, because it considered that there was 'no real demand' for integrated circuits and second, because it considered that entry could be achieved through licensing if markets did emerge (Scholz, 1974).

Philips has historically been noted as cautious in moving into new areas, perhaps due to its bias towards capital-intensive investment which would favour shifting into new markets only when demand had been assured. Early entry into integrated circuits would have been risky given uncertain demand and costly as capital investment in existing technology would have had to have been written down prematurely. Moreover, capital costs of integrated circuit production (which used the silicon planar process) were much higher than for its semiconductor predecessors, mainly because of the high costs of inspection/test equipment and air conditioning/filtering to produce an ultra-clean manufacturing environment (Golding, 1971: 101). At the same time, sales of discrete devices were buoyant, thereby reducing both the urgency and perceived need to move to a more radical technology.

Another factor which slowed Philips' entry into ICs was that its research laboratories favoured post alloy diffused transistors (PADT) in which there had already been substantial investment (Golding, 1971: 203). Consequently, Philips did not produce its first DTL ICs (for the UK computer manufacturer, Marconi) until 1965 while Siemens had begun production of digital ICs at the end of the 1960s.

Associated Electrical Industries – a large established UK valve producer – similarly did not keep up with the rapid technological developments in semiconductors and suffered major declines in market share. Thus, in 1958, AEI was second only to Mullard with 31 per cent of the transistor market in the UK (Attwood and Company, 1958: 8); by 1962 its share had fallen to 7 per cent (Golding, 1971: 179). AEI delayed entry into planar transistors until 1965 and was forced to withdraw due to price competition from Fairchild and Texas Instruments (Golding, 1971: 193). Similarly, AEI delayed entry into ICs, producing multi-chip versions in 1965 and introducing DTL ICs in 1967.

Plessey (another UK-based firm) produced the world's first linear integrated circuit in the late 1950s, although commercial production did not begin until 1965 (Golding, 1971: 217). Moreover, it continued to focus primarily on linear (rather than digital) designs in line with the preference of the UK military which accounted for around 80 per cent of its IC sales in 1968. However, demand for linear ICs did not rise to the levels expected. Plessey's line of digital ICs excluded both DTL and TTL but included RTL, ECL and MOS. However, RTL was technologically redundant while demand for both ECL and MOS did not become significant until very much later.

Effects of delayed entry on the large European firms

Delayed entry meant that a considerable technological (and economic) gap had opened up between US and European-based semiconductor firms. US military demand for (principally digital) integrated circuits had provided US firms with considerable opportunities to achieve significant technological learning, leading to major reductions in IC prices. Thus, for example, while the average unit prices of linear and digital ICs in 1964 were US $17.35 and US $30 respectively, by 1972 both had fallen to about US $1 (EIA, 1979). No such opportunities or experience generally characterised European firms. Consequently, US-based firms made major inroads into European semiconductor markets as well as stimulating demand for integrated circuits. By 1970, Texas Instruments had captured 25 per cent of the European integrated circuit market and 50 per cent of its TTL market (Malerba, 1985: 111).

Overall, then, the major European-based valve-producing firms suffered a major decline in the face of competition from the highly dynamic low-cost US-based merchant producers. In the UK, for example, Mullard's market share had plummetted from 49 per cent in 1962 to 23 per cent by 1967–8 (Golding, 1971). Moreover, Mullard's share in the crucial integrated circuit market was a mere 1 per cent in 1967 where it held ninth position (Golding, 1971: 180). However, there appeared to have been some recovery by the next year when Mullard had moved to third position, with Texas Instruments and Fairchild together accounting for 70 per cent of the market (*Electronic News*, 1968: 4–5). (According to Payne (1969), US firms held about a 75 per cent share of the UK integrated circuit, with the remainder accounted for by Marconi–Elliott, Ferranti, Plessey and Mullard.)

Entry problems of large European firms

European firms entered into technology licensing agreements for ICs with US companies (Table 7.3) for two main reasons. The first was to overcome production problems. For instance, manufacturing problems with its first DTL ICs led Philips to switch to WC200 DTL ICs produced under licence from Westinghouse in 1967 (Malerba, 1985: 13). The second was as a way of

CASE STUDY: STANDARD LOGIC

closing the technological gap. Overall, though, these efforts ran into problems. For instance, AEG–Telefunken produced TTL devices under licence
from Sylvania principally for internal use, but demand was too low and by the
end of the 1960s AEG had shifted to linear and custom ICs (Malerba, 1985:
114). Philips had switched from the Westinghouse DTL to Fairchild's 930
DTL (Malerba, 1985: 12). However, by this time DTL was being rapidly
superseded in the USA by TTL. In the late 1960s, Mullard (Philips' UK
subsidiary) switched to producing the 7400 TTL for GEC, but, GEC later
began to purchase these directly from Texas Instruments (Malerba, 1985: 113).

Table 7.3 Logic ICs and technology licensers for European firms

European firm	Technology	Licenser	State of licenser at end of 'logic war'
Philips	DTL (WC 200 series)	Westinghouse	Exited commercial IC market in 1968
	DTL (930 series)	Fairchild	Major loss of market share to TI
Radiotechnique	TTL (SUHL)	Sylvania	Closed semiconductor division, Dec. 1970
Mullard	TTL (54/74 series)	–	–
Marconi–Elliott	DTL (930 series)	Fairchild	⎫
	TTL (990 series)	Fairchild	⎬ Major loss of market share to TI
	TTL (9000 series)	Fairchild	⎭
AEG–Telefunken	TTL	Sylvania	Closed semiconductor division, Dec. 1970
SGS–Fairchild	TTL (900 series)	Fairchild	Major loss of market share to TI

Sources: Malerba, *The Semiconductor Business: The Economics of Rapid Growth and Decline*,
Pinter Publishers (1985: 113–15);Payne (1969: 75)

European firms suffered when their technological licensers lost the 'bipolar
logic war' to Texas Instruments. For example, Radiotechnique (Philips'
French subsidiary) produced SUHL ICs but was adversely affected by
Sylvania's decline in the semiconductor market (Malerba, 1985: 13).

Finally, the major European firms' entry into volume production coincided
with a downturn in semiconductor demand. Towards the end of 1970 prices of
TTL ICs in Europe were between one-half and one-quarter of their value at
the beginning of the year (Malerba, 1985: 112). Thus while Siemens manufactured TTL devices in the late 1960s, these were *specialised*, rather than
standard volume, devices primarily for in-house use. Rapid price falls during
the semiconductor recession of 1970–1 prohibited entry into the international
market and Siemens thus opted to purchase TTL devices on the open market
(Malerba, 1985: 114).

Small European firms and entry into ICs

In contrast to the above, a small number of European firms had rapidly
adopted planar technology, initially for the production of discrete components and then for integrated circuits. Three firms in the UK fell into this
category: Ferranti, Elliott–Automation and SGS–Fairchild (a subsidiary of
two Italian firms with a minority holding by Fairchild). These firms were

successful in digital IC markets in the 1960s. However, all delayed entry into TTL and were adversely affected by the defeat of Fairchild and the emergence of Texas Instruments as the winner in the 'logic war'.

Ferranti had initiated research into silicon semiconductors in 1953 and by the end of the 1950s produced a range of silicon diffused transistors. Experience of diffusion and oxide masking allowed Ferranti rapidly to absorb the planar and epitaxial processes (the foundations of integrated circuit fabrication). Ferranti was thus the acknowledged leader of UK integrated circuit manufacturers (Golding, 1971: 210).

In 1964, Ferranti produced its first commercial IC, Micronor I, a DTL device (based on RCA technology) on a government contract for a small computer for the Royal Navy. A faster DTL circuit, Micronor II, was developed very soon afterwards. However, Ferranti ran into four main problems. First, military demand for Micronor II was low due to the limited number of circuits available. Second, production difficulties with these devices resulted in small yields, hence high prices, and thus they were unattractive to the industrial and consumer markets. These problems were not resolved until two years later though their prices remained high. Third, by the time that Ferranti had overcome its production problems, the TIs 54/74 series had become available in the UK. Fourth, while Ferranti later developed its own TTL ICs which it sold in large quantities to ICL (the major UK computer manufacturer) between 1966 and 1970 (Malerba, 1985: 116), ICL subsequently switched to Texas Instruments for TTL. Ferranti was thus also forced to abandon the standard TTL market (Malerba, 1985: 116).

Elliott–Automation obtained a licence from Fairchild for the 930 DTL series in 1964 and later switched to the 990 TTL. (In October 1967, English Electric purchased Elliott–Automation and merged it with Marconi in July 1968.) While Elliott–Automation's market share in semiconductors was 3 per cent in 1967 and 1968 (Golding, 1971) it was much more successful in integrated circuits with an 11 per cent share of the UK market, placing it in third position after Texas Instruments (25 per cent) and SGS (21 per cent) (Golding, 1971: 180). However, it was adversely affected by Fairchild's defeat in the logic war.

SGS was set up as a joint venture between two Italian firms, Olivetti and Telettra, in 1958. Three years later, Fairchild acquired a 30 per cent stake in the company in return for the transfer of planar technology. Overseas subsidiaries were established in the early 1960s, the first being in the UK in 1962. SGS–Fairchild quickly adopted planar technology and rapidly entered digital integrated circuit production, with RTL in 1962 and (Fairchild's) DTL in 1964 (Malerba, 1985: 118). By the second half of the 1960s, SGS had the third largest share of the UK semiconductor market and was second only to Texas Instruments in the integrated circuit market, with 21 per cent in 1967 (Golding, 1971: 180). SGS performed less well in other European markets (Tilton, 1971; Pertile, 1975).

After it broke away from Fairchild in 1968 (Tilton, 1971) SGS suffered a decline in the volume digital logic market (Malerba, 1985), for a number of reasons. First, Fairchild's defeat in the bipolar logic war adversely effected SGS. Secondly, technical assistance and technology transfer from Fairchild subsequently decreased as SGS was then regarded as a competitor. Third, due to a lack of large-scale R&D investment in standard digital IC, as SGS had focused on linear and power ICs and non-standard devices. Thus, it fell to ninth position in the UK semiconductor market with just under a 3 per cent share (Golding, 1971).

By the early 1970s, both large and small European-based firms had been forced to exit the volume digital standard logic IC market and move into low-volume niche markets such as linear ICs and discrete semiconductor power devices. The large firms ran into problems principally as a result of delayed entry and an inability to respond quickly to the rapid and unpredictable shifts in integrated circuit technology. Smaller firms also faced difficulties despite earlier entry into integrated circuits. These were mainly due to a combination of the superior competitive position of the highly dynamic US-based merchant producers, which had gained considerable experience in their large domestic market, and the defeat of Fairchild (the technology licenser for many of these firms) in the logic war.

7.4 THE JAPANESE EXPERIENCE[4]

The previous section has shown that the large diversified valve-producing firms in both the USA and Europe had successfully negotiated entry into transistor production. However, generally these firms were subsequently unable to cope with the leap to integrated circuit technology which in its early history was characterised by a combination of rapid movement along, and sudden and unpredictable shifts to, new trajectories.

This course of events did not occur in Japan. Unlike their counterparts in the USA and Europe, Japanese valve-producing firms were successful in entering and *retaining* market leadership in semiconductors. Moreover, US merchant producers were not able to displace the predominance of Japanese firms in their domestic market. (Semiconductor imports did, however, increase over time, rising from 2 per cent of the market in 1959 to 10 per cent by 1968.) Two principal factors appear to have led to these results: first, prohibitive entry barriers to foreign firms and second, the rapid adoption and diffusion of new technological developments (such as the planar process) by Japanese firms.

Entry barriers to foreign firms

Generally, foreign firms were unable to establish wholly owned subsidiaries in Japan as the Japanese government banned direct foreign investment (DFI). Moreover, import controls reduced the level of direct competition in the domestic market from overseas firms. Restricted entry meant that US merchant firms were unable to challenge the supremacy of domestic firms. The only exception was Texas Instruments which was allowed a 50 per cent joint venture with Sony (delayed till 1968) on two conditions: first, that TI licensed its integrated circuit patents to a number of Japanese firms (NEC, Hitachi, Mitsubishi, Toshiba and Sony) and second, that it limit production to 10 per cent (at most) of the Japanese market. This delay allowed Japanese firms to accumulate substantial experience in both planar technology and integrated circuit production, making it more difficult for US firms subsequently to enter the domestic market.

Flexibility and rapid absorption of foreign technology

Unlike most of the European firms, Japanese firms were characterised by the rapid adoption and widespread diffusion of technological innovations. Thus, Nippon Electric produced the planar transistor in 1962 (a year after it was first commercially produced) under licence from Fairchild. This technology was diffused to other Japanese firms through sub-licences from Nippon Electric. In this respect, R&D expenditure was focused more on absorbing foreign know-how than on generating innovations (Tilton, 1971).

Tilton identified three factors which appear to have stimulated Japanese companies (especially the valve-producing firms) into monitoring and adopting technological developments generated elsewhere. First, the Japanese electronics industry was much smaller than its US and European counterparts in the immediate post-war period. Thus, electronics firms had less commitment to previous generations of technology and appear to have maintained a more receptive attitude to change.

Second, overseas markets for electronics goods (which incorporated a high proportion of semiconductor production) were of crucial importance and thus encouraged Japanese firms to monitor foreign technological developments closely and to 'adopt them as soon as economic conditions warrant' (Tilton, 1971: 155). Such markets were particularly important for the diversified valve-producing firms, as any reduction in exports would reduce their sales of both semiconductors and final electronic goods.

Third, there was intense competitive pressure on Japanese firms, both within domestic and foreign markets. Internal competition arose through the Japanese government's policy of licensing several firms with any particular technology or production techniques, thereby preventing firms from following monopolistic pricing policies. External pressure arose initially from US companies and Japanese firms were able to withstand this due to their lower wage costs. However, leading US merchant producers countered this advantage by setting up subsidiaries in countries with even lower costs, thereby encouraging Japanese firms to remain dynamically competitive.

Overall, then, a combination of high entry barriers into the Japanese market, the Japanese government's technology policy and the rapid take-up of the planar process by the large diversified Japanese valve-producing firms prevented the US-based merchant producers from mounting an effective challenge in the early history of integrated circuits. Moreover, early adoption of the planar process ensured that Japanese firms were not at a disadvantage *vis-à-vis* the US merchant suppliers as entry barriers were lowered. Thus, unlike their US and European counterparts, the large Japanese diversified valve producers were able successfully to negotiate entry into ICs.

7.5 TECHNICAL CHANGE IN STANDARD LOGIC ICs AND MARKET STRUCTURE

This section summarises technical change in standard logic and examines both market concentration and disruption in bipolar and MOS devices.

Two of the main technical performance characteristics of standard logic chips are speed and power dissipation. The speed of these devices is generally given in terms of the gate delay (i.e. the time taken for a particular gate to be switched 'on' or 'off') and is usually expressed in nanoseconds (nS) with the power dissipation in milliWatts (mW). Power dissipation of CMOS devices is generally much lower than with bipolar (or other MOS) technologies. Moreover, unlike bipolar, PMOS and NMOS, the gate delay of CMOS logic is frequency dependent.

Data on gate delays (i.e. speed) of standard logic were based primarily on those used by Swann (1986) and updated from the journals *Integrated Circuits International* and *Electronics*. These data were plotted to obtain changes in speed over time for the various competing technologies.

Estimates of annual worldwide sales of bipolar and MOS standard logic ICs were provided by Dataquest Europe and covered the period from 1979 to 1988 inclusive. Those data were used to calculate levels of concentration and disruption in the bipolar and MOS market.

Technical change in standard logic ICs

Figure 7.1 showed that gate delays of standard logic chips have undergone rapid improvements over time, with speeds increasing by a factor of around 1,000 over a period of about twenty-five years. The first part of this chapter showed that after the mid-1960s DTL was rapidly superseded by the faster and more reliable TTL and ECL circuits (with TTL dominating the bipolar logic market even though ECL achieved much faster gate delays). Texas Instruments (the market leader in TTL technology) further developed TTL to counter competition from other types of logic, introducing a faster TTL (Schottky TTL) in 1970 in response to the speed advantage of ECL and three years later bringing out a low-power version of TTL (low power Schottky) to meet competition from the evolving MOS technology (Langlois *et al.*, 1988: 12).

MOS-based circuits were introduced in the mid-1960s. These were generally slower than their biplar counterparts, by about two orders of magnitude. The early circuits were fabricated in PMOS technology, later superseded by NMOS which in turn was replaced by CMOS. While CMOS was initially even slower than NMOS, it had the advantage of negligible standby power consumption.

Gate delays in NMOS technology fell rapidly after their introduction in 1972, overtaking standard TTL in the mid-1970s and ECL logic in the late 1970s (Figure 7.1). CMOS technology also speeded up, but not as quickly. By the late 1980s, gate delays in all these technologies were beginning to converge.

Bipolar standard logic market

The first part of the chapter showed that the large, vertically integrated valve-producing firms that had previously dominated the electronics industry were generally unsuccessful in entering and keeping up with the rapid and unpredictable changes in integrated circuit markets and technology. Thus, in the 1960s, the early market leaders in bipolar standard logic (the first integrated circuits) were the merchant producers Texas Instruments, Fairchild and National Semiconductor.

The speed of bipolar standard logic increased very rapidly in the 1960s (Figure 7.1), with Texas Instruments pushing TTL while Motorola dominated the much smaller ECL market. Standard logic's share of the total IC market fell over time and by the late 1980s the latter accounted for about 25 per cent of the market. Moreover, within standard logic, MOS-based devices were increasing their share at the expense of bipolar chips (Table 7.4).

Table 7.4 Estimated worldwide shipments of standard logic ICs ($m)

Year	1979	1980	1981	1982	1983	1984	1985	1986	1987	1988
Bipolar	1,200	1,467	1,392	1,483	1,820	2,665	2,155	2,176	2,204	2,204
MOS	195	254	301	368	471	659	579	702	745	845
GaAs	–	–	–	–	–	1	1	5	7	11

Source: Dataquest Europe, Denham UK

In 1979, the four leading firms in the bipolar standard logic market were Texas Instruments, Fairchild, National Semiconductor and Motorola.[5] These companies continued to occupy the top four positions throughout the 1980s. Significantly, these were the major players in the 1960s. Texas Instruments, which had emerged as the market leader in TTL in the late 1960s, retained the leading position worldwide and accounted for around one-third of the total market in bipolar logic between 1979 and 1988.[6]

Market concentration over the period from 1979 to 1988 remained high and was remarkably stable. Thus the four-firm concentration was around 70 per cent in 1979 and steadily declined to 63 per cent by 1988 (Figure 7.2). (This

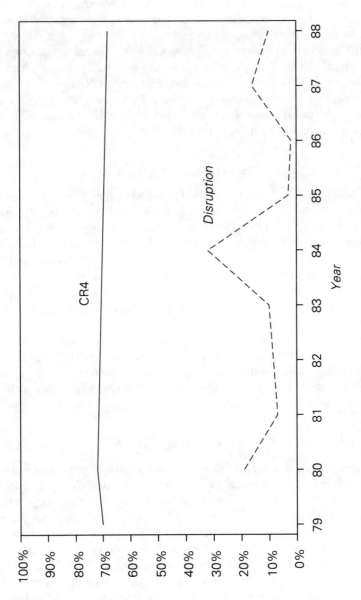

Figure 7.2 Concentration and disruption: bipolar logic
Source: Calculated with data from Dataquest Europe, Denham UK

level of stability is similar to the overall DRAM market when considered across a number of generations of device – see Chapter 6.) In 1986, concentration in the bipolar standard logic market increased due to the acquisition of Fairchild by National Semiconductor. This is not shown in Figure 7.2 as Fairchild and National Semiconductor are treated as separate firms in the calculation of four-firm concentration.

This high level of stability in the market was reflected in the low values of disruption. Market disruption was generally below 20 per cent with a peak of 30 per cent in 1984, principally due to the data from National Semiconductor and Fairchild being aggregated (Figure 7.2). Overall, though, this level of stability is unsurprising given the relatively small size and high level of maturity of the standard logic market.

MOS standard logic market

The MOS standard logic market developed a few years after its bipolar counterpart and is thus less mature. With the exception of Motorola, the market leaders in MOS technology were not among the major players in bipolar devices. This is not unexpected as late entrants to a market with high rates of technical change may seek to compete by establishing and moving along a different technological trajectory and thus destabilise the market shares of incumbents (see Chapter 4). Thus, in 1979, the top four positions were occupied by two US companies, Motorola and RCA, and two Japanese firms, Toshiba and NEC.

The MOS standard logic market was more turbulent than the bipolar logic market. The market became less concentrated from 1979 through to 1983 and the four-firm concentration fell from 77 per cent to 62 per cent and then was roughly stable (Figure 7.3). Disruption in MOS was higher than in the bipolar market.

7.6 CONCLUSIONS

The first part of this chapter showed that the early history of standard logic chips was marked by a combination of rapid technical change and an unclear vision of the future. The findings from other chapters would suggest that such characteristics mean that new and small entrants would be better placed than large established firms to use the rapid and unpredictable changes in technology to their competitive advantage. The development of standard logic chips fits in with this view. The previously dominant large US and European diversified valve-producing firms were unable to keep up with the new US-based merchant firms in an environment characterised by rapid and unpredictable shifts in technology and markets. Only the large Japanese diversified valve producers (which were less committed to previous generations of electronics technology, than their European and US counterparts) were able

156

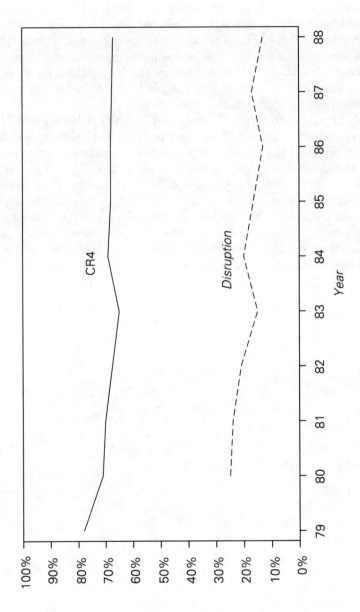

Figure 7.3 Concentration and disruption: MOS standard logic
Source: Calculated with data from Dataquest Europe, Denham UK

successfully to negotiate entry into integrated circuit technology, due to the rapid adoption of the planar process and high entry barriers which prevented US merchant semiconductor firms from competing directly in Japan.

The second part of the chapter showed that firms which had dominated the bipolar logic market in the early 1960s continued to do so from 1979 though to the end of the 1980s This is not surprising given the relative stability of the technology from the mid-1970s onwards compared to the dramatic and unpredictable changes that took place in the 1960s. Thus, the market was characterised by high and relatively stable levels of concentration and low levels of disruption through the 1980s

A competing trajectory had been set up in MOS technology which in its early years did not appear to be a strong competitor. However, rapid declines in the gate delays and the advantage of lower power consumption increased sales of these devices at the expense of bipolar chips. By the late 1980s, the speeds of these various technologies were beginning to converge. As expected, firms that did well in the MOS market were generally not the leaders in bipolar technology, as switching to and pushing a rival technology would undermine their existing technology base. Market concentration in MOS was still high though this declined faster than for bipolar devices. Disruption in the MOS market was considerably higher than for bipolar devices.

8

CASE STUDY: PC SOFTWARE

8.1 INTRODUCTION

The case of PC software illustrates very nicely the two polar extremes identified in the theoretical discussion and the previous case studies. This may seem surprising, for a perusal of the current PC software market suggests that it is dominated by large players, and that mergers are the order of the day to remain competitive. Looked at over a ten-year period, however, the software case does illustrate both the concentrating effects of rapid incremental change and the deconcentrating effects of radically new software product categories.

Incremental change has been very rapid in this market, with leading packages being upgraded every two years or less. Many commentators view these upgrades as being fairly predictable and incremental changes, although offering a large number of additional features. The model of Chapter 4 does still apply here, but the main mechanism that generates the dynamic-scale economies is not so much internal to the firm but arises from the network externalities around leading products. This, as we shall see, acts as a powerful force towards concentration in a particular segment in the software market. Upgrades would generally (though not invariably) observe retrospective compatibility – so that applications developed with Mark I would also run on Mark II – though frequently not vice versa. For this reason, much of the network around the earlier versions of the package would carry over to the upgraded version.

But as well as incremental change, the development of the PC software market in recent years has also seen a proliferation of new product categories. For much of this period, the leaders in one software category were not necessarily the market leaders in others. Indeed, some observers proposed the following rule: 'A firm's best product is its first one'. We shall discuss below the rationale for this argument, but note that if it applies the emergence of new software categories must essentially be a deconcentrating process. It can also be argued that while the rule had some truth until the late 1980s, the user community now pays sufficient attention to the interconnection of diverse applications software that the network externalities argument noted above increasingly applies to new software categories.

The remainder of this chapter looks in some detail at these two polar arguments. Section 8.2 looks at the concentrating effect of rapid incremental change in the spreadsheet software market and section 8.3 looks at that for word-processing software. Section 8.4, in contrast, looks at the deconcentrating effect of the rapid introduction of new software categories. Section 8.5 makes some concluding remarks and draws out the implications of this case study for the theoretical analysis of this book.

8.2 RAPID INCREMENTAL CHANGE IN THE SPREADSHEET SOFTWARE MARKET

In this section and the next, we explore how the rate of advance in software upgrades influences the development of market structure. We do this using two simulation models of the emergence of *de facto* standards which were constructed for the spreadsheet and word-processing markets (Swann and Lamaison, 1990a, 1990b). These models analyse the competition between the main products introduced in the PC spreadsheet and PC word-processing markets from 1982–7 and 1980–7 respectively.[1] The models recognise a fair amount of upgrade activity. We explore the effect of the rate of advance on the evolution of market structure by altering the extent of upgrades in our simulations.

We start with the spreadsheet case. The details of this simulation models are set out in Swann and Lamaison (1990a). The spreadsheet market model has been further developed in Swann and Shurmer (1992) and subjected to extensive sensitivity analysis. Here we simply give a broad outline of the models and then set out the simulations of how the rate of upgrade activity affects the market outcome.

Simulation model

Swann and Lamaison (1990a) developed a simulation model which analyses the emergence of *de facto* or 'market-defined' compatibility standards in the market for PC spreadsheet software. This simulation model is based on standard economic models of the emergence of *de facto* standards developed by Farrell and Saloner (1985, 1986), Katz and Shapiro (1985, 1986), and David (1985, 1987) – see also David and Greenstein (1990) for a valuable survey. However, our model has three valuable enhancements.

1 It can recognise an arbitrary diversity of consumer preferences towards intrinsic quality and network externalities, and thus allow for a solution with multiple standards.
2 It can handle cases where many competing products are introduced – in the simulations, we allow a total of fifteen product introductions.

3 It can allow for partial compatibility between generations of the same product – where the network externalities of one version carry over (at least in part) to the next generation – and no compatibility between completely different products.

In addition, it explores the role of pre-announcements as analysed theoretically by Farrell and Saloner (1986), and allows for various possible functional relationships between network externalities and installed base.

The spreadsheet market is one which in practice has been dominated by one product, Lotus 1–2–3. This was neither the first spreadsheet introduced nor (in the opinion of many) the highest performance product, but nevertheless it has achieved a dominant market position over a number of years. The simulation model is not capable of precisely reconstructing the observed patterns but goes some way to convey the flavour of competition in this market.

The *de facto* standards literature cited above shows that it is the network externalities around each product (as much as the intrinsic quality of the products) that influence consumer choice in any period. These network externalities are benefits that derive from using a technology with a wide installed base of users and which can be connected to a wide variety of other technologies. These consist of the reduced risk of buying a product which will become obsolete – the 'angry orphan' argument (David, 1985); the avoidance of translation or conversion costs; and explicit network effects such as the availability of add-on products, expertise to draw on, training courses and so on. Accordingly, there are strong bandwagon effects that determine the degree and form of standardisation in the market.

In our basic simulation model the consumer is assumed to have an indifference function of the following sort:

$$u_i = a_i + b_i \mu_j N_j + c_i Q_j \qquad (1)$$

Q_j, which could in principle be a vector, represents the intrinsic quality of product j, or 'value for money', where price is counted as a negative characteristic. N_j (a scalar) represents the installed base of product j. The μ_j is a 'network factor' for product j, so that network externalities are proportional to μN. The rationale for this network factor is that the ratio of externalities (add-ons, etc.) to user base is found to be higher for one particular package (Lotus 1–2–3) than for others. The parameters a_i, b_i, and c_i describe user i's indifference function.

For simplicity of exposition, the chapter assumes a normalised version of (1), where Q is taken to be a scalar:

$$u_i = \mu_j N_j + c_i Q_j \qquad (1a)$$

Measuring Q in this case is an exercise in weighting the various features of each product (including price, as noted) and the procedure used is described briefly in section 3.

In most of what follows, it is assumed that the relationship between network externalities and user base is linear (or indeed proportionate). This follows the assumption made in much of the theoretical literature. The chapter also explores what happens if network externalities are proportional to the logarithm of user base, as there are theoretical reasons to expect that this may be a more accurate representation of the relationship.

Pre-announcements of product launches are used to delay consumers' decisions and equally to discourage entry by rival firms (Farrell and Saloner, 1986). The model has been adapted to take account of pre-announcements as follows. In any period, currently uncommitted consumers have two options. The first is to buy one of the available products, in which case equation (1a) applies. The second is to postpone purchase, with a tentative plan to buy one of the pre-announced products not yet available. In this latter case the current (discounted) value of the income stream is:

$$u_i = [\mu_j N_j + c_i Q_j]/(1+r)^t \tag{2}$$

where t is the waiting period before the pre-announced product appears, assuming pre-announcement lags are reliable. The consumer will then make a choice after comparing the solution of (1a) or (2) as appropriate.

In the case of a postponement in anticipation of a forthcoming product, the decision is not binding as the consumer can reappraise the situation in the next period. If new products have been introduced or further pre-announcements have been made, the consumer could revise his plans. It is assumed therefore that the decision to wait does not get communicated publicly as a decision to back a particular forthcoming product, and so does not show up in the user base data.

In the model, it is assumed that consumers appear in a steady and increasing stream, defined by a (s-shaped) logistic growth curve:

$$n(t) = n_{max}/[1 + \exp\{-g(t-t^*)\}] \tag{3}$$

which may alternatively be written as:

$$n(t) = n(1).[1 + \exp\{-g(1-t^*)\}] / [1 + \exp\{-g(t-t^*)\}] \tag{3a}$$

where $n(t)$ is the number of new consumers arriving at time t, g is a growth rate parameter, n_{max} is the saturation level of new consumers, $n(1)$ is new consumer demand in period 1 of the simulation and t^* is the point of inflexion in the growth curve.

In the model, the intrinsic quality is taken to be predetermined, while the user base and so network externalities are dynamically endogenous: consumer choices in one period influence the user base (and so network externalities) in the next period. As is well known, this endogeneity gives such standard models their interesting path-dependent properties. This is most accentuated in the case of no diversity in consumer tastes: then single standards emerge

162

quickly and small changes in any of the model parameters can lead to a different standards outcome. A richer set of possibilities is opened up by allowing for some diversity in consumer tastes, for then outcomes are not so sensitive, though the process still has a similar character.

Accordingly, while it is assumed that all consumers have the same discount rates (r), we allow for consumers to differ in their relative valuation of intrinsic product quality and network externalities (this is the parameter c in equations 1a and 2). For some new (and younger) users, who value intrinsic quality, have little intellectual capital invested in existing products and accordingly have low switching costs, we can expect c to be relatively high. Conversely, for some well-established (and older) users, who have extensive intellectual capital invested in existing designs and correspondingly high switching costs, we can expect c to be relatively low. In particular, the distribution of c is assumed to be uniform over the range 0 to c_{max}.

Data used in spreadsheet simulations

From trade press sources we collated annual data on total spreadsheet sales over the years 1982–7 and used this data to calibrate a logistic curve describing the growth of new demand (see section 4). Data were collected on the announcement and introduction dates of the leading spreadsheet packages. We were able to define these to the nearest quarter. The announcement dates were taken to be the earliest dates given in *Software Users' Year Book* (1990) or where this was not available the first mention of each package found in the trade press. The introduction dates were taken to be the first review dates in the trade press. The rationale for this is that it is common for the trade press to publish a major review of a new product when it actually appears.

It was necessary to construct a one-dimensional measure of vertical quality and so an attempt has been made to place the packages in order on a scale 1...n. The four main quality characteristics mentioned in comparative trade press reviews of software packages are 'performance', 'ease of use', 'documentation' and 'value for money'. Data on these were obtained from several trade press reviews, and also data on spreadsheet size and special features incorporated (word-processing, graphs, communications, report generation, number of input file types, number of sort fields and so on). For fuller details of the calculations, reference is made to Swann and Lamaison (1990a).

Table 8.1 shows the resulting scalar quality ratings generated for each package (and upgrades) and the approximate introduction dates. There is inevitably a subjective element to the weighting of these features in trade press reviews, but the ratings have been checked with the comparative reviews in the trade press and no significant conflicts were found.

Table 8.1 Quality and introduction dates: spreadsheets

Products Product	Introduction date	Quality rating
A1	1982 Q2	1
A2	1983 Q3	2
A3	1984 Q2	8
A4	1986 Q4	10
B1	1983 Q3	3
B2	1986 Q4	6
B3	1987 Q1	9
C1	1983 Q4	4
C2	1986 Q4	6
D1	1985 Q1	9
D2	1986 Q2	11
E1	1987 Q1	12
F1	1984 Q2	7
G1	1986 Q2	5

Sources: Quality rating is the alternative rating in Swann and Lamaison (1990a)
Introduction date is first review date in Swann and Lamaison (1990a)

Simulations

In each case, the simulations took account of fifteen products over up to twenty-eight quarterly time periods. All the simulations were based on the following values for the logistic curve parameters: $n(1)$ (new consumers period 1) = £1.25 million; t^* (point of inflexion) = 1984 Q4; g (slope of growth curve) = 0.21. Note that these imply a maximum level of new consumer demand (n_{max}) of £13.8 million per quarter (= £55.2 million p.a.). Period 1, i.e. $t = 1$, is 1982 (I), while the latest simulation period (28) is 1988 (IV).

Four versions of the model are described, of increasing degrees of generality. Here, we use the most advanced version of the model. This has three particular features of interest.

First, it models partial gateways between upgrades, whereby each upgraded version of an existing product takes over a given percentage of the previous version's network. The upgraded version of the product enjoys a proportion of the network externalities accruing to the earlier version but the gateway does not work in the opposite direction. In other words, network externalities enjoyed by the first version of a software product can be passed down the line to all subsequent upgrades. In some cases we have assumed a gateway of less than 100 per cent because the upgrade does not necessarily ensure total compatibility.

Second, it allows for higher network factors for Lotus 1–2–3. It became clear that the importance of the network externalities surrounding it was not being recognised in simpler versions of the model. It was hypothesised that Lotus 1–2–3 enjoyed disproportionately large network externalities; that is, the network externalities per unit of installed base were higher than for other products. This was confirmed by data on two measures of network extern-alities: the numbers of add-ons and add-ins; and the number of training courses advertised.

Third, it models pre-announcements of products, and implements this by using the data on announcement dates and introduction dates described above. The model also explores the different results according to whether network externalities are a linear or logarithmic function of the installed base, but here we stick to the linear formulation.[2]

In other works, we have subjected the model to a fair degree of sensitivity analysis. Here we hold the majority of model parameters fixed and simply concentrate on the effect of varying three parameters:

1 the extent of gateways (from 25 per cent to 100 per cent);
2 the extent of the Lotus 1–2–3 network factor (1 to 2);
3 the rate of quality advance in upgrades (from 0 to twice the rate of advance given in Table 8.1).

The rate of quality upgrading and consequences for market structure

In the following simulations, the main focus is on the rate of quality advance in upgrades of the various software packages. This is summarised by a rate of advance parameter which is allowed to take values between 0 per cent and 200 per cent, and which is defined as follows. When it is set at 0 per cent, the upgrades are indistinguishable from the earlier version.[3] When it is set at 100 per cent, this implies that the quality of upgrades is equal to those numbers shown in Table 8.1. When it is set at 200 per cent, the upgrade from one version to the next is assumed to give a quality enhancement twice that shown in Table 8.1. For example, with a 100 per cent rate of advance, the four versions of Supercalc have quality scores of 1, 2, 8 and 10 respectively, while with a 200 per cent rate of advance the scores would be 1, 3, 15 and 19 respectively.

Two measures of concentration are considered. One is the share of the top package (including all upgrades) of the final installed base at the end of the simulation. The other is a count of the number of packages (again counting all upgrades in together with the original version) that achieve a positive installed base by the end of the simulation.

Figure 8.1 shows two simulations based on 100 per cent gateways. In one, the network factor for Lotus 1–2–3 is simply unity, meaning that the ratio of network externalities for this product is the same as that for all others. In the other, Lotus 1–2–3 is given a network factor of 1.75, meaning that the ratio of

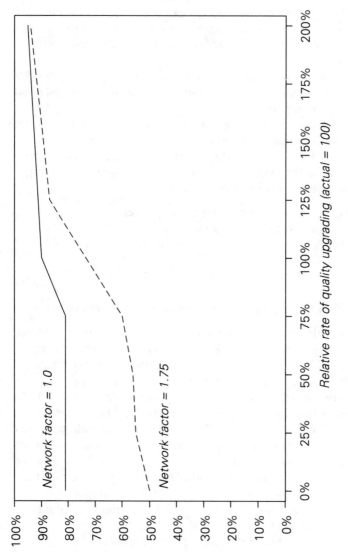

Figure 8.1 Rate of upgrading and degree of standardisation
Note: Upgrade gateways set at 100% throughout

network externalities to installed base for that product is higher than for other products.[4] The vertical axis is the percentage of the total installed base at the end of the simulation (i.e. 1988) accounted for by the leading package or what is, in effect, the *de facto* standard by the end of the race.

In the case of a unit 'Lotus' factor, the speed of upgrade does not make a huge difference. This is because Supercalc wins the race here, regardless of the speed of upgrading, and faster upgrading simply raises the Supercalc share from 81 per cent to 92 per cent. With the larger 'Lotus' factor, however, the effect of a faster rate of upgrading is much more substantial. This happens because with no upgrading the race is won by the product that has the greatest ability to generate network externalities (i.e. Lotus 1–2–3), while with rapid upgrading the race is won by the product that has the most upgrades (Supercalc).

As different packages have different numbers of upgrades, and as the identity of the winner can change as the rate of upgrading increases, we can find some unexpected results in the simulations. Table 8.2 shows a much wider group of simulations for different Lotus factors (1–2), a range of carry over percentages (25 to 100 per cent), and a range of upgrade rates (0 to 200 per cent).

With Lotus factors of 1.75 or 2, note that there can be a 'dip' in the share of the leading firm as the rate of upgrading increases. The reason for this unexpected dip is that the winner at a 0 per cent rate of advance is Lotus (strong on networks) while the winner at 200 per cent is Supercalc (strong on upgrades). At 100 per cent, the race is more closely contested and hence the market share of the winner is less. The pattern in terms of the number of packages with positive installed bases however, is much simpler: this number is always a decreasing function of the rate of upgrading.

8.3 RAPID INCREMENTAL CHANGE IN THE WORD-PROCESSING SOFTWARE MARKET

The same exercise was repeated with a simulation model of the word-processing software market, calibrated with data relating to the period 1982–7. A discussion paper (Swann and Lamaison, 1990b) describes that model in detail and also simulations which vary the basic model parameters. Here, as in the previous section, our attention focuses exclusively on the rate of upgrading and the extent of the gateway between successive upgrades of a package.

Simulation model

There are two main differences between the model used in this case and the one described in the previous section – apart, of course, from relating to different markets. The first is that in this case products are differentiated both along a vertical quality scale and along a horizontal quality spectrum. By vertical we mean those aspects of quality on which there is general agreement

Table 8.2 Sensitivity analysis: Concentration in PC spreadsheet software

		Installed base share of leading product (%)					Number of products with positive installed bases			
			Gateway					Gateway		
Network		25%	50%	75%	100%		25%	50%	75%	100%
factor	0%	81	81	81	81	0%	4	4	4	4
1.00	25%	81	81	81	81	25%	4	4	4	4
	50%	81	81	81	81	50%	4	4	4	4
	75%	81	81	81	81	75%	4	4	4	4
	100%	90	90	90	91	100%	3	3	3	3
	125%	91	91	91	92	125%	2	2	2	2
	150%	91	91	92	92	150%	2	2	2	2
	175%	92	92	92	92	175%	2	2	2	2
	200%	92	92	92	92	200%	2	2	2	2
	Rate of upgrade					Rate of upgrade				

			Gateway					Gateway		
Network		25%	50%	75%	100%		25%	50%	75%	100%
factor	0%	81	81	81	81	0%	4	4	4	4
1.25	25%	81	81	81	81	25%	4	4	4	4
	50%	81	81	81	81	50%	4	4	4	4
	75%	81	81	81	81	75%	4	4	4	4
	100%	86	87	88	89	100%	4	4	3	3
	125%	91	91	91	91	125%	2	2	2	2
	150%	91	91	91	91	150%	2	2	2	2
	175%	91	91	91	92	175%	2	2	2	2
	200%	91	91	92	92	200%	2	2	2	2
	Rate of upgrade					Rate of upgrade				

			Gateway					Gateway		
Network		25%	50%	75%	100%		25%	50%	75%	100%
factor	0%	77	77	77	77	0%	5	5	5	5
1.50	25%	77	77	77	78	25%	5	5	5	4
	50%	77	77	77	78	50%	5	5	4	4
	75%	77	76	77	78	75%	5	4	4	4
	100%	76	80	84	86	100%	4	4	3	3
	125%	90	90	90	90	125%	2	2	2	2
	150%	90	90	90	91	150%	2	2	2	2
	175%	91	91	91	91	175%	2	2	2	2
	200%	91	91	91	92	200%	2	2	2	2
	Rate of upgrade					Rate of upgrade				

Table 8.2 cont'd

		Installed base share of leading product (%)					Number of products with positive installed bases			
		Gateway					Gateway			
Network		25%	50%	75%	100%		25%	50%	75%	100%
factor	0%	51	51	51	51	0%	5	5	5	5
1.75	25%	51	51	55	56	25%	5	5	5	5
	50%	51	57	53	58	50%	5	5	5	4
	75%	57	49	59	62	75%	5	4	4	4
	100%	47	51	51	75	100%	3	3	3	3
	125%	88	88	88	89	125%	2	2	2	2
	150%	89	89	90	90	150%	2	2	2	2
	175%	90	90	90	91	175%	2	2	2	2
	200%	90	90	91	91	200%	2	2	2	2
	Rate of upgrade					Rate of upgrade				

			Gateway					Gateway		
Network		25%	50%	75%	100%		25%	50%	75%	100%
factor	0%	81	81	81	81	0%	5	5	5	5
2.00	25%	81	81	80	80	25%	5	5	5	5
	50%	81	80	79	79	50%	5	5	5	5
	75%	79	78	77	78	75%	5	5	5	4
	100%	73	71	67	74	100%	4	3	3	3
	125%	85	85	86	87	125%	2	2	2	2
	150%	88	88	88	89	150%	2	2	2	2
	175%	89	89	89	90	175%	2	2	2	2
	200%	89	90	90	91	200%	2	2	2	2

about what constitutes an improvement, while by horizontal we mean those aspects of quality where different consumers have a different optimum, and where there is no general agreement about what constitutes an improvement. The spreadsheet simulation model had only a vertical quality dimension to it. The second difference is that no attempt is made here to model pre-announcements, in contrast to the previous model. There is one other minor difference: here, no product enjoys a disproportionate network factor, and the ratio of network externalities to installed base is assumed to be the same for all products.

The word-processing market was dominated by one product (Wordstar) for the early part of the period under study, but in the last few years other products have achieved significant market shares.[5] Simulations which ignore the horizontal dimension do not seem to replicate events closely since (as we saw above) one product would in most cases tend to swamp the field – and all the more so as time progresses. Swann and Lamaison (1990b) found that a mixed horizontal/vertical model can do much better for this market, essentially because the horizontal dimension makes it easier for multiple standards to appear for different (horizontal) market segments.

Here, the consumer is assumed to have an indifference function of the following sort:

$$u = a + bN_j + cV_j - p \mid H_j - H^* \mid \tag{4}$$

where V_j and H_j represent the intrinsic quality (vertical and horizontal respectively) of product j (or value for money, where price is counted as a negative characteristic), N_j represents the network externalities of product j, and a, b, H^*, c and p are parameters of the user's indifference function. The a is an intercept term, while b and c are the marginal values of the network and vertical quality respectively. H^* describes the consumer's ideal horizontal quality, that is, the ideal product specification for that type of consumer, while p defines the utility penalty incurred by the consumer when a particular product design deviates from the ideal horizontal quality. As in section 8.2, we use (for simplicity of exposition) a normalised version of (4):

$$u = N_j + cV_j - p \mid H_j - H^* \mid \tag{4a}$$

As before, the simulation model assumes that all consumers have indifference functions as above (4a), but that consumers differ in their relative valuation of intrinsic qualities to network externalities and in their relative valuation of vertical and horizontal quality. In terms of the parameters of (4a), this means that we allow for a distribution of values for c and H^*, but assume a fixed value for p within any simulation. In the simulation model, c varies in the same way as before, while H^* is allowed to vary over the length of the horizontal quality spectrum – i.e. from one end to another. As before, uniform distributions are assumed for simplicity.

As argued above, for new (and younger) users who have little intellectual capital invested in these existing designs and who have low switching costs accordingly we can expect c to be high and b and p to be relatively low. Conversely, for well-established (and older) users who have extensive experience of existing designs and much intellectual capital invested in existing designs with accordingly high switching costs, we can expect c to be relatively low and b and p to be relatively high.

In all respects the model is the same as that in section 8.2 and needs no further elaboration. It incorporates partial gateways, and it is assumed that market demand again follows a logistic curve – though, of course, with different parameters. Network externalities are taken to be proportional to user base.

Data used in word-processing simulations

From trade press sources we collected data on sales of word-processing packages and used this to calibrate the logistic curve describing the growth of new demand (see below). Data were collected on introduction dates (to the nearest quarter) of the main word-processing packages and their upgrades. As before, these were taken as the dates the package was first reviewed in the trade press.

The vertical measure of quality was generated as before. This was based on reviews of packages in the trade press, with 'performance', 'ease of use', 'documentation' and 'value for money' the four main quality attributes. These are the characteristics most often mentioned in comparative reviews and seem to be used in these reviews to rank the products. This is described in detail in Swann and Lamaison, 1990b.

In calculating the horizontal measure, it was recognised that word processors varied not only in terms of 'performance', as measured above, but also in their individual character and suitability for different types of uses. Some, for example, were designed for secretarial/commercial applications while others are more suitable for author/technical use. The horizontal rank was determined in two stages. First, a figure was constructed which listed all the features mentioned in reviews for each product. These features were then classified into secretarial/commercial, neutral, author/technical. Scores on a scale of 0 to 3 were then awarded and totals for each category were calculated. The relative spread of these scores was then examined and used to position each product on a six-point horizontal scale from 0 (secretarial/commercial) to 5 (author/technical).

Figure 8.2 summarises the results of the vertical and horizontal quality ranking exercises in a two-dimensional characteristics diagram.

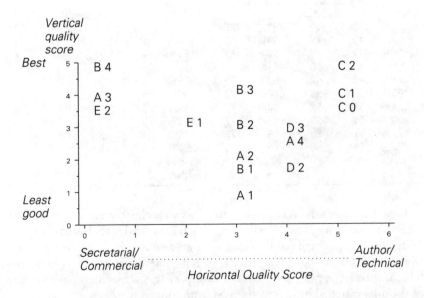

Figure 8.2 Vertical versus horizontal quality: word-processing packages

Simulations

In each case the simulations track the performance of fifteen products. We make use of one base-case set of parameters (see Swann and Lamaison, 1990b for the results of variations around this base-case simulation). The logistic curve parameters are: $n(1)$ (new consumer demand period 1) = 0.4 (£ million); t^* (point of inflexion) = 1984 Q3; b (slope of growth curve) = 0.18. Note that these imply a maximum level of new consumer demand (n_{max}) of £10.6 million per quarter (= £42.4 million p.a.). The simulations are performed for fifteen products over thirty-two quarterly periods from 1980: I (period 1) to 1987: IV (period 32).

The simulations use an 11*11 grid of consumer types, uniformly distributed over the range ($0 \leq c \leq c_{max}$) and $0 \leq H^* \leq 5$. In the base case, $c_{max} = 20$, $p = 50$.

The rate of vertical quality upgrading in word-processing software

As before, we simply report here the results obtained by varying two parameters: the extent of the gateway between successive upgrades (from 25 per cent to 100 per cent) and the rate of vertical quality upgrading (from 0 to twice the rate of advance shown in Figure 8.2).

Table 8.3 Sensitivity analysis: concentration in PC word-processing software

	Installed base share of leading product (%)					Number of products with positive installed bases			
	Gateway					Gateway			
	25%	50%	75%	100%		25%	50%	75%	100%
0%	49	49	54	62	0%	4	4	4	4
25%	49	49	58	65	25%	4	4	4	4
50%	49	50	64	68	50%	4	4	4	4
75%	48	62	66	69	75%	5	5	4	4
100%	57	58	67	72	100%	5	5	5	4
125%	55	58	68	72	125%	5	5	5	5
150%	54	59	67	72	150%	5	5	5	5
175%	54	60	66	72	175%	5	5	5	5
200%	55	60	65	70	200%	5	5	5	5
Rate of upgrade					Rate of upgrade				

Table 8.3 shows the results obtained. It is a much simpler table than 8.2 as there is no network factor. As before, the share of final installed base enjoyed by the leading package (counting in all upgrades) is seen to rise as the rate of advance rises from 0 per cent to 100 per cent. Thereafter it levels out or even falls. Surprisingly, perhaps, the number of packages achieving a positive share of the final installed base actually rises from four to five.

In short, while there is some evidence here that an increase in the rate of vertical quality improvement leads to greater concentration, the picture is less pronounced than in the spreadsheet case. The reason almost certainly lies in the inclusion of horizontal differentiation in this model. This means that the market is more segmented, and that the attractiveness of a product to its immediate niche is affected less by vertical quality improvements in products from another niche.

Indeed, just as the existence of a horizontal quality dimension reduces the concentrating effects of vertical quality improvement, so we see in the next section that the rapid extension of the horizontal dimension – by the proliferation of new software categories – is in fact deconcentrating.

8.4 NEW SOFTWARE CATEGORIES

Quite soon after the introduction of the IBM PC in December 1981, three main operating system standards came to the fore in the PC market. Until that time the market was very fragmented, with almost as many operating systems as hardware systems and little standardisation. The appearance of a standard gave the market the sort of stability on which a large number of third party software houses could build.

As a result, the 1980s saw a rapid proliferation of new software packages for the PC standard, with many of them produced by newly formed and often small companies. At the end of the 1980s, this process was continuing but with the larger software houses starting to dominate again. Nevertheless, the picture during most of the 1980s appears to be one of deconcentrating technological change.

We argue here that this arises for two reasons, which we return to analyse below. First, some of the new software categories represent more radical product innovation than the sorts of incremental improvement found in the upgrade paths described above. Second, a firm which had already had success in one software category would usually find the switch to another software category harder than a newcomer. We shall argue that this second point reflects both the relative inertia of established firms in the face of unanticipated technological change and the fact that established firms tend to experience a degree of lock-in to existing product designs.

Deconcentrating effects of new software categories: cluster analysis

The *PC World* (1987) survey, reproduced in Juliussen and Juliussen (1988) lists the leading products in each of twenty-seven software categories for the PC[6]. While these do not represent an exhaustive market share breakdown in each category, they allow us to explore the extent to which leaders in one category have success in other categories.

For each pair of product categories, these data allow us to compute the extent of overlap among the leading firms. The basic idea is as follows.

Consider two software categories, 1 and 2. If there is only one firm (A) that is a market leader in both category 1 and category 2, the overlap between the two categories will be measured as the smaller of A's market shares in 1 and 2. The rationale for using this minimum – rather than the average – as the measure of overlap is easily seen. Suppose A has 5 per cent of category 1 (and only just qualifies as a market leader) but 75 per cent of category 2. In effect there is a very limited market share overlap between categories 1 and 2, and the minimum (5 per cent) rather than the average (40 per cent) gives a more honest reflection of this. However, if the two software categories (1 and 2) are combined to form a cluster, it obviously makes sense to say that A's share of the combined market is the (weighted) average of its shares in categories 1 (5 per cent) and 2 (75 per cent) respectively.

The 27*27 matrix of pairwise category overlaps can easily be computed, but it is a bit hard to interpret. A natural way to summarise these overlaps is, of course, by cluster analysis. The overlap metric described above is a natural one to use to describe clusters in this case.[7] The first (pairwise) cluster would be the pair of software categories with the largest overlap. The second cluster would be that with the next largest overlap, and could comprise either a second pair of categories or a new cluster formed of an existing sub-cluster and another software category. The third and subsequent clusters, in turn, could be a pair or a new cluster comprising an existing sub-cluster and another category, or two existing sub-clusters.

Figure 8.3 shows the clusters obtained by grouping categories in turn using this overlap metric.[8] The horizontal axis is the overlap measure so a reading of 20 per cent for a cluster implies that there is a 20 per cent overlap between the constituent categories. There is a downward bias here which arises because, as noted above, we do not have a comprehensive breakdown of 'market shares' for each software category. Suppose that we have data on the top four in two different categories, and that in each case they together account for 60 per cent of the market, then obviously the overlap measure cannot exceed 60 per cent, even if the four leaders are the same and the distribution of market shares among the four is identical.

Investment and personal management software come out as the two closest categories, though neither of these two categories have market leaders very close to those in other categories. Spreadsheets, financial analysis software and integrated packages form quite a close cluster, meaning that the market leaders are relatively similar in each of these markets. This is not perhaps surprising as one of the leading financial analysis packages is in fact a spreadsheet and indeed one of the market leaders in spreadsheets also has a popular integrated package.

The largest cluster at an overlap metric of 20 per cent comprises word-processing software, word-processing support tools, desktop management, programming languages, operating environment (e.g. operating systems) and training. These are some of the more traditional software areas in which some

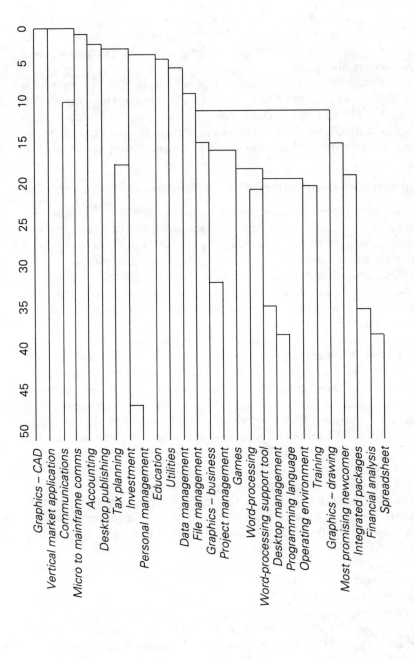

Figure 8.3 PC software clusters by market share overlap

Source: Based on cluster analysis using data from 'World Class PC Celebration', *PC World*, 5(11), October 1987. This data is reprinted with the permission of *PC World*

of the large software producers have a prominent position. Reducing the overlap measure to 15 per cent brings in file management software, business graphics, project management software and, surprisingly perhaps, games. This large cluster joins up with the rather different spreadsheet cluster at 11 per cent, but the only other cluster at that level is the investment/personal management/tax planning group.

All other categories in the top half of Figure 8.3 appear to have very little overlap, either with each other or with these main clusters. This suggests that the leadership of these sub-markets is of a very different composition from those of the main clusters. The proliferation of these software categories can be seen as a deconcentrating force in the development of the software market.

Deconcentration from the perspective of three core software categories

Of course, what Figure 8.3 does not show are the dates at which these new software categories emerged and hence the sequence from the most traditional sectors to the newest. In fact, it turned out to be rather difficult to pin down these dates without a more extensive historical analysis than was possible for the present case study.[9] Instead, we take three core software categories (spreadsheets, word-processing, and operating systems) and explore how the proliferation of new categories is deconcentrating from the perspective of these particular sub-markets.

For each of these three core categories in turn, and using the same overlap metric, we sort the other categories into descending degree of overlap with the core category. We then plot graphs of the share of those firms that form the top three in the core category as other (increasingly distant) software categories are added to the core category (Figure 8.4). In spreadsheets (SPSH) and operating systems (OS), the top three account for over 80 per cent and in word-processing (WP) about 70 per cent. But as extra categories are added to the cluster (in descending order of their overlap with the core category), these figures fall, quite sharply in the case of operating systems (OS) though less sharply in the case of spreadsheets and word-processing software.

This means that the top three in the spreadsheet market are quite well represented in other categories; taking the best fourteen categories, these three firms account for about 40 per cent. Conversely, the top three in the operating systems (OS) market are less well represented elsewhere; taking the best fourteen categories they account for less than 20 per cent. The top three in word-processing take an intermediate position.

These graphs are obviously constructed in such a way that they are bound to slope downwards. As we add categories which have little or no overlap with the core category, the share of the original top three in the composite market thus created is bound to fall. The real issue is how rapidly it falls, and it is here apparent that shares fall off steadily in all cases but especially so with operating system software.

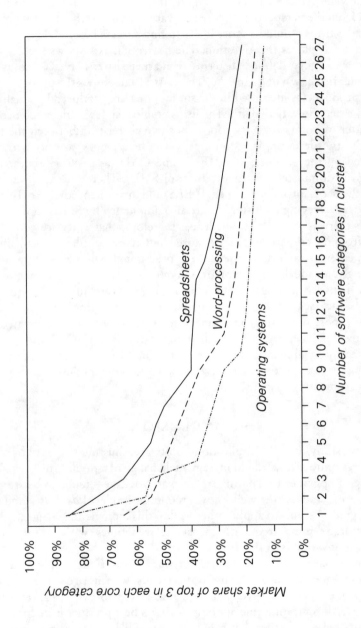

Figure 8.4 Deconcentrating effect of proliferating software categories

Source: Based on cluster analysis using data from 'World Class PC Celebration', *PC World*, 5(11), October 1987. This data is reproduced with the permission of *PC World*

Market share of top 3 in each core category

Number of software categories in cluster

Spreadsheets

Word-processing

Operating systems

We conclude this section by asking whether the new categories that have relatively little overlap with the core categories are more likely to be populated by the newer, smaller firms in the sample. If these are the radical innovations (viewed from the perspective of core software categories) the thesis would be that smaller firms would be more likely to find success here.

Figure 8.5 explores this question. The horizontal axis shows the distance between a category defined in terms of market share: it is 100 minus the overlap metric shown in Figure 8.6. The vertical axis shows the proportion of leading products (as identified in the survey) that are produced by small and medium enterprises, here defined as firms employing fewer than 500 people. The scatter of points suggests a loose positive correlation between the two. Spreadsheets, for example, counting as a core category are not strongly populated by the products of SMEs, while CAD (as a specialised area of graphics) is dominated by the products of SMEs. There are, however, two clear outliers, personal management (PERS) and investment software (INVE), which form a very tight cluster but are also dominated by SMEs[10].

While there is some loose evidence, therefore, that software categories distant from the core categories are more likely to be populated by small and medium enterprises (SMEs), these SMEs need not also be new. There is, not surprisingly, a wide dispersion of growth rates in this industry, so that quite a few new firms are no longer SMEs while many SMEs are quite old. Figure 8.6 illustrates the lack of correlation between these two indices. The NEW category ('most promising newcomer' items of software) is dominated by new firms but they are not small. Conversely, the GAME category is dominated by small firms but they are not young.[11] In some cases, of course, the young firms are also small (CAD, etc.), while in others the older firms are also large (operating systems, OS).

8.5 CONCLUSIONS

This case study of PC applications software illustrates the two polar hypotheses quite nicely. Rapid incremental change of a predictable sort – the sequence of upgrades to a particular software package – tends to be steadily concentrating. Indeed, the well-known economic model of *de facto* standards (with upgrades) seems to apply rather well to this incremental change. As the software trade press frequently observes, sometimes with regret, much software innovation is of this sort.

But there have been more radical software innovations that spawn new software categories. This sort of innovation tends to be more deconcentrating. Indeed, some observers have suggested that in the software market a particularly deconcentrating rule applies: 'A firm's best product is its first one'. We discuss below whether that rule is still plausible. First, we note that if it applies, a market leader in segment A (say) can never expect the same success in another market segment that it has enjoyed in A. This must mean either that

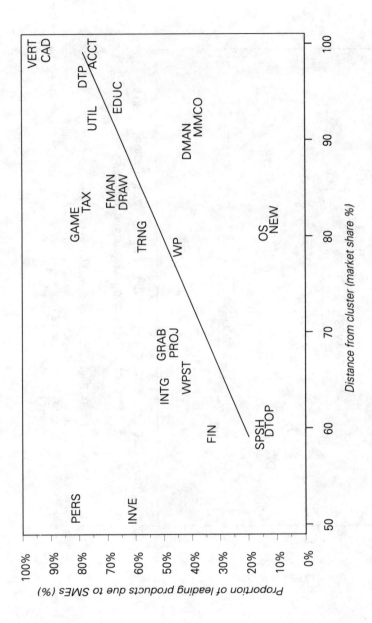

Figure 8.5 Disruptiveness and niches for SMEs: PC software

Source: Calculated from data in: 'World Class PC Celebration', *PC World*, 5(11), October 1987, this data is reprinted with the permission of *PC World*; and data from the book, *The Computer Industry Almanac 1989* by Juliussen and Juliussen, Copyright © 1988, published by Brady, a division of Prentice Hall Computer Publishing, used by permission of the publisher.

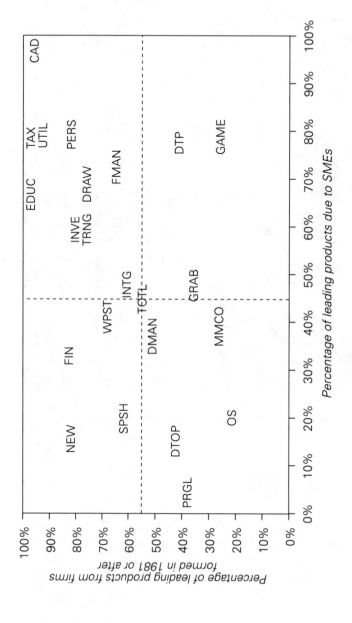

Figure 8.6 SME niches and new firm 'bias' in PC software

Source: Calculated from data in: 'World Class PC Celebration', *PC World*, 5(11), October (1987), this data is reprinted with the permission of *PC World*; and data from the book, *The Computer Industry Almanac 1989* by Juliussen and Juliussen, copyright © 1988, published by Brady, a division of Prentice Hall Computer Publishing, used by permission of the publisher.

market segments for new software categories are less concentrated than earlier markets (which seems implausible) or that a new entrant will be the market leader in a new market segment.

But why should 'a firm's best product be its first one'? The argument is in three steps.

1 some users tend to use a number of software products together, so that material is passed to and fro between one package and another (Lamaison, 1991);
2 A successful product in one segment will have a certain 'look and feel' and the wise producer will seek to ensure that his offerings in other segments have a similar 'look and feel' so that the buyer of suites of programs is likely to buy them all from one source;
3 while the producer is wise to exploit these network externalities (and switching costs), it does mean running the risk of applying a user interface originally designed for one environment to another environment for which it is less suitable.

In short, the producer of a market leader in segment A is so constrained in its user interface that it has to settle for a second-best design for market segment B (viewed as a stand-alone product) and hence it will not achieve such market success with that second product.

It may be asked whether the network externalities to the market leader in segment A do not more than offset the design constraint on the product from segment B? And if they do not, why does the producer let himself be constrained? The answer is that, in the short to medium term, these network effects do provide offsetting benefits; in the long term the design constraint becomes more and more serious. Yet incumbents dare not distance themselves from their existing network in the short term. These observations introduce some interesting dynamics into the economics of software production.

9

CASE STUDY: BIOTECHNOLOGY

9.1 INTRODUCTION

Earlier chapters examined the effects of rapid technology change and the development of market structure in the various microelectronics markets, thus it is not clear whether the findings are applicable to other sectors. This chapter is an attempt to examine these issues for biotechnology.

The rest of this chapter is in five parts. Section 9.2 gives some background to biotechnology, the nature of innovation in this area and biotechnology markets. This is followed in section 9.3 by details of the diagnostics market (with a focus on kits for detecting infection of human immunodeficiency virus). Next, section 9.4 outlines the methodological approach of this case study, and section 9.5 the main findings. Conclusions and policy implications are drawn out in section 9.6.

9.2 BIOTECHNOLOGY

Biotechnology has been defined as 'the application of biological organisms, systems and processes to manufacturing and service industries' (ACARD, 1980). Biotechnology is a set of process technologies which not only have wide applications covering a variety of industrial sectors and markets but are expected to open up a range of new (and unforeseen) possibilities in the future.

Historical development of biotechnology

Biotechnology can be conveniently divided into three generations or phases of development (Sharp, 1985). First-generation biotechnology generally refers to the use of biological organisms principally in the processes of fermentation (for example, brewing alcoholic beverages, the use of yeast in the production of bread and so on) and dates back to prehistory. Biotechnology in this phase was more a craft than a science.

Second-generation biotechnology emerged in the 1930s with the advent of petrochemicals and antibiotics such as penicillin. This phase relied on screening naturally occurring and artificially modified (for example, by chemical or X-ray mutagenesis) biological products.

Third-generation biotechnology (also referred to as the 'new biotechnology') emerged in the 1970s with the advent of technologies based on recombinant DNA (rDNA) and monoclonal antibodies (MAb) and differed from earlier generations in being closer to a science than a craft. Thus, while first- and second-generation biotechnology were largely based on trial and error – and have been termed 'molecular roulette' (Walsh, 1990) – third-generation biotechnology allows the systematic and deliberate introduction of changes at the level of the genetic code.

Biotechnology and innovation

Due to its generic nature, third-generation biotechnology (hereafter referred to simply as biotechnology) is considered to be strategically important, with potentially revolutionary and pervasive impacts on a worldwide scale (OTA, 1984). Leadership in biotechnology is thus seen as crucial for long-term success in the world markets and technology of the twenty-first century. Consequently, competitive pressures at the leading edge of biotechnology are expected to be intense, with innovatory capacities playing a key role in technological and market leadership. The OTA put it thus:

> The United States, at first through new firms and now with the combined efforts of the established companies, has the ability to maintain its lead by continuing to innovate at a pace equal to or faster than its competitor countries.

(OTA, 1984: 98)

In the 1970s, technological innovation in biotechnology was largely driven and dominated by university-based research institutions as well as new (small) start-up firms (Sharp, 1985; Dibner, 1988). During this period, the large established firms that had been pre-eminent in second-generation biotechnology (e.g. pharmaceutical companies, brewing firms, petrochemical producers and so on) generally followed a policy of providing investment capital to the new biotechnology firms which provided a window on technological developments (Sharp, 1985). It was only in the 1980s that many large established companies began to commit substantial resources to build up in-house facilities and expertise (OTA, 1984). Thus, the rapid increase in the number of new start-ups in the 1970s was followed by a marked slowdown in the 1980s (Dibner, 1988).

Biotechnology is, in effect, a double-edged sword, providing both opportunities and threats to established companies in a variety of sectors. Opportunities arise, for example, through the possibility of manufacturing existing products at lower cost or producing new ones with enhanced or novel characteristics. Threats are posed by new entrants. The precise nature of

183

technological development and competition varies between the different product sectors.

Biotechnology markets

The OTA (1984) divides biotechnology applications into seven broad groups: pharmaceuticals, plant and animal agriculture, speciality chemicals and food additives, environmental applications, commodity chemicals and energy production, and finally, bioelectronics.

Biotechnology is widely considered to be most advanced in the pharmaceuticals market, in which such techniques are held to be at the leading edge. The conventional wisdom regarding future development in this sector (as outlined by Sharp, 1985) is as follows. Biotechnology is potentially highly destabilising. However, in the long run, new entrants will not be able to displace the dominant role of the established pharmaceutical firms for two main reasons. The first is the high entry barriers in the industry (e.g. regulatory approval resulting in long lead times from product invention to market approval). The second is that the new entrants lack 'complementary assets' (e.g. marketing and distribution networks, links to regulatory bodies and so on) required for market success[1].

On the other hand, the biotechnology firms have expertise, knowledge and skills in this new technology base. Such synergies have led to co-operative agreements between established firms and the new biotechnology companies. At the same time, there has been a proliferation of new biotechnology companies, specifically established to exploit this new technology, contributing to market deconcentration. This situation is not expected to last. Over time the established large companies will regain leadership and thus lead to market reconcentration.

It is not clear, however, whether such prognostications will hold across all pharmaceutical (or other biotechnology) markets as there are considerable variations in entry barriers and the complementary assets required within and between such markets. Pharmaceuticals cover a wide range of products but can be broadly divided into two categories: therapeutics and diagnostics.

Therapeutics markets are highly regulated and present major problems for new entrants. The regulatory regime for diagnostics depends on whether these are *in vitro* or *in vivo* products, with the latter stringently controlled. Thus, market entry is easier for companies producing *in vitro* diagnostics – a market segment characterised by high levels of activity by new biotechnology firms (Dibner, 1988; OTA, 1984) and higher rates of technology change than in therapeutic products.

In order to examine a market where there is greater potential for success on the part of new entrants using high rates of technology change as a competitive weapon against incumbent firms, this case study focuses on the less regulated and more open *in vitro* diagnostics sector of pharmaceuticals. The next section gives a detailed account of one of the single largest biotechnology-based diagnostic markets, the detection of exposure to the human immunodeficiency virus (HIV).

9.3 DIAGNOSTICS

Diagnostics are available for a variety of diseases and conditions. In 1987, worldwide sales of biotechnology drugs and diagnostic tests were estimated to have reached about $400 million and $300 million respectively (*Economist*, 1988). Within the diagnostics market, tests for AIDS (i.e. infection with human immunodeficiency virus) accounted for some $60 million (*Economist*, 1988). The focus here is on diagnostic kits for infection by the human immunodeficiency virus (HIV) and their use in mass screening markets for blood.

Human immunodeficiency virus

HIV is a human retrovirus which attacks the immune system and culiminates in acquired immune deficiency syndrome (AIDS). The first AIDS cases were identified in 1981 in the USA where young homosexual males were found to have parasitic (viral or fungal) infections along with Karposi's sarcoma (a rare skin tumour).

Two main subgroups of HIV have been identified: HIV–1 and HIV–2. HIV–1 was first isolated by the Pasteur Institute (France) and termed LAV – lymphadenopathy associated virus in 1983, followed by researchers in the USA (who used the term HTLV–III – human T-cell lymphotrophic virus. HIV–2 was reportedly isolated by the Pasteur Institute in 1985. HIV–1 infection is principally confined to Europe and the USA. HIV–2 is more prevalent in West Africa but is considered to be increasing in Europe (Gottfried and Urnovitz, 1990: 35; Weiss, 1988: 219). The main methods of horizontal transmission of HIV are by intimate sexual contact, involving an exchange of body fluids, and blood-to-blood contact. Vertical transmission can occur through transplacental transfer of maternal infection.

The pathogenesis of HIV

HIV infection has generally been characterised by three main stages: primary, latent and acute infection. In the first stage of primary infection, antigen concentration increases over time, reaches a peak and then declines (or disappears).

The second stage, latent infection, is associated with seroconversion (i.e. the appearance of IgG and IgM antibodies to HIV in the sera of infected individuals). Two principal markers in this phase are antibodies to core and envelope proteins of HIV, p24 and gp160 respectively. The period between infection with the virus and seroconversion is termed the 'window period'. The window period for infection by HIV through contaminated blood (and sexual contact) is generally considered to be around one month. In some instances, individuals who have been infected with HIV appear not to seroconvert (i.e. not to display any antibodies). Confirmation of HIV infection for this group is by detection of the antigen.

In the third stage, acute infection, the virus reappears and increases in concentration while antibody levels decline. This is generally regarded as a poor prognostication leading to suppressed immune response in which the individual becomes increasingly prone to opportunistic infections and is characterised by AIDS or AIDS-related complex (ARC).

Performance characteristics of tests

The suitability of diagnostic kits depends on a number of key technical and economic characteristics. Technically the most important factors are sensitivity, specificity and speed, though other parameters which may also be taken into account are ease of use, shelf life and reliability of supply. From an economic perspective, the cost of the kit is the most important factor.

Sensitivity

Generally, the results of a diagnostic assay (i.e. test) can be positive or negative.[2] If the result of the test is positive and the disease is present, this is termed a true positive. Similarly, if the result is negative and the disease is not present, this is called a true negative. However, a positive result where the disease was not present would give rise to what is termed a false positive. Conversely, a negative result with the disease present is called a false negative.

Sensitivity can be defined as the number of true positives detected by the test divided by the sum of true positive and false positive results. An assay which had a sensitivity of 95 per cent would detect 95 out of 100 cases where the disease was present.

In certain situations the result may be equivocal, i.e. borderline between positive and negative. To take such results into account some authors (e.g. Parry et al., 1990) add the number of equivocal results to both the numerator and denominator in their calculation of sensitivity.

Specificity

The specificity of a test is a measure of its accuracy in giving a negative result when the disease is not present. Thus, specificity can be defined as the number of true negatives divided by the sum of the true negatives and false positives.[3] A specificity of 80 per cent would mean that the assay would give a negative result in eight out of ten tests where the disease was not present (and a false positive in two out of ten cases).

Speed

The speed requirements of any test depend on the exact nature of the application. For example, a clinic or doctor's surgery may need an individual test which provides a result within the consultation time of the patient, e.g. within ten minutes or so. Institutions (e.g. blood banks) which have a high throughput of samples to be tested may find it acceptable to have tests which take longer (e.g. in the order of hours) but allow a high number of screening tests to be carried out simultaneously. Confirmatory tests may be acceptable even if they take a long time.

Ideally, a diagnostic test should have both high sensitivity and specificity. Generally, mass screening markets (such as blood products) require very low values of false positives (i.e. 0.1 per cent or less) in order to avoid having to discard such donations or carry out a large number of high-cost confirmatory tests. Over the last five years, however, the level of false positives with HIV kits has fallen to around 0.1 per cent and mass blood-screening institutions have now become more concerned with avoiding of false negatives.

The sensitivity and specificity of any given diagnostic kit will vary with the sample population under test. Performance data for HIV are generally based on tests carried out in four types of samples: low-risk populations (i.e. blood donor markets), high-risk populations (e.g. drug abusers), known positives (which can be weak or strong) and seroconversion panels.

Seroconversion panels refer to a series of blood samples taken at intervals from individuals either already infected or at a high risk of contracting HIV. Thus, the time series of samples contain different levels of antibodies to HIV. Seroconversion panels are generally used by the various virus reference laboratories throughout Europe and are also available commercially. Manufacturers can also commission regional blood transfusion centres to carry-out sensitivity and specificity studies on their kits.

Performance data will vary depending on the type of population sample used. There may also be variation within any given type of population (for example, test results from blood donors in different countries may give different values of sensitivity and specificity). Such variation makes comparisons between the performance of various kits problematical. In practice, the exact methodological details of the sensitivity or specificity data for various kits are not always given by the manufacturer.

Detection of HIV infection

Methods of identifying individuals with HIV infection fall into three main categories:

1 the detection of antibodies to HIV in blood serum and certain other body fluids such as saliva;
2 testing for HIV protein and glycoprotein in body fluids and in culture; and
3 the direct detection of HIV RNA by gene probes.

By the end of 1990 the market for HIV diagnostics had become dominated by antibody detection tests. These tests use the presence of antibodies to characterise exposure to HIV. Thus, individuals who have HIV but do not have antibodies to the virus, either because they are still in the first stage of the infection (i.e. have not yet seroconverted) or they are seronegative for some other reason, will not be picked up with these tests.

HIV diagnostic markets

Worldwide sales of AIDS diagnostic kits grew from zero in 1984 to more than US $100 million in 1989 (Gottfried and Urnovitz, 1990: 35). HIV diagnostic markets can be grouped into three categories of tests depending on their application: screening, confirmatory and monitoring. Screening tests represent the single most important market due to its sheer size and this is where most development effort has been concentrated.

Screening tests

Screening tests for HIV can be divided into two markets: blood and blood-based products, and the identification of HIV-infected individuals, e.g. healthcare and applicant suitability market (Gottfried and Urnovitz, 1988: 214).

HIV diagnostic kits were first developed for the blood transfusion market to prevent the spread of HIV infection through the transfusion of contaminated blood. All these tests are antigen based (obtained either through cell culture or recombinant DNA technology) which is used to detect the presence of antibodies to HIV. The first test kit for HIV antibodies (Abbott Anti-HTLV III) was licensed by the US Federal Drug Administration in March 1985 (Weiss, 1988: 218) at which time seven other companies were also aiming to produce such kits. HIV kits for screening blood in the UK market were first utilised about six months later.

The blood transfusion market has been dominated by ELISA[4] (enzyme-linked immunoassay) kits which use automated equipment. While the cost per test in the UK has been between 50 and 70 pence, the capital costs for the automated ELISA test readers (and associated equipment) are high. Such high equipment costs are considered to constrain take-up of ELISA kits in developing country markets.

A recent development has been the appearance of relatively fast individual tests which give results typically in five minutes (though some may take around thirty minutes). In principle, such tests may be used in situations requiring rapid tests (e.g. doctor's surgeries and accident wards in hospitals) or in the over the counter (OTC) market. However, the OTC market is unlikely to be significant in the near future as a result of concern about the implications of uncontrolled access to HIV diagnosis without the complementary counselling services or the potential for misuse of such tests to discriminate against HIV-positive individuals.[5]

Overall, such tests are considered more suitable than ELISA kits for developing country markets where the high capital costs of ELISA readers, for example, preclude their use for blood screening.

Confirmatory tests

Early screening tests are not considered very accurate (they had a high incidence of false positives). Confirmatory tests are therefore used to filter results which are positive on repeat testing by screening tests. The best known and most common test in this category is the 'Western Blot' (based on gel electrophoresis). For many years this was regarded as the 'gold standard' and is the only confirmatory test licensed by the US Federal Drug Administration. However, it is costly (US $45 per test in the mid-1980s), time consuming (taking around sixteen hours) and requires considerable skill to carry out. Improvements in the performance of ELISA tests and disagreements in recent years as to what contitutes a positive Western Blot has undermined its role as a confirmatory test.

Radioimmunological assays (RIA) are more sensitive but involve even more complex and time-consuming procedures than the Western Blot. As a result the latter has historically become more widely accepted.

Overall, while confirmatory tests are considered highly accurate they are unsuitable for volume screening markets due to their higher cost, complex procedures and time-consuming nature.

Monitoring tests

Tests to determine the disease stage of a patient and monitor the progress of the HIV infection are beginning to emerge. These are based on monoclonal antibody technology (to detect the antigen directly, or measure the levels of various types of cell) as well as gene probes (to detect, and localise HIV nucleic acid). The focus here is on the mass blood-screening market (i.e. antigen-based tests), which accounts for the bulk of HIV testing.

9.4 METHODOLOGY

Diagnostic testing in the blood-screening market is carried out on a large scale, with blood products generally being used within twenty-four hours of collection. There are four main requirements of any test: high speed, accuracy (i.e. high sensitivity and specificity), ease of performance and low cost.

Technical data on sensitivity, specificity and time to carry out the test were obtained from UK Public Health Reference Laboratory reports assessing HIV diagnostic kits, and medical and clinical biology journals (principally *Biotechnology, Trends in Biotechnology* and *Clinical Microbiology*). Additional data on the technical performance, price and date of product launch of HIV diagnostic kits marketed over this period were obtained from the companies identified in the Public Health Reference Laboratory reports (Appendix). In effect, the sensitivity and specificity data have been obtained by pooling a variety of original sources (e.g. seroconversion panels, blood donor populations, high risk groups and so on).

Market share data on HIV diagnostic kits for blood screening by the UK National Blood Transfusion Service from October 1985 to August 1990 inclusive were supplied by the Manchester Transfusion Centre. (The number of donations screened in 1990 has been extrapolated to an annual basis from data for January to August inclusive.)

Market share data were used to calculate measures of both concentration and changes (i.e. disruption) in the market over time. Initially, the four-firm concentration (CR4) was calculated, but this was so close to 100 per cent that the CR1 and CR3 were also calculated. To examine changes in market leadership over time, the CR1 and CR3 were also calculated for firms which had dominated the early (and similarly for those that dominated a later) period of the market. Market disruption in any one year was calculated by summing the absolute values of the change in market share for each *firm* from the previous year.[6] (Disruption is given at the firm level unless stated otherwise.)

Supplementary and more qualitative information, such as the reasons for switching from one generation of diagnostic kit to another, was obtained through telephone interviews with some of the manufacturers.

9.5 TECHNOLOGICAL CHANGE AND MARKET STRUCTURE FOR HIV DIAGNOSTIC KITS

Technological trajectories of HIV diagnostic kits

HIV diagnostic kits can be classified into three different technological generations based on changes in the production of the antigen (which detects antibodies to HIV) used in these kits.

First-generation kits utilised the viral lysate obtained by extracting the virus from infected cells. These were based on culture techniques to grow the virus which was then purified and coated on to a suitable substrate (e.g. beads or microtitre wells) in the kit. These kits were only possible once the virus had been isolated (around 1983–4) by French and US researchers. Virus from the French cell line was made available to various research laboratories and five

US companies, and was used to develop commercial diagnostic kits (Mortimer and Clewley, 1987: 133). However, there were problems in producing virus lysate-based kits as the virus was not very easy to grow and had a tendency to mutate, thus giving rise to batch-to-batch variations in yield.

Second-generation kits used recombinant DNA technology to synthesise those viral core and/or envelope proteins that produced an early immunological response. These kits sometimes incorporated the term 'recombinant' in their name. Second-generation kits were considered to have higher specificities than those based on the purified virus as well as being able to detect antibodies against particular HIV antigens (Newmark, 1988: 761). In addition, production and use of these kits were considered safer as they did not require working with HIV. The move to these recombinant protein-based kits appears to have been due to advantages to manufacturers.

Third-generation kits incorporated synthetic polypeptides for the detection of different antibodies to HIV. Some of these kits used a combination of both second- and third-generation technology; for example, having a recombinant protein (to detect HIV–1 virus) and a synthetic polypeptide (for HIV–2). These have been classified as belonging to third-generation technology by virtue of involving synthetic polypeptides in their design.

The first diagnostic kits for HIV were available in the UK market in early 1985 (Table 9.1). By 1990, at least 37 kits had been launched on the UK market, 24 of which were for the detection of HIV–1 (by 14 companies) and 13 for the combined detection of HIV–1 and 2 kits (produced by 10 firms) (Table 9.2).

With the exception of the first HIV–1 kits, where many companies entered the market within a few months of one another, generally the first products in any generation of technology have been introduced by the largest companies, with delayed entry by small firms.[7] Thus, the pharmaceuticals giant Abbott was the first to market recombinant technology-based kits for HIV–1 and HIV–1 and 2, followed by Dupont (a large non-pharmaceuticals company) in the case of the former and by Hoffmann La Roche in the latter case. The first

Table 9.1 First commercial introduction of HIV diagnostic kits into the UK market

Antibodies detected	Generation of kit	Introduction date
HIV 1	1st (viral lysate)	Early 1985
	2nd (recombinant protein)	Aug. 1987
	3rd[1] (synthetic polypeptide)	Late 1986[2]
HIV 1/2	1st (viral lysate)	End 1988
	2nd (recombinant protein)	Dec. 1988
	3rd (synthetic polypeptide)	Dec. 1988

Notes:
1 The first 'third generation' kit was marketed before a 'second generation' one
2 Approximate launch date by the Olympus Optical Company in the West German market

191

Table 9.2 Firms with HIV diagnostic kits in the UK market 1985–90

Kit generation To detect:	*HIV–1*	*HIV–1 and 2*
1st (viral lysate)	Organon Teknika Ortho Diagnostics/Litton Dupont Abbott Wellcome Diagnostics Electronucleonics Mercia Diagnostics Behring Amersham International Pharmacia Fujiregio/Mast Diagnostics	Diagnostic Pasteur
2nd (recombinant protein)	Abbott Dupont Wellcome	Abbott Roche
3rd (synthetic polypeptide)	Olympus Optical Company Pharmacia Lab-Systems	Dupont Pharmacia Behring IAF Biochem Wellcome

small company to produce a recombinant HIV–1 kit was Wellcome which entered a year later than Abbott. Similarly, Dupont appears to have been the first to market a third-generation combined HIV–1 and 2 kit, followed a few months later by two large pharmaceutical companies (Pharmacia and Behring) and a year later by Wellcome. However, getting a product on to the market quickly does not appear to have given the first innovator a particular advantage in terms of market share in blood-screening applications.

Just over two-thirds (i.e. 17) of the 24 HIV–1 kits introduced over the period 1985 to 1990 were based on first-generation technology. In terms of the first-generation-based kits, four companies (Abbott, Organon Teknika, Dupont and Wellcome) each accounted for three products, two (Diagnostics Pasteur and Pharmacia) producing two kits while the remainder only marketed one kit each. Over time, the number of HIV–1 kits marketed has declined (Figure 9.1) and shifted to combined HIV–1 and 2 kits (Figure 9.2).

Combined HIV–1 and 2 kits first came on to the UK market around 1988 and a total of thirteen kits had been introduced by 1990. Nine were based on third-generation technology, three on second-generation and one on first-generation technology (Figure 9.2).

The number of new entrants into second- and third-generation technology-based (HIV–1 and combined HIV–1 and 2) diagnostic kits generally peaked

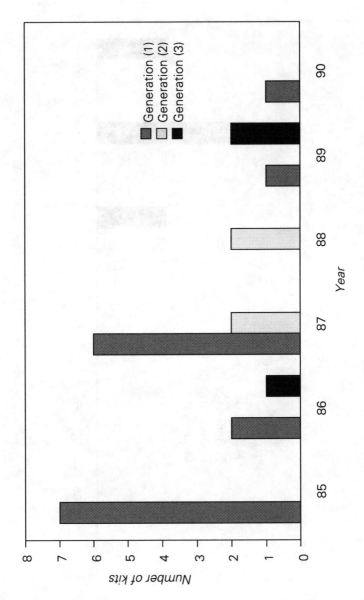

Figure 9.1 Introduction of HIV–1 kits by year, 1985–90

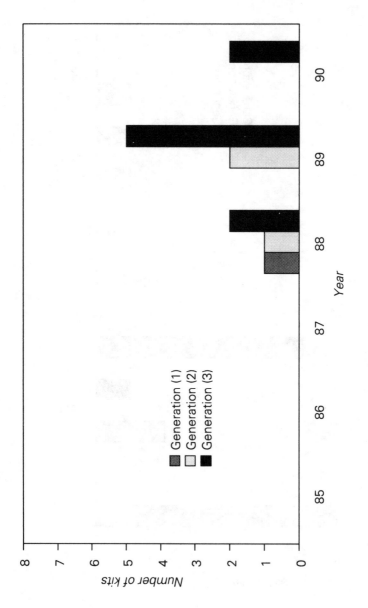

Figure 9.2 Number of new HIV–1 and 2 kits by year, 1985–90

very quickly and then fell to zero. This may suggest that rapid technology change was being used as a competitive weapon to prevent subsequent entry. It may be significant that, generally, very few companies seem to produce kits in all three technologies. Thus, Abbott and Roche do not yet appear to have marketed third-generation technology kits, while other companies such as Lab Systems, Olympus and IAF Biochem have only produced third-generation-based products. Diagnostics Pasteur (a company connected to the Pasteur Institute which isolated HIV–1 and HIV–2 two years before others) does not appear to have moved from first-generation technology.

Overall, the HIV diagnostic kit market has increased in concentration over time both in terms of the number and size of firms in the market (Table 9.2). Thus, while fourteen firms produced kits detect HIV–1, only eight (generally large companies) were marketing the new HIV–1 and 2 kits. In effect, the number of small firms in the market has sharply declined over time, with only Wellcome successfully managing the transition to HIV–1 and 2 kits.

Technological development in HIV ELISA diagnostic kits for blood transfusion screening markets appears to have been remarkably rapid. Thus, while the first-generation kits (based on cell culture techniques) were marketed in early 1985, second- and third-generation kits (both based on recombinant DNA technology) to detect HIV–1 had already appeared fewer than two and a half years later. Moreover, new kits based on each of these three generations of technology later emerged for the detection of HIV–1 and HIV–2.

Improvements in the technical performance (i.e. speed, sensitivity and specificity) of HIV–1 kits appear to have taken place very rapidly. Thus, around the beginning of 1985 the fastest diagnostic kits based on first-generation technology took around three hours to perform, with ninety or so samples screened at a time (Figure 9.3). By mid-1985 this had fallen to two hours with very marginal improvements taking place in subsequent kits. Similarly, both the sensitivity and specificity of these tests increased from about 99 per cent to 100 per cent within a few months of the introduction of the first kits. However, there was a wide range in the values of these parameters. Thus, the worst performing kit had a sensitivity of around 96 per cent, while the minimum value of specificity was just under 87 per cent.

The next type of HIV–1 kit for this market was based on third-generation technology, introduced by Olympus Optical which had thereby leapfrogged recombinant protein (i.e. second-generation) designs. The performance of these third-generation kits appears to have involved a marked trade-off between the level of sensitivity and specificity. Thus, while the first kit in this series combined a slightly higher speed (100 minutes) than viral lysate-based designs and a high specificity (99.5 per cent) it appeared to have an extremely low sensitivity (around 75 per cent). This would lead to an extremely high level of false positives. Further kits appear to have been slightly slower and showed a dramatic jump in sensitivity (between about 98 and 100 per cent) though at the cost of significantly lower specificities. None of these kits

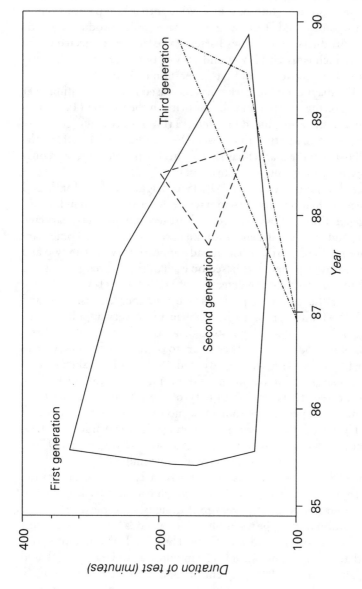

Figure 9.3 Speed of HIV–1 diagnostic kits, 1985–90

appears to have been utilised in the blood-screening market. The speed of third-generation combined HIV–1 and 2 kits was around 120 minutes, while their sensitivity and specificity ranged from 99 to 100 per cent.

Second-generation technology-based HIV–1 kits were a little slower (with a test time of around 150 minutes) than the fastest first-generation kits but speeded up slightly over the next twelve months (with a 125-minute test time). These kits were similar to the third-generation based kits in terms of a trade-off between sensitivity and specificity. Thus, while the first HIV–1 kit (in mid-1987) had a very low sensitivity (around 93 per cent) but high specificity (100 per cent), one introduced a year later was highly sensitive (100 per cent) but with a reduced specificity (just under 97 per cent). For combined HIV–1 and 2 kits, sensitivities ranged from 99 to 100 per cent, though the specificities appeared to be around 94 per cent.

According to these data, there appears to have been little difference in the performance of kits based on any of the three generations of technology. However, according to the manufacturers (Martin, 1990; Scott, 1990), second-generation kits gave much lower values of false positives (i.e. had higher specificities) than the first-generation kits. It is likely, then, that the data suggesting sensitivities or specificities of 100 per cent for viral lysate kits were based on small sample sizes (such as seroconversion panels, or known positives) rather than the more representative results obtained from studies on blood donor populations. Ideally, comparisons of kit performance for blood-screening markets require that test data are based on blood donor populations. This may be problematical; for instance, such data were not available for many of the commercial kits launched on the UK market.

Technical change and market structure in blood screening

The UK Blood Transfusion Service started to screen all blood donations for HIV from October 1985. About 2.8 million donations are routinely screened every year (Figure 9.4).

Between 1985 and 1990, four types of kits were used to screen blood donations (Table 9.3): first- and second-generation kits for HIV–1 and second- and third-generation kits for HIV–1 and 2. No third-generation kit for HIV–1 appears to have been used. This is not surprising given the very low sensitivity (around 75 per cent) of the first third-generation HIV–1 kit produced.

The time between utilisation of the next type of kit was around two years though both second- and third-generation kits for the detection of HIV–1 and 2 were introduced simultaneously, in 1989. This suggests that the pace of innovation may be speeding up. Overall, though, a two-year new product introduction time appears to have been less than that observed for dynamic random access memory chips (DRAMs) – the leading edge products in the highly dynamic semiconductor industry (see Chapter 6).

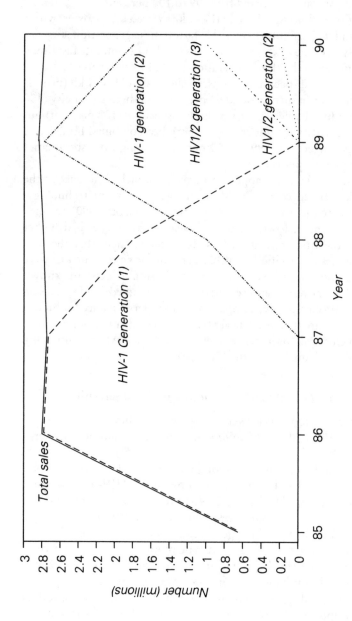

Figure 9.4 Sales of HIV diagnostic kits to the UK Blood Transfusion Service, 1985–90

CASE STUDY: BIOTECHNOLOGY

Table 9.3 Stages in the product life cycle of HIV diagnostic kits in the UK blood screening market

Stage		HIV–1 kits		HIV 1/2 kits	
		1st generation	2nd generation	2nd generation	3rd generation
I	Introduction	1985	1987	1989	1989
II	Early growth	1986	1988	1990	1990
III	Late growth	1986	1989		
IV	Maturity	1986	1989		
V	Rapid decline	1987	1989		
VI	Stagnation	1989			

Note: No 3rd generation HIV–1 kit or 1st generation HIV 1/2 kit appear to have been taken up in the UK blood screening market.

The market for HIV diagnostic kits for blood screening has been highly concentrated with the CR4 remaining at 100 per cent (Figure 9.5). However, there has been some shift in market leadership over time. Thus, the collective market share of the top four firms in 1987 had dropped from 100 per cent to about 90 per cent by 1990. Market disruption has been particularly pronounced at the kit level (rising to over 170 per cent in 1987, for example) but very much lower (around 25 per cent at most) at the firm level.

The following examines changes in market shares and disruption in more detail. This will show, first, that high market disruption is a result of the displacement of one generation of kit by the next and second, that one firm (Wellcome Diagnostics) appears both to have successfully made the transition to each new generation of kit and continued to retain a dominant market position.

First-generation kits for HIV–1 began to be used in the blood-screening market in October 1985 and accounted for the total market until 1987. Four companies, Wellcome, Organon Teknika, Dupont and Ortho Diagnostics, supplied the entire market (Table 9.4). Abbott had been the first to produce an HIV kit commercially, receiving FDA approval for the US market in March 1985, but this kit had a high level of false positives and thus was not taken up in the UK blood-screening market.

Table 9.4 Companies supplying HIV kits to the UK blood transfusion service

HIV–1		HIV–1 and 2	
1st generation	2nd generation	2nd generation	3rd generation
Wellcome (1985)	Wellcome (1988)	Abbott (1990)	Wellcome (1990)
Organon (1985)	Dupont (1988)		Behring (1990)
Dupont (1986)	Abbott (1989)		
Ortho (1987)			

Note: Year of entry into market is given in parentheses

199

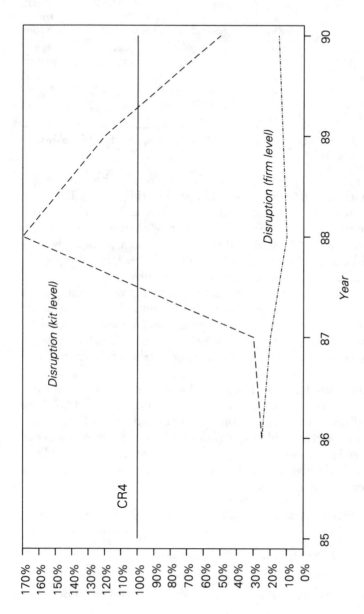

Figure 9.5 Concentration and disruption in the HIV market, 1985–90

Market concentration was extremely high with the CR1 (one firm concentration) rising from just under 80 per cent in 1985 to 100 per cent by 1989. Wellcome successfully retained the leading position until 1989 when it appears to have completely switched over to a second-generation HIV–1 kit. Organon Teknika increased its share in the final stages of the life cycle of first-generation kits. Generally, market disruption was low (gradually declining from around 25 per cent in 1986 to about 10 per cent in 1988) but jumped dramatically in 1989 with the switch of market leader from Wellcome to Organon Teknika.

Second-generation kits for HIV–1 began to be adopted in 1987 and were supplied by three companies, Wellcome, Dupont and Abbott. By 1989, second-generation kits had more or less completely displaced first-generation kits. Wellcome again retained its position as the market leader in recombinant DNA technology-based kits, building up its share from around 70 per cent in 1988 to nearly 90 per cent by 1990. Market disruption over this period declined from nearly 30 per cent to just over 10 per cent.

Kits to detect both HIV–1 and HIV–2 became available at the end of 1988. Diagnostics Pasteur appears to have been the first company to introduce such a kit. This was based on viral lysates (i.e. first-generation-based technology) using purified HIV–1 and HIV–2 viruses in the kit.[8] This kit combined high sensitivity (100 per cent) with a slightly lower specificity (just under 98 per cent). No other firms appear to have utilised viral lysates in their kits and instead relied on second- or third-generation technology. These recombinant DNA-based kits appeared to have sensitivities of 100 per cent (or close to 99 per cent for the worst performing kits), though third-generation kits had higher specificities (99.8 per cent) than second-generation devices (around 94 per cent). Rapid technological improvements again seem to be concentrated in the first few months after the introduction of the first product. Thus, the steepest decline in test time occurred within six months of the first product's introduction. Similarly, while the specificity of the second-generation-based kits showed no improvement ten months after the first kit had been launched.

A first-generation (i.e. based on viral lysates) kit to detect both HIV–1 and HIV–2 became available at the end of 1988, followed a few months later by both second- and third-generation technology kits. However, combined kits were not used to any significant extent in the blood-screening market until some three years later when they began to displace the second-generation HIV–1 kits (Figure 9.4). Sales of combined HIV–1 and 2 kits based on third-generation technology rose fastest, followed (though quite some way behind) by second-generation kits, while first-generation kits were not taken up at all. These third-generation kits were produced by Wellcome and Behring, with the former accounting for the vast majority of the market. Abbott's kit was based on second-generation technology and appears to have been less successful.

Market trends in terms of changes in concentration or disruption for the combined HIV–1 and 2 market cannot be given as these kits were only adopted a year or so ago.

Overall, four firms (Wellcome, Organon Teknika, Dupont and Ortho Diagnostics) supplied the UK blood transfusion service with first-generation technology diagnostic kits for the detection of HIV–1 (Table 9.4). By 1990, kits for the combined detection of HIV–1 and 2 had been taken up by the transfusion service from three suppliers (Wellcome, Abbott and Behring). However, only one of the initial four firms (Wellcome) continued to supply this institutional market, joined by two large companies (Abbott and Behring). Thus, while this market was highly concentrated in the early years, it appears to have become even more concentrated over time (Table 9.4). (The shift from HIV–1 to HIV–1 and 2 kits appears to have contributed a shake-out in the market.)

Recent and possible future technological developments

At the end of 1990, the market for HIV diagnostics was dominated by antigen-based kits. Further technological developments in these kits have been to increase their sensitivity (to identify infected individuals earlier) as well as to develop other combined detection kits (such as HIV and hepatitis B). However, not only is HIV highly mutagenic (which has made the development of therapeutics and vaccines especially difficult) but it is considered to be increasing its rate of mutation in unpredictable directions. Thus, it is likely that new types of kit will continually be required to detect infection.

Moreover, the existence of a window period (and some infected individuals who do not produce antibodies) with HIV infection means that other types of kit will be required. One possibility is that developments in antigen-based HIV diagnostics may, in the longer term, be undermined by gene probe trajectories which are beginning to open up.

Gene probes operate at a more fundamental (i.e. DNA) level than antibody capture technology. As antibodies are produced in response to antigens, gene probes would allow detection at an earlier stage than antibody-based diagnostics. Historically, one major drawback of gene probes has been the problem of detecting such small amounts of DNA. In 1985, however, a technique of gene amplification, polymerase chain reaction (PCR), removed this obstacle. This technique was patented by Cetus and made available to other firms under licence. In January 1988, the application of PCR to viral sequences of HIV–1 was reported to have decreased the time required for determining infection from three or four weeks using traditional virus isolation to within three days (Ou et al., 1988).

As yet, such probes are still at the laboratory stage and are both complex and time consuming to perform. However, a competing trajectory appears to have recently opened up with antibody-based kits to detect HIV antigens.

A further technological development is the shift to increasing levels of automation for HIV diagnosis, an area targetted for expansion by Abbott.

9.6 CONCLUSIONS AND POLICY IMPLICATIONS

The 'new' (or third-generation) biotechnology is considered strategically important, with wide-ranging and potentially revolutionary impacts across a variety of sectors. Technological leadership in biotechnology is thus perceived to be a prerequisite for future competitiveness in international and domestic markets. In the 1970s, technological innovation in biotechnology was driven principally by small new start-ups. However, by the 1980s, large firms were also becoming significant players in biotechnology markets, especially pharmaceuticals. Within pharmaceuticals, small firms have been most active in *in vitro* diagnostics, a market characterised by lower entry barriers and regulation than therapeutics.

This case study has examined the rates of technology change and the development of market structure in HIV diagnostics used for mass screening of blood by the UK transfusion service. This is the single largest *in vitro* diagnostics market. Six principal conclusions can be drawn from this study.

First, antigen-based HIV diagnostic kits used in the UK blood-screening market have been characterised by remarkably high rates of technological development since their introduction in 1985. These kits have changed both in the way in which the antigen is manufactured and the range of virus strains that can be detected simultaneously.

The technology used to produce the antigen used in these kits can be categorised into three generations. First-generation devices used a viral lysate (derived from traditional cell culture techniques). Second-generation kits represented a major technological discontinuity through the use of rDNA technology to synthesise particular virus proteins. Third-generation technology was a further development of rDNA techniques but involved the synthesis of specific virus polypeptides. (Some kits have used a combination of synthesised viral proteins and polypeptides for antibody capture.)

In parallel with developments in antigen production, diagnostic kits have been developed to extend the range of virus strains that can be detected. Thus, while the first kits were designed for the detection of antibodies to HIV–1, later ones allowed the combined detection of HIV–1 and HIV–2. Further development along this trajectory would lead to the introduction of other types of combined detection kits (some manufacturers have already introduced kits which detect HIV-1 and hepatitis B for the blood-screening market).

Second, improvements in the technical performance of new generations of kit seem to take place principally within six months or so of the first product introduction. Third, each new generation of product has been characterised by rapid firm entry which quickly tails off to zero. Such a pattern would be expected in a market where firms were using high rates of technology change to deter further entrants.

Fourth, the research suggests that rapid technology change in terms of producing a *new generation* of kit is being used as a competitive weapon rather than technical change *within* any one generation. This suggests that delayed entry may be a considerable handicap. At present, new product introduction seems to be principally driven by the large established companies. Further developments (such as increasing the level of automation) are expected to be pioneered by the larger firms. That large firms have played a leading role in innovation suggests that the vision of the future regarding technological development of HIV kits has been fairly clear. Despite this, the blood-screening market has continued (so far) to be dominated by Wellcome. Discussion with firms suggests that other factors (such as quality of service) are also important in capturing market share. This needs further investigation.

Fifth, biotechnology-derived diagnostic kits are generally referred to in the literature as being based on monoclonal antibody technology (or rDNA technology such as gene probes which directly detect the antigen). Thus, estimates may be given of monoclonal antibody (and the much smaller gene probe) diagnostic markets. Kits for determining whether an individual has been exposed to HIV are generally included in the category of monoclonal antibody diagnostics. However, diagnosis of HIV infection in such kits is through detection of antibodies to HIV. These antibodies are 'captured' (i.e. detected) by the kit as it contains HIV antigen coated onto a substrate (e.g. microtitre plates). Essentially, these kits are antigen-based devices in which technical change has been driven by recombinant DNA rather than monoclonal antibody technology. (While such kits may sometimes also utilise monoclonal antibodies, this is not a key aspect of their operation.) Thus, such kits should be reclassified under rDNA technology markets.

Sixth, very little quantitative work seems to have been carried out to map technological change in biotechnology products. This study has indicated some of the most important technical performance characteristics of diagnostic tests (sensitivity, specificity and speed). Time series data on these parameters for other diagnostic products would be useful, to provide information on the rate of performance improvements across a range of products. In addition, work needs to be carried out to identify parameters suitable for examining performance changes in non-diagnostic markets, for example, therapeutics. In this respect, it is necessary to identify key performance parameters for therapeutic products. This may not be especially difficult as there are very few biotechnology-based therapeutics on the market, the best known being human insulin, interferons, tissue plasminogen activator (tPA) and interleukin 2 (IL–2). In the cases of IL–2 and tPA, a key parameter is the half life of the product. The appropriateness of half life as one performance indicator for other products needs to be examined. Overall, such studies of technology change across a diverse range of biotechnology products and markets are a prerequisite for informed policy making in the area.

APPENDIX

Information requested from firms manufacturing/marketing HIV diagnostic kits:

(a) the full name of each kit
(b) market for kit (blood screening, STD clinics and so on)
(c) time taken to carry out the test
(d) format (i.e. number of tests in kit, e.g. 12 × 8)
(e) sensitivity (plus definition and methodology)
(f) specificity (plus details as above)
(g) kit type (e.g. ELISA, MAb and so on)
(h) generation of kit (1st, 2nd and so on)
(i) shelf-life
(j) detection of antibodies to HIV–1 or both HIV–1 and 2
(k) gene products detected for HIV–1 and HIV–2 (e.g. gp160)
(l) approximate cost of kit (over time)
(m) cost of equipment to use kit
(n) date and country of first product launch
(o) date of product launch on the UK market
(p) date of product withdrawal from UK market.

10

CONCLUSIONS

We start with a brief résumé of the main thesis advanced in the book. We then explore some of the implications of this study and some unresolved questions.

10.1 RÉSUMÉ

We can return to the central hypotheses set out at the start of the book, where two contrasting but not incompatible propositions were set out. The first was that rapid change which is consistent with a widely accepted vision of the future for a technology and market will tend to be concentrating. The second was that radical change which conflicts with widely held visions will tend to be deconcentrating.

Chapter 2 saw that these two propositions are each supported by fairly extensive literature, but that there is generally little overlap between these two bodies of literature. Much of the theoretical economics literature on the effects of rapid technology change on market structure tends to find arguments for persistent dominance and hence supports the concentrating thesis. The empirical economic literature is split: much stresses the concentrating effects of innovation, but more recently some has found evidence in support of the reverse effect.

Early sociological and organisational behaviour literature on this issue commonly stresses the organic–mechanistic distinction (Burns and Stalker, 1961). Organic firms can adapt more easily to radical change than can mechanistic firms, and hence this perspective tends to support the deconcentrating thesis. But more recently, it is well recognised that bureaucratic organisations can cope well with change, even rapid change, for which they can establish routines.

Chapters 3 and 4 argued that the reconciliation of these apparently diverse streams lies in the concept of organisational or corporate visions. Having a clear (and accurate) technological vision allows the organisation to plan the organisational routines required to allow it to cope with rapid technological change. In short, the vision makes change – even rapid change – along the anticipated trajectory incremental rather than radical. Chapter 3 examined the concept of technological vision in much more detail, while Chapter 4 examined a model of rapid technological change and the development of market structure in which the closeness of the vision to the actual outcome is instrumental in determining the effect of change on the evolution of market structure.

If the match is close, rapid change tends to be concentrating, and the faster it is the faster concentration will grow. If, conversely, the match is poor, rapid change tends to be deconcentrating, and the faster the change the faster the deconcentrating trend. The model suggests that the large multi-divisional firm tends to do worse than smaller mono-divisional firms when the rate and direction of change is uncertain. There is one exception, however. If different divisions have different technological visions, but expertise learnt in one division can benefit other divisions – that is, internal absorptive capacity is strong – then the multi-divisional organisation can outperform smaller mono-divisional firms, even in a very uncertain environment.

Chapters 5 to 9 sought to assess the empirical relevance of these arguments by studying five case studies of how rapid technological change impacts upon market structure.

The microprocessor case (Chapter 5) illustrated the two polar hypotheses very neatly. The microprocessor was a radical innovation, incompatible with the prevailing vision of technological development in the semiconductor industry of the late 1960s, which foresaw a future of localised customisation of components. The innovator was a very young firm, formed as a spin-off from one of the industry leaders, and this development was markedly deconcentrating as the established industry leaders were slow to adapt to this radical change in the technological trajectory. Later in the life cycle of the microprocessor, however, rapid change was concentrating, because the pioneer was able to consolidate its market leadership in microprocessors by rapidly developing its technology along a well-articulated technology – for which its organisation was well adapted.

While the early generations of memory chips were produced by smaller firms, the memory case (Chapter 6) illustrates the concentrating hypothesis nicely. The leading trajectory of technological development in memory chips is one of exponentially increasing capacity per chip, and this has been well understood and mapped in the industry from the 1970s. Confident in that vision, firms have invested heavily in chip fabrication equipment, which has made the industry exceptionally capital intensive and also acted as a substantial entry barrier. In the 1980s all the small US merchant producers were shaken out of the market due to a combination of high rates of technological development and price falls in semiconductor markets (aggravated by the 1991–2 recession). Continued technological development meant that by the late 1980s even the large US merchant semiconductor producers had been forced out of the market. Overall, production of leading edge

DRAMs has increasingly become dominated by the very large diversified Japanese firms. There is, however, entry of a special sort in the production of any particular generation of chip, when technological advance in that component slows down and low-cost entrants (especially from the NICs) take over a maturing sub-market. This does not disturb the concentrating trend in the memory market as a whole, however, because when this happens the leading edge firms have already moved up to the next generation, where sales are growing.

The standard logic case (Chapter 7) exhibits three phases. In the first phase (1960s), the technological developments in standard logic followed a series of rapid but unpredictable shifts. The large diversified firms were unable to cope with these developments successfully (made more difficult as many had not realised the strategic potential of integrated circuits and had thus delayed entry). Thus, the technological and market leadership shifted to the small US merchant producers. In phase 2, however, steady change within a particular technology reinforced the existing pattern of market leadership. And in phase 3, the more radical jump from one semiconductor technology to another led to a quite different pattern of market leadership.

The conclusions of the software case (Chapter 8) are similar to phases 2 and 3 of the standard logic case. Using two simulation models of the spreadsheet software and word-processing software markets, we found that a faster rate of upgrade activity tended to lead to greater degrees of concentration. Conversely, the proliferation of new software categories was essentially deconcentrating.

In the biotechnology case study (Chapter 9), there is intense competition to bring diagnostic kits to market. Thus, technological development has focused primarily on new generations of product; technological improvement within a generation is limited and has little effect on market structure. New generations of diagnostics kits have been pioneered by the large companies which have also been responsible for further innovation (e.g. combined detection kits, increased levels of automation and so on). This would suggest that the vision of the future regarding technological development of HIV kits was reasonably clear. However, the blood transfusion market in the UK has continued to be dominated by one small UK company, though its market share has declined.

10.2 IMPLICATIONS

Broadly speaking, the empirical evidence in Chapters 5 to 9 is supportive of the thesis set out in Chapters 1 to 4. What then are the implications of this thesis? Here we examine seven main issues and then in the final section set out some unresolved questions and issues for further research.

Visions as a strategic asset

We have shown above that the firm faces a crucial strategic choice in setting its technological vision. There is a clear trade-off between the scope of a corporate vision and the scale economies that can be realised. A narrowly defined vision offers an obvious competitive strength over a limited range of outcomes, at the risk of exposing the firm's weaknesses in the face of different technological challenges. Conversely, a broad vision (if manageable) allows the firm to compete in a wider range of outcomes, but nowhere gives the firm a particular edge. These points are so obvious, perhaps, that they hardly need stating. Yet it is still more usual to see the construction of technological visions as an exercise in (passively) forecasting the future, whereas it is really making a strategic choice.

One special example of this arose in Chapter 4. In some cases, firms will promote a diversity of visions within the one organisation – perhaps on a divisional basis. We saw in the simulation model of Chapter 4 why such a strategy could have considerable payoffs but only if the firm has engineered a substantial internal absorptive capacity. Essentially this internal diversity of vision is an insurance policy against the technology taking an unexpected turn.

Firms face another strategic decision about how widely they disseminate their visions. To do so in house seems straightforward enough, but should the vision be marketed outside the organisation? We saw in Chapters 3 and 5 that there were clear circumstances in which the fact that a vision was marketed outside the company contributed to the success of that vision.

In short, a firm's vision of the future of the technologies in which it operates and plans to operate is a valuable strategic asset, and, like any such asset, needs careful management. In addition, the construction and management of technological visions go hand in hand with organisational structuring and restructuring, for as argued above any structure has an implicit vision and severe tensions will emerge if the implicit vision is at odds with the emergent explicit technological vision.

We have said little here about how firms should manage these assets, and how they should in practice construct their technological visions. Nor have we said anything about how the technological vision relates to the broader mission statement for the organisation (Campbell *et al.*, 1990). These issues are really too intricate for proper treatment here. Moreover, such an analysis really calls for longitudinal case research, or at least detailed interview work with current decision makers. Given the broad brush historical approach used here, that was not really practicable. A striking example of such work, however, is Metcalfe and Boden (1993).[1]

The social desirability of a diversity of visions

The second main implication of this study is that, in one important sense, a diversity of technological visions has a similar effect on technological development as a thriving small firm sector. With a limited number of rigid and restrictive technological visions held in a few large companies, the path within which technologies can develop is fairly limited. Faced with a radically challenging new technology, this group would not adapt well to the challenge and the opportunity would be lost, perhaps to overseas competitors.

Small firms of organic structure are, it is argued, much better placed to adapt to such an unexpected technological opportunity even if it does not lie within their starting vision. The existence of a thriving small firm sector is one way of ensuring that such opportunities are not immediately lost. Alternatively, if there is a wide diversity of visions amongst a group of large firms, then for any radical technological development, one firm at least will not have too far to move to rise to the challenge. In that sense, a diversity of technological visions and a thriving small firm sector are substitutes for each other: they both act as a partial insurance policy against lost technological opportunities.

This has a straightforward analogy with Feyerabend's philosophy of science. While the Kuhnian paradigm asserts that research follows well-recognised programmes (rather like our widely accepted visions), and while some in that tradition argue that it is desirable that scientific research should do this, Feyerabend (1978) argues that this is neither descriptively correct, nor prescriptively desirable. In contrast, Feyerabend argues that the range of facts discovered depends on the theories in use. A restricted range of theories will be very efficient at uncovering a certain class of data, but they will miss other data. This happens because scientific data are, in a sense, answers to questions posed by theories; a restricted range of theories will ask a restricted range of questions and hence generate a restricted set of data.

It is easy to see how this reasoning can be applied, loosely at least, to argue for the social desirability of a diversity of technological visions. The range of technological opportunities that a market will be able to exploit will, we argue above, depend on the range of visions held by the different firms in that market. A restricted range of visions will be very efficient at reacting to some technological opportunities, but will miss others.[2]

Excess clustering in technological visions – in the same way as excess clustering of ice-cream sellers on a beach (Hotelling, 1929) – may be socially undesirable but can still be the competitive outcome. This suggests that public policy might have a role to play in conditioning the range of visions held about the future of a technology (see below). But just as we speak of a socially optimal degree of product variety, which will commonly be less than infinite, so there will be an optimum diversity of technological visions. It would not be difficult to sketch out a model to analyse this, though we do not attempt it here.

Small companies and radical technological change

The preceding argument suggests that when small companies are successful in areas of rapid change, it will be areas of technological development outside the mainstream vision. These may be niche markets but they may also be the more radical technological changes, and some of this latter group may be especially important. For this reason, we may find that even when small firms are sparsely represented in markets with rapid technology change (Patel and Pavitt, 1991), the innovations for which they are responsible are disproportionately important. The microprocessor is undoubtedly one such case. The PC is another.[3]

If a government's aim is to maximise the rate of exploitation of technological opportunities in markets with rapid change – and we recognise that there is a substantial 'if' here – small firms are an insurance policy in such markets. They can be relied on to pursue technological opportunities that are missed by the larger firms. From this limited perspective the actual success of small firms is less significant. If there is sufficient diversity in the technological visions of large established firms in a market that that are not missing technological opportunities, small firms will not perform well. But from the perspective of a technological maximiser, that may not matter too much. A simple corollary of this is that governments should be less concerned about the success of small firms in a particular technology market when that technology's development is following a clear and generally accepted vision.

In practice, this insurance policy function is quite common, even if the small firm (as an independent agent) is short lived. It is very common in markets of the sorts analysed here that small firms realise the radical innovations and are then bought up by larger concerns anxious to build up their expertise in radically different technologies. The fact that the large firm has this 'buy later' option certainly limits the damage such firms suffer from having restricted technological vision.

Merger policy

These last two points have a natural implication for merger policy, though this is a point that is very seldom raised in the discussion of mergers. Unless the management of the new firm formed after merger actively chooses to preserve the earlier diversity of vision, then post merger there must be a reduction in the diversity of technological visions. We have argued above that the preservation of diversity has a positive social value and hence the reduction in diversity associated with merger has a social cost.

Traditionally, economists are sceptical about the social returns to conglomerate merger. Horizontal mergers could have some obvious efficiency gains,[4] but conglomerate mergers involving quite distinct businesses are unlikely to generate such synergies. Socially valuable synergies can, however, emerge from the merger between firms whose lines of business have been quite separate in the past but which are now confluent.[5] This line of argument would tend to favour the merger of confluent businesses, but in the present context the merged firm would need to harmonise technological visions across organisations in order to exploit these synergies realistically. Yet that leads on to the reduction of diversity raised above.

In short, the conglomerate mergers that might lead to exploitable synergies are more likely to involve a reduction in the diversity of visions than are those conglomerate mergers with few synergies.

Catching up and forging ahead

The study has an interesting implication for the catching up/forging ahead debate. It is constantly remarked that the skills required to be an imitator (and catch up) are different from those required to be an innovator (and to forge ahead).

Putting these ideas in the present context, it could be argued that those catching up have a very clear vision of where to go – the leaders have shown them the way. If our central thesis is accepted, a mechanistic structure capable of substantial economies of scale (static and dynamic) and low unit costs would be well adapted for catching up but much less well suited for forging ahead until, and unless, a clear and credible vision of the as yet uncharted is established. As regards forging ahead, there are cases where the organic firm is at an advantage.

Yet there are some reservations to these arguments. The vision of those catching up will certainly be clear if they follow a strict and literal catch-up strategy. If, however, their strategy is to aim for where they expect the technology leader to be (rather than where the leader has just been) then the follower needs to create a technological vision in the same way as the leader.

Catching up in the memory market – in the days when that was still possible! – might simply involve setting the corporation's sights on the technology leader, because of the pervasive and long-lived trajectory of exponentially increasing capacity per chip. Catching up in other contexts, however, may require the follower to look ahead in the same way as the leader. This would be true, for example, in the PC software market where even incremental innovation (in the form of upgrades) involves the use of additional product characteristics that may not be used by the technology leader at the time of strategy formation.

Experience in the semiconductor market, and the success of Japanese firms in catching up, is instructive. In the early 1980s, Japanese electronics firms began to catch up with US semiconductor companies in memory chip technology. Soft error problems and the downturn in memory chips caused by the 1981–2 recession adversely affected US merchant semiconductor producers. Overall, Japan has been phenomenally successful not only in catching up with the world's technological leaders but in moving ahead in a growing number of areas. Freeman (1987) argues that Japan's success is based on the development of a particular institutional and social framework, a 'national system of innovation', which is ideally suited to the emerging information and communication technology paradigm. A key element is the formulation of long-term visions of the future – generated, for example, by Japan's Science and Technology Agency using the Delphi method – broadly to map out the direction of change in technologies and the economy. Thus, Japan's system of technological forecasting allowed the importance of information technology to be identified early, with the aim of shifting the economy to knowledge intensive industries in the early 1970s (Freeman, 1987: 84).

Overall, the widespread diffusion of such visions gives firms 'sufficient confidence to make their own long-term investments in research, development, software, equipment and training' (Freeman, 1987: 89). Given the importance of visions in Japan, it is not surprising that within semiconductor markets Japanese firms have been most successful in memory chips (with their relatively clear, predictable path of development) but have made little impact in leading edge microprocessor markets (which historically have not been amenable to technological leapfrogging by large firms).

Large Japanese electronics firms could, in principle, run into problems now that they have caught up with and overtaken the technological leaders in memory chips. This is because, as stressed above, the strategies for staying ahead and pushing the international technology frontier forward are likely to be quite different from those required to catch up with the technological leaders. In this respect, visions of the future into uncharted territory are problematic.

In practice, Japanese firms are in the process of actively responding to these new challenges and restructuring their memory chip divisions to position themselves for a new phase of innovation. Thus, Japanese DRAM manufacturers have started to reorganise and strengthen their research and development systems. At the same time, these firms are setting up in-house facilities to produce capital equipment formerly purchased from outside specialist suppliers. From the late 1980s, these large Japanese firms moved into a new phase characterised by intense competition between one another and from both the newly industrialising economies (principally South Korean) and the re-emerging US and European firms.

Other implications for business strategy

The case studies described above suggest that there are at least four generic sorts of strategy for successfully competing in a radically new technology subject to rapid technological change:

1 success as a pioneer followed by sustained performance over the life cycle;
2 success as a pioneer followed by take-over by a larger organisation in the growth phase of the product life cycle;
3 entry when vision is clear and the market is still growing; and
4 entry towards the maturity phase when technological change is slowing and low-cost production is the key.

The most striking example of (1) here is Intel in microprocessors or Apple in personal computers. Strategy (2) appears to be very important in biotechnology, where very long lead times in bringing innovations to market may make it hard for small pioneers of radical innovations to follow strategy (1). Strategy (3) was followed by IBM in the PC market, and the IBM PC became a *de facto* standard very rapidly. Strategy (4) is used very effectively by some semiconductor producers from the NICs when the market for a particular generation of memory chip is approaching maturity, though in saying that we do not imply that this is the only entry strategy used by such producers.

Other implications for technology policy

We discussed in Chapter 3 to what extent corporate technological visions are a public good. The conclusion was that in some important respects they are, but in some they are not. While they certainly refer to tacit and uncodified knowledge bases within the firm, they have to be articulated in a reasonably clearly codified form to be assimilated right across the firm (or division), and *a fortiori* to be disseminated outside the organisation. As such, the vision represents replicable information, which can indeed be reproduced at low marginal cost.

In that sense there is a clear public policy aspect to this. The Office of Technology Assessment in the USA does play a very important role in setting out what are generally accepted to be the prevailing technological visions in a wide variety of sectors, and disseminating them to a wide audience. MITI has played an important (some would say vital) role in co-ordinating the same activity in Japan.

10.3 UNRESOLVED QUESTIONS AND FURTHER RESEARCH

Econometric studies and data on the rate of technology change

The first observation is really composed of two points. When this research project was conceived in 1988, one author briefly considered the possibility of assembling a collection of data on the rate and direction of technology change (measured directly, as in Chapters 5 to 9) across a number of industries, with a view to carrying out a more systematic econometric study of how the speed and direction of technological change impacts on the development of market structure. This possibility was soon rejected as unrealistic for reasons we discuss below.

Of course, a number of studies have done this using patent statistics, R&D data or innovation counts as a measure of the rate of change. As noted at the start, these measures, while undoubtedly invaluable for mapping the rate of technological change across industries, do not really allow us to assess whether changes are consistent with visions or not.[6] To do that requires data on the development of technologies in a characteristics or technological space.

Such data are not in principle hard to define or measure. Rather it is the sheer labour intensity of assembling historical series on such data that is so daunting. Few studies manage to cover more than a few technologies at a time. It is perhaps instructive to compare the ease with which sectoral comparisons of price inflation can be obtained – such data being routinely generated by government statistical agencies – with the difficulty of making sectoral comparisons of quality 'inflation' – the latter rarely, if ever, being generated by official statistical bodies.[7]

The two points then are these. First, such an econometric study using direct measures of the rate and direction of technological change would be very valuable. Second, it can only be done if direct measures of the rate and direction of change can be routinely collected, and that is something needing a fair amount of effort to co-ordinate.

Are PC software and microprocessors special cases?

Those imbued with case work on these two industries at the formative stage of their development (early 1980s and early 1970s respectively) cannot help but come away with an optimistic impression about what start-up firms can hope to achieve in high technology markets. But are these very special examples, and quite atypical of what might be expected elsewhere?

We have already remarked on the findings of Patel and Pavitt (1991) which stress the dominant role of large firms in patenting activity worldwide. Have large firms got better at adapting to unexpected change? Or are they sufficiently quick at assimilating radically new technologies after development by others that nothing much represents a seriously competence-destroying form of technological change? Or is it simply a composition effect: among the population of large firms is there a sufficient diversity of visions that there will always be one large firm whose vision is close enough to the actual that apparently radical change is to it simply incremental?

The relevance of the small firm/large firm distinction

In practice, the debate about the relative merits of small and large firms is becoming much more complex because of the growing amount of collaboration taking place between firms of different sizes. Thus, for instance, the synthetic peptide used in many of the HIV diagnostic kits was supplied by a specialist firm. Such collaboration may take various technological forms such as technology transfer, joint (research or production) ventures and so on (Georghiou and Barker, 1993). Moreover, such collaboration is not limited to between small and large companies. Thus, for instance, Japanese firms are transferring DRAM technology where they have a lead to various US firms in exchange for microprocessor or other advanced technology. The models described above say little about collaboration, and that is an important area for future work.

Application to other areas

Finally, we conclude that it would be valuable to extend this analysis to some other case studies. The following look promising:

1 transistors, where there was a radical jump from valve technology, then a shift in transistor technology from germanium to silicon;
2 typewriters versus computer printers;
3 printers, with the daisy wheel versus dot matrix, dot matrix versus inkjet, and inkjet versus laser printers;
4 medical electronic equipment versus biotechnology-based products;
5 computer games, where there has been change within a particular technology, and threats from new generations of technology, e.g. virtual reality; and
6 other biotechnology areas, in particular plant and animal agriculture, and speciality chemicals.

NOTES

1 INTRODUCTION

1 The extensive work of Keith Pavitt and associates (e.g. Patel and Pavitt, 1992) is perhaps the outstanding example of this.

2 EMPIRICAL AND THEORETICAL MOTIVATION

1 Let I define innovation and C define concentration, and assume that each causal effect operates with a lag of one period, so that:

$I_t = I_0 + aC_{t-1}$ and $C_t = C_0 + bI_{t-1}$.

The long-run solution for this (see chapter 4, section 2) generates the following derivatives with respect to exogenous shifts in innovative activity (I_0) and concentration (C_0):

$$dI/dI_0 = dC/dC_0 = 1/(1-ab) \; ; \; dI/dC_0 = a/(1-ab); \; dC/dI_0 = b/(1-ab)$$

An exogenous increase in innovative activity will have a positive multiplier effect on further innovation of $1/(1-ab)$, as long as $0<ab<1$ and regardless of the sign of a and b; the effect on concentration will be positive if $b>0$ and negative if $b<0$. An exogenous increase in concentration will lead to a similar positive multiplier effect on concentration, regardless of the signs of a and b; the effect on innovation will be positive if $a>0$ and negative if $a<0$.

The dynamic paths of this very simple model are surprisingly rich, especially for composite exogenous changes in C and I. See section 4.2.

2 We use the term without implying a value judgement: many economists would consider continually increasing concentration a bad thing.

3 Particularly here we are referring to the arguments of Feyerabend (1978). In a number of papers, Metcalfe and Boden (1990, 1991, 1993) have produced a fascinating account of the linkage between concepts in the philosophy of science, the firm's strategic paradigm and economic performance.

4 The term was coined by Merton (1973), following the passage in St Matthew's Gospel.

5 Further support for this comes from a study of technological change and engine plant development. See Abernathy (1976, 1978), Abernathy et al. (1983) and Clark (1983).

6 Carlsson (1989b) discusses the concept of flexibility in greater depth.

7 Marx and Engels, *Communist Manifesto*, 1848. We cannot give a full account of this here, but see Rosenberg's essay 'Karl Marx on the economic role of science' in his book *Perspectives on Technology* (Rosenberg, 1976a).

8 We cannot begin to survey the very large body of literature on patent races here but two important and accessible contributions are those of Harris and Vickers (1985) and Vickers (1986).
9 I am grateful to Paul David for this insight.
10 See also Klepper and Grady (1989).
11 Williamson (1985) is a more recent statement of the development of transaction cost economics, while Kay (1982, 1984) uses transaction cost economics to examine issues of corporate strategy.
12 Freeman and Perez (1988) advance the concept of a techno-economic paradigm to describe the most pervasive technologies that influence firms in all industrial sectors. These are broader than the paradigms referred to by Dosi and others.
13 Copyright © Harwood Academic Publishers GmbH. We are grateful to Harwood Academic Publishers for permission to reproduce it here.

3 THE STRATEGIC ROLE OF VISIONS OF THE FUTURE FOR TECHNOLOGIES AND MARKETS

1 It can be shown that once the fundamental line width of chip photolithography (in microns) and the quality of each lithography step (faults per square centimetre) are set, the unit cost per chip is relatively easy to calculate. See Wise *et al.* (1980) or Swann (1986), and the references therein, for a further discussion of this. Investment plans that could reasonably expect to deliver a fabrication process with these two fundamental parameters would be read by industry rivals as a credible commitment to produce at that unit cost.
2 Tossing a coin gives a 'random' outcome, we say, and yet in principle one could write down a model of the flight of the coin which, conditional on the starting position of the coin, could predict the outcome. In some sense the outcome is not random in an absolute sense but subject to details and complexities of which we are ignorant.
3 At the time the law was articulated, Moore was at Fairchild Corporation.
4 With the hindsight of the early 1990s, this view about the ease of software reprogramming now seems overoptimistic, as is evidenced by the software crisis talked about in some circles. Indeed, custom design was never fully replaced, and has continued to take a steady share of the total semiconductor market.
5 As noted before, Intel, the originator of the microprocessor, was one of the many new 'Fairchildren'; these companies made a mark in areas of radical product innovation, the inference being that such new product areas were too challenging for the Fairchild organisation to assimilate, so that these technologies would only see the light of day through spin-off companies. The genealogy of 'Fairchildren' is shown in Rothwell and Zegveld (1982: 30–1).
6 We use the sense of equilibrium used by Peter Skott and in no sense imply a static model. For Skott (1983), the equilibrium of a model is simply its solution(s), or the set of values for the variables that are mutually consistent. A model with no equilibrium, in this sense, is a model with no internally consistent solution, and that is arguably not a very interesting model.
7 Reference to Phelps (1967) and Friedman (1968).
8 A more familiar way of writing the logistic curve is in the form: $S_t = S_{max}/[1 + \exp\{a - bt\}]$. At t^*, the point of inflexion, $S_t^* = S_{max}/2$, and hence it is readily apparent that $a - bt^* = 0$. Using this to substitute for a, the logistic can easily be rewritten: $S_t = S_{max}/[1 + \exp\{-b(t-t^*)\}]$. Now solve this at time $t = 0$ to obtain: $S_0 = S_{max}/[1 + \exp\{+bt^*\}]$. With a little rearrangement, this yields the following expression: $b = \ln[(S_{max}/S_0) -1]/t^*$. Substituting that into the last general expression for the logistic gives: $S_t =$

$S_{max}/[1 + \exp\{-\ln[(S_{max}-S_0)/S_0].(t-t^*)/t^*\}]$, and that can be rewritten in the final form: $S_t = S_{max}/[1 + \{(S_{max}-S_0)/S_0\}^{-(t-t^*)/t^*}]$, as in the text.

9 The reason for rejecting the logit formulation in this case is very simple: the expression $\exp\{T\}$ rapidly becomes too large to store in a computer when T gets large!

10 The starting number can have an effect on some other aspects of the technological path, however.

11 This was essentially the argument we made in Swann (1986). It could be argued that the incentive for investment in many areas of microelectronics was primarily to stay in the game, while the rewards from opening up new markets requiring the highest level of technology were of secondary importance.

4 THEORETICAL CONNECTIONS BETWEEN RAPID TECHNOLOGICAL CHANGE AND THE DEVELOPMENT OF MARKET STRUCTURE

1 Peters (1988) argues that some firms, at least, can learn to flourish in unstable or chaotic conditions.

2 Copyright © Harwood Academic Publishers GmbH. We are grateful to Harwood Academic Publishers for permission to reproduce it here.

3 There is the additional question of what the vision adjusts towards? It could be the actual centre of gravity (i.e. T) if that is known: if it is not, the vision might be adjusted towards the most successful design in the previous period, or perhaps to some rather more systematic estimate of T (where that is unknown), or some sort of optimum adjustment could be introduced. We have not been able to address any of these interesting possibilities in this book.

4 Swann (1986) analyses this issue at some length. For any one consumer, the trade-off between price and desired quality is defined by their indirect utility function, so in principle any quality change can always be converted into an equivalent price change. The only exceptions arise in the case of discontinuities, such as lexicographic preferences. However, if one conversion is to be applied to all consumers they must either have very similar preferences, which is a strong and usually unwarranted assumption, or else there must be a straightforward way of physically modifying products (at a cost) so that they can be upgraded to the desired quality. Ironically, if the logit discrete choice function is to satisfy aggregation conditions, it effectively rules out any random diversity in different consumers' marginal willingness to pay for quality. So in effect, if one is already using logit as a market share model, no additional strong assumptions are required to convert quality differences into price equivalents.

5 CASE STUDY: MICROPROCESSORS

1 Sections 5.2 and 5.3, and the data for Figures 5.2–5.7 draw on Swann (1986).

6 CASE STUDY: MEMORY CHIPS

1 This situation began to change in the early 1980s when AT&T announced its entry into the open market for DRAMs.

2 In the early history of semiconductors, the electronics market was dominated by large diversified vertically integrated corporations but nearly all were unable to

make the transition to semiconductors successfully and subsequently lost techno-logical leadership to the emerging merchant firms; see, for example, Tilton (1971) and Malerba (1985).

3 SRAMs can be divided into two groups based on their speed: 'slow' or 'fast'. The principal focus is on the speed of the devices and therefore examines the fast SRAM market.
4 These were not the actual prices for each size of memory chip but were calculated by averaging over different speeds, lot size, and military and commercial specification devices.
5 See Tilton (1971).
6 The historical review of the 4K DRAM is largely based on OTA (1983).
7 Based on data from Dataquest Europe, Denham, UK.
8 Calculated with data from Dataquest Europe, Denham, UK.
9 Calculated with data from Dataquest Europe, Denham, UK.
10 IBM started purchasing 16K DRAMs on the open market in the spring of 1978 to meet unexpectedly high demand for its new (model 4341) computer (Durniak, 1979: 88).
11 Calculated with data from Dataquest Europe, Denham, UK.
12 Note, though, that the graph of changes in access time does not distinguish between the single and multiple power supply 16K devices.
13 Calculated with data from Dataquest Europe, Denham, UK.
14 NEC and a number of other Japanese producers have generally been characterised in this way, though over time it has become clear that they possess significant innovative capacities and thus – at least in the memory segment – fall into both the category of innovators and low-cost volume producers.
15 Based on data from Dataquest Europe, Denham, UK.
16 Based on data from Dataquest Europe, Denham, UK.
17 Calculated with data from Dataquest Europe, Denham, UK.
18 Calculated with data from Dataquest Europe, Denham, UK.
19 Calculated with data from Dataquest Europe, Denham, UK.
20 Calculeted with data from Dataquest Europe, Denham, UK.
21 *Integrated Circuits International* 6(2), 19 (April 1982).
22 *Integrated Circuits International* 7(1), 16 (March 1983).
23 *Integrated Circuits International* 5(11), 2–3 (January 1982).
24 *Integrated Circuits International* 6(9), 18 (November 1982).
25 *Integrated Circuits International* 6(6), 1–2 (August 1982).
26 Calculated with data from Dataquest Europe, Denham, UK.
27 *Integrated Circuits International* 6(8), 18 (October 1982).
28 *Integrated Circuits International* 6(12), 18 (February 1983),
29 Calculated with data from Dataquest Europe, Denham, UK.
30 Calculated with data from Dataquest Europe, Denham, UK.
31 *Integrated Circuits International* 7(7), 17–18 (September 1983).
32 *Integrated Circuits International* 7(6), 10–11 (August 1983).
33 *Integrated Circuits International* 9(7), 6 (September 1985).
34 *Integrated Circuits International* 9(9), 17 (November 1985).
35 *Integrated Circuits International* 9(9), 17 (November 1985).
36 *Integrated Circuits International* 10(11), 11 (January 1987).
37 Dataquest Europe, Denham, UK.
38 In 1983, AT&T had announced its intention to be the first US producer of the 256K chip for the open market.
39 *Integrated Circuits International* 7(9), 7 (November 1983).
40 *Integrated Circuits International* 7(7), 8 (September 1983).
41 *Integrated Circuits International* 9(12), 2 (February 1986).

42 *Integrated Circuits International* 9(6), 2 (August 1985).
43 *Integrated Circuits International* 9(6), 2 (August 1985).
44 *Integrated Circuits International* 10(3), 12 (May 1986).
45 *Integrated Circuits International* 10(1), 12 (March 1986).
46 *Integrated Circuits International* 9(6), 14 (August 1985).
47 *Integrated Circuits International* 9(9), 16 (October 1985).
48 *Integrated Circuits International* 9(7), 17 (September 1985).
49 *Integrated Circuits International* 9(10), 19 (December 1985).
50 *Integrated Circuits International* 9(4), 2 (June 1985).
51 *Integrated Circuits International* 9(11), 2 (January 1986).
52 *Integrated Circuits International* 10(4), 13 (June 1986).
53 *Integrated Circuits International* 10(5), 14 (July 1986).
54 *Integrated Circuits International* 10(10), 13 (December 1986).
55 *Integrated Circuits International* 11(2), 10 (April 1987).
56 *Integrated Circuits International* 11(4), 16 (June 1987).
57 Another Korean firm, Hyundai, signed a licensing agreement with Inmos for the 256K DRAM in early 1985 (*Integrated Circuits International* 9(1), 16 (March 1985)) though this does not appear on Dataquest statistics of worldwide production of this device.
58 Calculated with data from Dataquest Europe, Denham, UK.
59 *Integrated Circuits International* 11(5), 16 (July 1987).
60 *Integrated Circuits International* 10(10), 14 (December 1985).
61 Dataquest Europe Denham UK.
62 *Integrated Circuits International* 11(4), 17 (June 1987).
63 *Integrated Circuits International* 7(5), 11 (July 1983).
64 *Integrated Circuits International* 8(9), 11–12 (November 1984).
65 *Integrated Circuits International* 9(4), 3 (June 1985).
66 In association with Philips, which was to focus on SRAMs.
67 *Integrated Circuits International* 8(10), 20–21 (December 1984).
68 *Integrated Circuits International* 9(6), 18 (August 1985).
69 *Integrated Circuits International* 8(11), 9–10 (January 1985).
70 *Integrated Circuits International* 8(12), 10 (February 1985).
71 *Integrated Circuits International* 9(4), 15 (June 1985).
72 Calculated with data from Dataquest Europe, Denham, UK.
73 Dataquest Europe, Denham, UK.
74 *Integrated Circuits International* 12(4), 12 (June 1988).
75 Another view is that Japanese suppliers deliberately constrained production to maintain higher prices in the 256K market. However, cutbacks in capital investment by Japanese firms to reduce trade friction with the USA would also have slowed down the move to the 1Mb DRAM.
76 *Integrated Circuits International* 9(11), 12 (January 1986).
77 Calculated with data from Dataquest Europe, Denham, UK.
78 Calculated with data from Dataquest Europe, Denham, UK.
79 *Integrated Circuits International* 12(12), 8 (March 1988).
80 *Integrated Circuits International* 12(3), 10 (May 1988).
81 *Integrated Circuits International* 12(3), 9 (May 1988).
82 Calculated with data from Dataquest Europe, Denham, UK.
83 Calculated with data from Dataquest Europe, Denham, UK.
84 For example, the capital cost of a plant capable of producing a minimum of 1,500 wafer starts per day was estimated to have risen from US $10 million in 1975 to US $60 million by 1985 (ICE, 1982: 60).
85 Calculated with data from Dataquest Europe, Denham, UK.
86 Calculated with data from Dataquest Europe, Denham, UK.

87 Calculated with data from Dataquest Europe, Denham, UK.
88 Calculated with data from Dataquest Europe, Denham, UK.
89 Based on data from Dataquest Europe, Denham, UK.
90 Calculated with data from Dataquest Europe, Denham, UK.
91 Dataquest Europe, Denham, UK.
92 Dataquest Europe, Denham, UK.
93 *Integrated Circuits International* 9(9), 20 (November 1985).
94 Calaculated with data from Dataquest Europe, Denham, UK.
95 Calaculated with data from Dataquest Europe, Denham, UK.
96 *Integrated Circuits International* 6(3), 18 (May 1982).
97 Calaculated with data from Dataquest Europe, Denham, UK.
98 Dataquest Europe, Denham, UK.
99 Dataquest Europe, Denham, UK.
100 Inmos was sold to Thomson in the late 1980s
101 *Integrated Circuits International* 10(8), 5 (November 1986).
102 *Integrated Circuits International* 12(1), 10 (March 1988).
103 *Integrated Circuits International* 12(3), 14 (May 1988).

7   CASE STUDY: STANDARD LOGIC

1 A spin-off from Fairchild in 1961.
2 An applications engineer from Texas Instruments – which had its own TTL family – stated, for example, that around 80 per cent of computer designs required TTL (*Electronics*, 1967: 179).
3 The 54/74 series was in three temperature ranges: 54 series (for military applications) from −55 to +125 C; 64 series for industrial markets from −40 to +85 C; 74 series temperature range from −20 to +70 C.
4 This section is based principally on Tilton (1971).
5 Dataquest Europe, Denham, UK.
6 Dataquest Europe, Denham, UK.

8   CASE STUDY: PC SOFTWARE

1 Readers will note that as the IBM PC was not introduced until December 1981, the word-processing model predates the IBM PC. The reason for this is that Wordstar, a key product in that market, was introduced for other PC standards (e.g. CP/M) before the IBM standard arrived. That is arguably at least a factor in Wordstar's success in this market. In the spreadsheet market, while it is true that Visicalc was introduced before the appearance of the IBM PC (on CP/M and Apple II), Visicalc was not a major success in the IBM PC market, and it is neglected in the simulation model.
2 The logarithmic version seems more plausible, while the linear version fits the data better!
3 In that case, the upgrade will always be uncompetitive unless the gateway is equal to 100 per cent, in which case all users would be indifferent between the original and the upgrade. For the simulations, we simply look at the market share of (all versions of) the leading product, so it does not matter how consumers are divided between original and upgrade.
4 The empirical evidence discussed in Swann and Lamaison (1990a) suggests that special network factors for Lotus 1–2–3 might be up to two or even three times that for other leading products.

5 Indeed, at the time of writing, market leadership has changed considerably.

6 This user survey does not exactly give market share and market size data, but to a first order of approximation the data can be interpreted as such.

7 This leads to a slightly different procedure than in more conventional cluster analysis based on standard metrics (such as the Euclidean distance). But as noted, we consider this metric the most appropriate. Moreover, experiments with conventional cluster analysis gave very similar results.

8 This is a weighted clustering procedure in the following sense. At each stage, after the next cluster has been identified, the share of each firm in that new cluster must be computed. In computing the share of a firm in two categories combined, the relative size of each constituent market is taken into account. Thus, if two categories have sales X_A and X_B, and firm 1 has market share M_A and M_B respectively, then firm 1's market share of the combined category A+B is, in an obvious notation, $(M_A X_A + M_B X_B)/(X_A + X_B)$, rather than $[M_A + M_B]/2$. However, in working out the overlap, the market shares in each sub-market are treated unweighted.

9 There are at least three problems here. First, while it is easy to establish the earliest introduction date among the current generation of products, that does not necessarily indicate the start of that category as other (now unsuccessful or deleted) products may predate that. Second, many of the software categories predate the PC, and indeed custom software for such an application would be available some way back. Third, the 'soft' nature of the product makes it hard to place software products unambiguously in one category. Thus, the ubiquitous spreadsheet is undoubtedly a popular financial analysis program, though obviously not in the same way as the more specialist programs for money management. This ambiguity also makes it hard to pin down starting dates for these categories.

10 A regression of the proportion of SMEs (% SME) on the distance from the cluster (D) omitting the two outliers gives the following result:

$$\% \text{ SME} = -0.64 + 0.015\ D;\ R^2 = 55\%;\ df = 22$$
$$(0.003)$$

11 This may seem surprising, as games software would appear to be the domain of the one-man start-up. Remember, however, that this is the MSDOS PC market, and not the 'games computer' market. The smaller, older firms here are, in fact, publishers.

9 CASE STUDY: BIOTECHNOLOGY

1 For more details on complementary assets see Teece (1986).

2 The following is based on Buchan et al. (1990).

3 Following the procedure for sensitivity, equivocal results are generally added to both the numerator and denominator.

4 Sometimes abbreviated to EIA.

5 In November 1989, the UK government amended the Health and Medicines Bill so that these kits could only be sold to licensed laboratories (Green, 1989).

6 See chapter 4 for a more detailed explanation.

7 Analysis is made more complicated by the trends towards globalisation of innovation (see Freeman, 1990; Pisano et al., 1988) involving, for instance, collaborative ventures such as a large foreign company marketing its products through a small domestic firm (for example, Fujirebio with Mast Diagnostics).

8 Significantly, Diagnostics Pasteur had been set up by the Pasteur Institute, an organisation with a long trajectory of expertise in culture technology which had

been the first to isolate HIV–1 (in 1983) and HIV–2 (in 1985), two years before others.

10 CONCLUSIONS

1 Bosworth and Wilson (1993) analyse how different companies make differing use of scientists and engineers in constructing their technological visions. Lonie *et al.* (1993) show how a sufficiently charismatic product champion can override financial constraints and impose his vision on the company if the culture is sufficiently receptive.

2 In turn, it is tempting to apply the arguments of Chapters 1 to 4 to research institutions. This would suggest that large institutions tend to have powerful visions which enable them to pursue mainstream research programmes very efficiently, but they are much less adaptable than the small institution in the face of a radical breakthrough in the subject. Casual empirical evidence lends some support to this argument.

3 The first PCs produced in the mid-1970s were introduced by small firms. IBM did not enter that market until later (December 1981). Before 1980, relatively few large firms were in this business, for example Tandy (Radio Shack in the USA). Apple was, of course, a 1970s start-up firm, its first product being the Apple PC.

4 This argument in favour of horizontal mergers is usually offset by the anti-competitive effects of such merger.

5 Natural examples here would include the merger of publishing and IT businesses.

6 Data on innovation counts do perhaps come the closest, as such counts tend to be based on important discrete innovations rather than continuous incremental improvements. Of course, the technological content of patents could in principle be used for such an exercise, but not the patent count.

7 Triplett (1990) gives a fascinating, if rather depressing, 'autopsy' of the use of hedonic methods in adjusting price indices. It is clear that we have some way to go before statistical agencies feel comfortable with quality indices. Yet in the case of the technologies studied in this book it is almost impossible to make any meaningful analysis of the macroeconomics of those industries without some information on the rate of quality improvement observed. To some extent there is an element of Habermas' *unsurveyability* here. One of us has argued elsewhere (Swann, 1990a) that incremental quality improvement often takes the form of a continuing expansion of characteristics space, in which the number of varieties marketed increases rapidly over time. In that reference, it was suggested that product variety maps have a fractal character, with a high fractal dimension except perhaps in the maturity phase of a product life cycle.

REFERENCES

Abernathy, W. (1976) 'Production process structure and technological change', *Decision Sciences 7*, 607–19.

—— (1978) *The Productivity Dilemma: Roadblocks to Innovation in the Automobile Industry*, Baltimore, MD: Johns Hopkins University Press.

Abernathy, W. and Clark, K. (1985) 'Mapping the winds of creative destruction', *Research Policy 14*, 3–22.

Abernathy, W., Clark, K. and Kantrow, A. (1983) *Industrial Renaissance*, New York: Basic Books.

ACARD (1980) *Biotechnology: Report of the Joint Working Party (The Spinks Report)*, Advisory Council for Applied Research and Development (ACARD) with Advisory Board for the Research Councils (ABRC) and the Royal Society, London: HMSO.

Acs, Z. and Audretsch, D. (1987) 'Innovation, market structure and firm size', *Review of Economics and Statistics 69*, 576–674.

—— (1989) 'Small firm entry in US manufacturing', *Economica 56*, 255–66.

—— (1991) 'Innovation and technological change: an overview', in Z. Acs and D. Audretsch (eds) *Innovation and Technological Change: An International Comparison*, Hemel Hempstead: Harvester Wheatsheaf.

Altman, L. (1978) '65-k Memories won't slight performance' *Electronics*, 51(4), 80, 82.

Altschuler, A., Anderson, M. Jones, D. T., Roos, D. and Womack, J. (1985) *The Future of the Automobile*, Cambridge, MA: MIT Press.

Aoki, M. (1986) 'Horizontal vs vertical information structure of the firm', *American Economic Review 76*(5), 971–83.

Attwood, W. & Co. (1958) 'Survey of the UK Transistor Market', unpublished market research report, Semiconductors Ltd, cited in Golding, A. M. (1971) 'The semiconducter industry in Britain and the United States: a case study in innovation, growth, and the diffusion of technology', D.Phil. thesis, University of Sussex.

Audretsch, D. (1992) 'The technological regime and market evolution: the new learning', *Economics of Innovation and New Technology 2*(1), 27–35.

Auerbach, P. (1988) *Competition: The Economics of Industrial Change*, Oxford: Basil Blackwell.

Baldwin, W. L. and Scott, J. T. (1987) *Market Structure and Technological Change*, London: Harwood Academic Publishers.

Barley, S. R. (1986) 'Technology as an occasion for structuring: evidence from observation of CT scanners and the social order of radiology departments', *Administrative Science Quarterly 31*, 78–108.

Bayliss, G. *et al.* (1987) *Public Health Laboratory Service and Department of Health and Social Security Evaluation of Four Commercial Anti-HIV Kits*, report no. STD/

87/38, London: Department of Health, NHS Procurement Directorate, Supplies Technology Division.

Blair, J. M. (1948) 'Technology and size', *American Economic Review* 38, 121–52.

—— (1972) *Economic Concentration: Structure, Behaviour and Public Policy*, New York: Harcourt Brace Jovanovich.

Borrus, M., Millstein, J. E. and Zysman J. (1983) 'Trade and development in the semiconductor industry, Japanese challenge and American response, in J. Zysman and L. Tyson (eds) *American Industry in International Competition*, London: Cornell University Press.

Bosworth, D. and Wilson, R. (1993) 'Qualified scientists and engineers and economic performance', in P. Swann (ed.) *New Technologies and the Firm*, London: Routledge.

Branch, B. (1972–3) 'Research and development and its relations to sales growth', *Journal for Economics and Business* 25, 107–11.

—— (1974) 'Research and development activity and profitability: a distributed lag analysis', *Journal of Political Economy* 82, 999–1,011.

Braun, E. and MacDonald, S. (1978) *Revolution in Miniature*, Cambridge: Cambridge University Press.

Bright, J. R. (1968) *Technological Forecasting for Industry and Government: Methods and Applications*, Englewood Cliffs, NJ: Prentice-Hall.

Buchan, H., Gray, M., Hiu, A. and Coulter, A. (1990) 'A testing question', *The Health Service Journal* 100(5,190), 328–9.

Burns, T. and Stalker, G. (1961) *The Management of Innovation*, London: Tavistock.

Bylinksy, G. (1981) 'Japan's ominous chip victory' *Fortune*, 104(12), 52–7.

Byte (1982) Editorial on IBM PC, 7 (1), 6 (January 1982).

Campbell A., Devine, M. and Young, D. (1990) *A Sense of Mission* London: The Economist Books.

Capece, R. P. (1979) 'Memories', *Electronics* 52 (22), 124–34.

Carlsson, B. (1984) 'The development and use of machine tools in historical perspective', *Journal of Economic Behaviour and Organisation* 5, 91–114.

—— (1989a) 'The evolution of manufacturing technology and its impact on industrial structure: an international study', *Small Business Economics* 1, 21–38.

—— (1989b) 'Flexibility and the theory of the firm', *International Journal of Industrial Organisation* 7, 170–204.

Carrell, S. (1968) 'International report on microelectronics', in M. Goldberg (ed.) *Impact of Microelectronics, II: Proceedings of the Second Conference on the Impact of Microelectronics*, Washington, DC: Electronics Industries Association and IIT Research Institute, cited in Tilton, J. (1971) *The International Diffusion of Technology: The Case of Semiconductors*, Washington, DC: Brookings Institution.

Cawson, A., Haddon L. and Miles, I. (1993) 'The heart of where the home is: the innovation process in consumer IT products', in P. Swann (ed.) *New Technologies and the Firm*, London: Routledge.

Chandler, A. D., Jr (1962) *Strategy and Structure*, Cambridge, MA: MIT Press.

—— (1977) *The Visible Hand: The Managerial Revolution in American Business*, Cambridge, MA: Belknap Press.

Chase Econometrics (1980) *US and Japanese Semiconductor Industries: A Financial Comparison*, cited in OECD (1985) *The Semiconductor Industry: Trade Related Issues*, Paris: Organization for Economic Co-operation and Development.

Child, J. (1984) *Organisation: A Guide to Problems and Practice*, 2nd edn, London: Harper & Row.

Clark, K. (1983) 'Competition, technical diversity and radical innovation in the US auto industry', in R. S. Rosenbloom (ed.) *Research on Technological Innovation, Management and Policy*, Greenwich, CT: JAI Press.

226

REFERENCES

Clewley, J. (1989) 'The polymerase chain reaction: a review of the practical limitations for human immunodeficiency virus diagnosis', *Journal of Virological Methods* 25, 179–88.

Cohen, W. M. and Levin, R. C. (1989) 'Empirical studies of innovation and market structure', in R. Schmalensee and R. Willig (eds.) *Handbook of Industrial Economics*, Amsterdam: North-Holland.

Cohen, W. M. and Levinthal, D. A. (1989) 'Innovation and learning: the two faces of R&D', *Economic Journal* 99, 569–96.

—— (1990) 'Absorptive capacity: a new perspective on learning and innovation', *Administrative Science Quarterly* 35(1), 128–52.

Cole, B. (1975) 'Low-power Schottky making its move', *Electronics* 48(21), 45–6.

Comanor, W. S. (1964) 'Research and competitive product differentiation in the pharmaceutical industry in the United States', *Economica* 31, 372–84.

Coombs, R. (1988) 'Technological opportunities and industrial organisation', in G. Dosi, C. Freeman, R. R. Nelson, G. Silverberg and L. Soete (eds) *Technical Change and Economic Theory*, London: Pinter Publishers.

Daft, R. L. (1982) 'Bureaucratic vs non-bureaucratic structure and the process of innovation and change', in S. B. Bacharach (ed.) *Research in the Sociology of Organisations* 1, 129–66, Greenwich, CT: JAI Press.

Dasgupta, P. and Stiglitz, J. E. (1980a) 'Uncertainty, industrial structure and the speed of R&D', *Bell Journal of Economics* 11, 1–28.

—— (1980b) 'Industrial structure and the nature of innovative activity', *Economic Journal* 90, 266–93.

David, P. A. (1985) 'Clio and the economics of QWERTY', *American Economic Review Proceedings* 75(2), 332–6.

—— (1987) 'Some new standards for the economics of standardization in the information age', in P. Dasgupta and P. Stoneman, (eds.) *Economic Policy and Technological Performance*, Cambridge: Cambridge University Press.

David, P. A. and Greenstein, S. (1990) 'The economics of compatibility standards: an introduction to recent research', *Economics of Innovation and New Technology* 1(1/2), 3–41.

Dibner, M. (1988) *Biotechnology Guide USA*, New York: Macmillan.

Dosi, G. (1982) 'Technological paradigms and technological trajectories: a suggested interpretation of the determinants and directions of technical change', *Research Policy* 11(3), 147–62.

—— (1984) *Technical Change and Industrial Transformation*, London: Macmillan.

—— (1988) 'The nature of the innovative process', in G. Dosi, C. Freeman, R. R. Nelson, G. Silverberg and C. Soete (eds) *Technical Change and Economic Theory*, London: Pinter Publishers.

Dosi, G., Freeman, C., Nelson, R. R., Silverberg, G. and Soete, L. (1988) *Technical Change and Economic Theory*, London: Pinter Publishers.

Downie, J. (1958) *The Competitive Process*, London: Duckworth.

Durniak, A. (1979) 'Memory pinch threatens profits', *Electronics* 52(22), 88–9.

Dutton, J. and Thomas, A. (1985) 'Relating technological change and learning by doing', in R. D. Rosenbloom (ed.) *Research on Technological Innovation, Management and Policy* 2, 187–224, Greenwich, CT: JAI Press.

Economist (1976) 'Microprocessors; the thumb nail brain', *The Economist* 260(6,936), 52–3.

Economist (1979) 'Innovative Intel', *The Economist* (7,085), 94–95.

Economist (1988) 'Survey: biotechnology', *The Economist* 307(7,548), 1–22.

EIA (1979) *Electronic Market Data Book*, Washington, DC: Electronic Industries Association.

Electronic Design News, various issues, 1974–85.

REFERENCES

Electronic News (1968), pp. 4–5, 30 September, cited in J. Kraus (1971) p. 235.

Electronics, various issues, 1969–89.

Electronics (1967) 'The swing to TTL becomes a stampede', *Electronics* 40(9), 179–82.

Electronics (1970) 'Sylvania closes semiconductor division' *Electronics* 43(21), 46.

Ettlie, J. E., Bridges, W. P. and O'Keefe, R. D. (1984) 'Organisational strategy and structural differences for radical vs incremental innovation', *Management Science* 30, 682–95.

Farrell, J. and Saloner, G. (1985) 'Standardization, compatibility and innovation', *RAND Journal of Economics* 16(1), 70–83.

—— (1986) 'Installed base and compatibility: innovations, product pre-announcements, and predation', *American Economic Review* 76, 940–55.

Feyerabend, P. (1978) *Against Method*, London: Verso.

Fisher, F. M., McGowan, J. J. and Greenwood, J. E. (1983) *Folded, Spindled and Mutilated: Economic Analysis and US vs IBM*, Cambridge, MA: MIT Press.

Fitzroy, F. R. and Kraft, K. (1991) 'Firm size, growth and innovation: some evidence from West Germany', in Z. Acs and D. Audretsch (eds.) *Innovation and Technological Change: An International Comparison*, Hemel Hempstead: Harvester Wheatsheaf.

Flaherty, M. T. (1980) 'Industry structure and cost-reducing investment', *Econometrica* 48, 1,187–209.

Freeman, C. (1965) 'Research and development in electronic capital goods', *National Institute Economic Review*, 34, 40–91.

—— (1982) *The Economics of Industrial Innovation*, 2nd edn, London: Frances Pinter.

—— (1987) *Technology Policy and Economic Performance*, London: Frances Pinter.

—— (1990) 'Networks of innovators: a synthesis of research issues', paper at International Workshop on Networks of Innovators, Montreal, Canada.

Freeman, C. and Perez, C. (1988) 'Structural crises of adjustment, business cycles and investment behaviour', in G. Dosi, C. Freeman, R. R. Nelson, G. Silverberg and L. Soete (eds) *Technical Change and Economic Theory*, London: Pinter Publishers.

Friedman, M. (1968) 'The role of monetary policy', *American Economic Review* 58(1), 1–17.

Gardiner, P. (1986) 'Design trajectories for airplanes and automobiles during the last 50 years: robust and lean designs', in C. Freeman (ed.) *Design, Innovation and Long Cycles in Economic Development*, London: Frances Pinter.

Georghiou, L. and Barker, K. (1993) 'Management of international collaboration', in P. Swann (ed.) *New Technologies and the Firm*, London: Routledge.

Georghiou, L., Metcalfe, J. S., Gibbons, M., Ray, T. and Evans, J. (1986) *Post Innovation Performance: Technological Development and Competition*, London: Macmillan.

Geroski, P. A. (1990) 'Innovation, technological opportunity and market structure', *Oxford Economics Papers* 42, 586–602.

—— (1991) *Market Dynamics and Entry*, Oxford: Basil Blackwell.

Geroski, P. A. and Pomroy, R. (1990) 'Innovation and evolution of market structure', *Journal of Industrial Economics* 38(3), 299–314.

Gill, J. (1990a) 'The speed of technology change and development of market structure: 3: memory chips', Centre for Research in Innovation, Culture and Technology (CRICT) discussion paper, Uxbridge: Brunel University.

—— (1990b) 'The speed of technology change and development of market structure: 4: standard logic', CRICT discussion paper, Uxbridge: Brunel University.

—— (1990c) 'The speed of technology change and development of market structure: 5: biotechnology – a case study of HIV diagnostics', CRICT discussion paper, Uxbridge: Brunel University.

Golding, A. M. (1971) 'The semiconductor industry in Britain and the United States: a case study in innovation, growth, and the diffusion of technology', D.Phil. thesis, University of Sussex.

Gort, M. (1962) *Diversification and Integration in American Industry*, Princeton, NJ: Princeton University Press.

Gort, M. and Kanakayama, A. (1982) 'A model of diffusion in the production of an innovation', *American Economic Review* 72, 1,111–20.

Gort, M. and Klepper, S. (1982) 'Time paths in the diffusion of product innovations', *Economic Journal* 92, 630–53.

Gottfried, T. and Urnovitz, H. (1990) 'HIV–1 testing: product development strategies', *Trends in Biotechnology*, 8, 35–40.

Grabowski, H. G. (1968) 'The determinants of industrial research and development: a study of the chemical, drug and petroleum industries', *Journal of Political Economy* 76, 292–306.

Grabowski, H. G. and Mueller, D.C. (1978) 'Industrial research and development, intangible capital stocks, and firm profit rates', *Bell Journal of Economics* 9, 328–43.

Green, K. (1989) 'HIV OTC-test ban', *Biotechnology Insight* 4–5.

Hamberg, D. (1967) 'Size of enterprise and technical change', *Antitrust Law and Economics Review* 1, 43–51.

Hannan, M. T. and Freeman J. (1977) 'The population ecology of organisations', *American Journal of Sociology* 83, 929–64.

—— (1984) 'Structural inertia and organisational change', *American Sociological Review* 49, 149–64.

Harris, C. and Vickers, J. (1985) 'Patent races and the persistence of monopoly', *Journal of Industrial Economics* 33, 461–81.

Hay, D. A. and Morris, D. J. (1991) *Industrial Economics and Organization*, Oxford: Oxford University Press.

Hayes, R. H. and Abernathy, W. J. (1980) 'Managing our way to economic decline', in G. A. Steiner and J. B. Minor (eds) *Management Policy and Strategy*, 2nd edn, New York: Macmillan.

Hippel, E. von (1979) 'A customer active paradigm for industrial product idea generation', in M. J. Baker (ed.) *Industrial Innovation*, London: Macmillan.

—— (1980) 'The user's role in industrial innovation', in B. Dean and J. Goldhar (eds) *Management of Research and Innovation*, Amsterdam: North-Holland.

Hobday, M. (1992a) 'A note on the semiconductor industry: cumulative learning, asymmetries and policy implications', mimeo, Brighton: SPRU, University of Sussex.

—— (1992b) 'External operations in the European semiconductor industry: corporate strategies, government policies and competitiveness', mimeo, Brighton: SPRU, University of Sussex, prepared for the Institute Français des Relations Internationales (IFRI), Paris.

Horowitz, I. (1962) 'Firm size and research activity', *Southern Economic Journal* 28, 298–301.

Hotelling, H. (1929) 'The stability of competition', *Economic Journal* 39, 41–57.

ICE (1979) *Status 1979*, Scottsdale, AZ: Integrated Circuit Engineering Corporation.

ICE (1982) *Status 1982*, Scottsdale, AZ: Integrated Circuit Engineering Corporation.

ICE (1984) *Status 1984*, Scottsdale, AZ: Integrated Circuit Engineering Corporation.

ICE (1985) *Status 1985*, Scottsdale, AZ: Integrated Circuit Engineering Corporation.

ICE (1991) *Status 1991*, Scottsdale, AZ: Integrated Circuit Engineering Corporation.

Integrated Circuits International (ICI), various issues (detailed in notes to Chapters 6 and 7), Oxford: Elsevier Advanced Technology.

Jantsch, E. (1972) *Technological Planning and Social Futures*, London: Cassell/ Associated Business Programmes.

Jones, H. and Twiss, B. C. (1978) *Forecasting Technology for Planning Decisions*, London: Macmillan.

REFERENCES

Juliussen, E. and Juliussen, K. (1988) *The Computer Industry Almanac 1989*, New York: Brady.

Kamien, M. I. and Schwartz N. L., (1982) *Market Structure and Innovation*, Cambridge: Cambridge University Press.

Katz, B. and Phillips, A. (1982) 'Innovation, technological change and the emergence of the computer industry', in H. Giersch (ed.) *Emerging Technology*, Tübingen: J. C. B. Mohr.

Katz, M. and Shapiro, C. (1985). 'Network externalities, competition and compatibility', *American Economic Review* 75(3), 424–40.

—— (1986). 'Technology adoption in the presence of network externalities', *Journal of Political Economy* 94, 822–41.

Kay, J. (1983) *Foundations of Corporate Success*, Oxford: Oxford University Press.

Kay, J. and Willman, P. (1993) 'Managing technological innovation: architecture, trust and organisational relationships in the firm', in P. Swann (ed.) *New Technologies and the Firm*, London: Routledge.

Kay, N. (1982) *The Evolving Firm: Strategy and Structure in Industrial Organisation*, London: Macmillan.

—— (1984) *The Emergent Firm: Knowledge, Ignorance and Surprise in Economic Organisations*, London: Macmillan.

—— (1988) 'The R&D function: corporate structure and strategy', in G. Dosi, C. Freeman, R. R. Nelson, G. Silverberg and L. Soete (eds) *Technical Change and Economic Theory*, London: Pinter Publishers.

Klemperer, P. (1987) 'Markets with consumer switching costs', *Quarterly Journal of Economics* 102, 375–94.

Klepper, S. and Grady, E. (1989) 'The evolution of new industries and the determinants of market structure', *RAND Journal of Economics* 21, 27–44.

Kraus, J. (1973) 'An economic study of the US semiconductor industry', Ph.D. thesis, Graduate Faculty of Political and Social Science, New School for Social Research, USA.

Lamaison, H. (1991) 'Standards in PC Software: Questionnaire Report' unpublished paper, Brunel University.

Langlois, R. N., Pugel, T. A., Haklisch, C. S., Nelson, R. R. and Egelhoff, W. G. (1988) *Microelectronics: An Industry in Transition*, Boston: Unwin Hyman.

Lonie, A., Nixon, W. and Collison, D. (1993) 'Internal and external financial constraints on investment in innovative technology', in P. Swann (ed.) *New Technologies and the Firm*, London: Routledge.

McKelvey, B. and Aldrich, H. (1983) 'Populations, natural selection, and applied organisational science', *Administrative Science Quarterly* 28, 101–28.

Malerba, F. (1985) *The Semiconductor Business: The Economics of Rapid Growth and Decline*, London: Frances Pinter Publishers.

Mansfield, E. (1962) 'Entry, gibrat's law, innovation and the growth of firms', *American Economic Review* 52, 1,023–51.

—— (1968a) *Industrial Research and Technical Innovation*, New York: Norton.

—— (1968b) *The Economics of Technical Change*, New York: Norton.

—— (1983) 'Technological change and market structure', *American Economic Review* 73, 205–9.

—— (1984) 'R&D and innovation; some empirical findings', in Z. Griliches (ed.) *R&D, Patents, and Productivity*, Chicago: University of Chicago Press for the National Bureau of Economic Research.

Martin, I. (1990) Personal communication, Product Manager, Abbott Diagnostics, Maidenhead, UK.

Martino, J. P. (1983) *Technological Forecasting for Decision Making*, 2nd edn, Amsterdam: North-Holland/Elsevier Science Publishers.

REFERENCES

Menge, J. A. (1962) 'Style change costs as a market weapon', *Quarterly Journal of Economics*, 76, 632–47.
Mensch, G. (1979) *Stalemate in Technology: Innovations Overcome the Depression*, Cambridge, MA: Ballinger.
Merton, R. K. (1973) *The Sociology of Science*, Chicago: Chicago University Press.
Metcalfe, J. S. and Boden, M. (1990) 'Strategy, paradigm and evolutionary change', unpublished paper, University of Manchester.
—— (1991) 'Innovation strategy and the epistemic connection', *Journal of Scientific and Industrial Research* 50, 707–17.
—— (1993) 'Paradigms, strategies and the evolutionary basis of technological competition', in P. Swann (ed.) *New Technologies and the Firm*, London: Routledge.
Mortimer, P. and Clewley, J. (1987) 'Serological tests for human immunodeficiency virus', in M. Gottlieb, D. Jeffries and D Mildman (eds) *Current Topics in AIDS*, vol. 1, London: Wiley & Sons.
Mortimer, P. *et al.* (1985) *Public Health Laboratory Service and Department of Health and Social Security Evaluation of Five Commercial Anti-HTLV III/LAV Assay Kits*, report no. STB/85/40, London: Department of Health and Social Security, Scientific and Technical Branch.
—— (1986) *Public Health Laboratory Service and Department of Health and Social Security Evaluation of Ten Commercial Anti-HTLV III/LAV Assay Kits*, report no. STB/86/14, London: Department of Health and Social Security, Scientific and Technical Branch.
Mowery, D. C. (1983) 'Industrial research and firm size, survival and growth in American manufacturing, 1921–46: an assessment', *Journal of Economic History* 43, 953–80.
Mueller, D. C. and Tilton, J. E. (1969) 'Research and development costs as a barrier to entry', *Canadian Journal of Economics* 2(4), 570–9.
Mukhopadhyay, A. K. (1985) 'Technological progress and change in market concentration in the US, 1963–77', *Southern Economic Journal* 52, 141–9.
Nelson, R. R. and Winter, S. G. (1977) 'In search of a useful theory of innovations', *Research Policy*, 6(1), 36–77.
—— (1978) 'Forces generating and limiting concentration under Schumpeterian competition', *Bell Journal of Economics* 9, 524–48.
—— (1982) *An Evolutionary Theory of Economic Change*, Cambridge, MA.: Harvard University Press.
Nelson, R. R., Winter, S. G. and Schuette, H. L. (1976) 'Technical change in an evolutionary model', *Quarterly Journal of Economics* 90, 90–118.
Newmark, P. (1988) 'Europe getting into the HIV-testing act', *Biotechnology* 6, 761.
Nonaka, I. and Yoneyama, S. (1991) 'The semiconductor industry: organisation and strategy for 1M DRAM development', mimeo, Japan: Nomura School of Advanced Management.
Noyce, R. N. (1977) 'Microelectronics', *Scientific American* 237(3), 62–9.
OECD (1985) *The Semiconductor Industry: Trade Related Issues*, Paris: Organization for Economic Co-operation and Development.
OTA (1983) *International Competitiveness in the Electronics Industry*, Washington, DC: Office of Technology Assessment, US Department of Commerce.
OTA (1984) *Commercial Biotechnology*, Washington, DC: Office of Technology Assessment, US Congress.
Ou, C.-Y., Kwok, S., Mitchell, S., Mack, D., Sninsky, J., Krebks, J., Feorino, P., Warfield, D. and Schochetman, G. (1988) 'DNA amplification for direct detection of HIV1 in DNA of peripheral blood mononuclear cells', *Science* 239, 295–7.
Panesar, B. (1990) *Personal communication*, Texas Instruments, Bedford: UK.

REFERENCES

Parry, J. *et al.*, (1990a) 'Sensitivity of six commercial enzyme immunoassay kits that detect both anti-HIV–1 and anti-HIV–2', *AIDS* 4(4), 355–60.

—— (1990b) *An Evaluation of Twelve Commercial Anti-HIV Kits*, report no. STD/90/27, London: Department of Health, NHS Procurement Directorate, Supplies Technology Division.

Patel, P. and Pavitt, K. (1991) 'Large firms in the production of the world's technology: an important case of non-globalisation', *Journal of International Business Studies* 22, 1–21.

Patel, P. and Pavitt, K. (1992) 'The innovative performance of the world's largest firms: some new evidence', *Economics of Innovation and New Technology* 2(2), 91–102.

Pavitt, K. (1979) 'Technical innovation and industrial development: the new causality', *Futures* 11(6), 458–70.

—— (1991) 'Key characteristics of the large innovating firm', *British Journal of Management* 2(1), 41–50.

Pavitt, K. and Wald, S. (1971) *The Conditions for Success in Technological Innovation*, Paris: OECD.

Pavitt, K., Robson, M. and Townsend, J. (1987) 'The size distribution of innovating firms', *Journal of Industrial Economics* 35, 297–316.

Payne, M. (1969) 'The American challenge in chip', *Electronics* 44(2), 74–8.

PC World (1987) 'World class PC celebration', *PC World* 5(11), cited in E. Juliussen and K. Juliussen (1988), *The Computer Industry Almanac 1989*, 3.29–3.40, New York: Brady.

Perez, C. (1983) 'Structural change and the assimilation of new technologies in the economic and social system', *Futures* 15, 357–75.

Perez, C. and Soete, L. (1988) 'Catching up in technology: entry barriers and windows of opportunity', in G. Dosi, C. Freeman, R. R. Nelson, G. Silverberg and L. Soete, *Technical Change and Economic Theory*, London: Pinter Publishers.

Pertile, R. (1975) L'industria dell'informatica e dei componenti elettronica: analis; delle prospettive e proposte di intervento', Rome: ISPE cited in Malerba, F. (1985) *The Semiconductor Buiness: The Economics of Rapid Growth and Decline*, London: Frances Pinter Publishers.

Peters, T. (1988) *Thriving on Chaos*, New York: Alfred A. Knopf.

Petritz, R. L. (1978) 'Technology of ICs: past, present and future', *Microelectronics Journal* 9(1), 27–36.

Phelps, E. S. (1967) 'Phillips curves, expectations of inflation and optimal unemployment over time', *Economica*, 34, 254–81.

Phillips, A. (1956) 'Concentration, scale and technological change in selected manufacturing industries, 1899–1939', *Journal of Industrial Economics* 5, 179–93.

—— (1966) 'Patents, potential competition and technical progress', *American Economic Review*, 56, 301–10.

—— (1971) *Technology and Market Structure: A Study of the Aircraft Industry*, Lexington, MA: Heath, Lexington Books.

Piore, M. and Sabel, C. (1984) *The Second Industrial Divide*, New York: Basic Books.

Pisano, G., Shen, W. and Teece, D. (1988) 'Joint ventures and collaboration in the biotechnology industry', in D. Mowery (ed.) *International Ventures in US Manufacturing*, Cambridge, MA: Ballinger.

Porter, M. (1980) *Competitive Strategy*, New York: Free Press.

Ravenscraft, D. and Scherer, F. M. (1982) 'The lag structure of returns to research and development', *Applied Economics* 14, 603–20.

Reinganum, N. (1985) 'Innovation and industry evolution', *Quarterly Journal of Economics* 99, 81–99.

Roberts, E. (1979) 'Stimulating technological innovation: organizational approaches', *Research Management* 22(6), 26–30.

232

REFERENCES

Robson, M. and Townsend, J. (1984) *Users' Manual for ESRC Archive File on Innovations in Britain since 1945*, Brighton: SPRU, University of Sussex.

Rogers, E. M. (1982) 'Information exchange and technological innovation', in D. Sahal (ed.) *The Transfer and Utilisation of Technical Knowledge*, Lexington, MA: D. C. Heath.

Rosenberg, N. (1969) 'The direction of technological change: inducement mechanisms and focusing devices', *Economic Development and Cultural Change*, 18, 1–24 (Reprinted in Rosenberg, W. (1976a), *Perspective on Technology*, Cambridge: Cambridge University Press.)

—— (1976a) *Perspectives on Technology*, Cambridge: Cambridge University Press.

—— (1976b) 'On technological expectations', *Economic Journal* 86, 523–35. (Reproduced in Rosenberg, W. (1982) *Inside the Black Box*, Cambridge: Cambridge University Press.)

—— (1982) *Inside the Black Box*, Cambridge: Cambridge University Press.

Rothwell, R. and Zegreld, W. (1982) *Innovation and the Small and Medium Sized Firm*, London: Frances Pinter.

Sahal, D. (1981) *Patterns of Technological Innovation*, New York: Addison Wesley.

—— (1985) 'Technology guide-posts and innovation avenues', *Research Policy* 14(2), 61–82.

Salop, S. and Scheffman, D. (1983) 'Raising rivals' costs', *American Economic Review* 73, 267–71.

Saviotti, P. P. and Metcalfe, J. S. (1984) 'A theoretical approach to the construction of technological output indicators', *Research Policy* 13.

Saviotti, P. P. and Trickett, A. (1992) 'Evolution of helicopter technology: 1940–86', *Economics of Innovation and New Technology* 2(2), 111–30.

Scherer, F. M. (1980) *Industrial Market Structure and Economic Performance*, 2nd edn, Boston: Houghton Mifflin.

—— (1984) *Innovation and Growth: Schumpeterian Perspectives*, Cambridge, MA: MIT Press.

Schmalensee, R. (1978) 'Entry deterrence in the ready to eat breakfast cereals industry', *Bell Journal of Economics* 9, 305–27.

—— (1982) 'Product differentiation advantages of pioneering brands', *American Economic Review* 72, 349–65.

Scholz, L. (1974) 'Technologie und innovation in der industriellen produktion', inaugural dissertation, University of Munich, cited in Malerba, F. (1985) *The Semiconductor Business: The Economics of Rapid Growth and Decline*, Madison: University of Wisconsin Press.

Schumpeter, J. A. (1954) Capitalism, Socialism and Democracy, 4th edn, London: Unwin University Books.

Scott, J. (1990) Personal communication, Wellcome Diagnostics, Dartford, UK.

Sharp, M. (1985) 'The New Biotechnology', Sussex European Papers no. 15, Brighton: SPRU, University of Sussex.

Simon, H. (1985) 'What do we know about the creative process?', in R. L. Kuhn (ed.) *Frontiers in Creative and Innovative Management*, Cambridge, MA: Ballinger.

Singh, A. and Whittington, G. (1975) 'The size and growth of firms', *Review of Economics Studies* 42, 15–26.

Skott, P. (1983) 'An essay on Keynes and general equilibrium theory', Thames Polytechnic: Thames Papers in Political Economy.

Software Users' Year Book (1990) London: VNU Business Publications.

Stinchcombe, A. L. (1965) 'Social structure and organisations', in J. G. March (ed.) *Handbook of Organisations*, Chicago: Rand McNally.

Stonebreaker, R. J. (1976) 'Corporate profits and the risk of entry', *Review of Economics and Statistics* 58, 33–9.

233

Swann, P. (1985) 'Product competition in mircoprocessors', *Journal of Industrial Economics* 34(1), 33–54.

—— (1986) *Quality Innovation: An Economic Analysis of Rapid Improvements in Microelectronic Components*, London: Frances Pinter.

—— (1987) 'Industry standard microprocessors and the strategy of second source production', in H. L. Gabel (ed.) *Product Standardization and Competitive Strategy*, Amsterdam: Elsevier/North–Holland.

—— (1990a) 'Product competition and the dimensions of product space', *International Journal of Industrial Organisation* 8(2), 281–95.

—— (1990b) 'Technology pre-announcements in the international market for microprocessors', unpublished paper (revised), Centre for Business Strategy, London Business School.

—— (1992) 'Rapid technology change, "Technological Visions", Corporate Organisation and Market Structure', *Economics of Innovation and New Technology* 2(2), 3–25.

Swann, P. and Lamaison, H. (1990a) 'Vertical product differentiation, network externalities and market-defined standards: simulation of the PC spreadsheet software market', CRICT discussion paper, Uxbridge: Brunel University.

—— (1990b) 'Horizontal product differentiation, network externalities and market-defined standards: simulation of the PC wordprocessor software market', CRICT discussion paper, Uxbridge: Brunel University.

Swann, P. and Shurmer, M. (1992), 'An analysis of the process generating *de facto* standards in the PC spreadsheet software market', unpublished paper, Centre for Business Strategy, London Business School.

Taylor, H. *et al.* (1987) *Public Health Laboratory Service and Department of Health and Social Security Evaluation of Six Commercial Anti-HIV Kits*, report no. STD/87/16, London: Department of Health, NHS Procurement Directorate, Supplies Technology Division.

Teece, D. (1986) 'Profiting from technological innovation: implications for integration, collaboration, licensing and public policy', *Research Policy* 15(6), 285–305.

—— (1988) 'Technological change and the nature of the firm', in G. Dosi, C. Freeman, R. R. Nelson, G. Silverberg and L. Soete (eds) *Technical Change and Economic Theory*, London: Pinter Publishers.

Teece, D., Pisano, G. and Shuen, A. (1991) 'Firm capabilities, resources and the concept of strategy', CCC Working Paper no. 90-8 (revised), Berkeley, California: University of California at Berkeley, Center for Research in Management.

TI (nd) *Schottky TTL*, Texas Instruments Application Report, Bedford, UK.

Tilton, J. (1971) *The International Diffusion of Technology: The Case of Semiconductors*, Washington, DC: Brookings Institution.

Tirole, J. (1988) *The Theory of Industrial Organization*, Cambridge, MA: MIT Press.

Triplett, J. E. (1990) 'Hedonic methods in statistical agency environments: an intellectual biopsy', in E. R. Berndt and J. E. Triplett (eds) *Fifty Years of Economic Measurement*, National Bureau of Economic Research Studies in Income and Wealth, vol. 54, Chicago: University of Chicago Press.

Tushman, M. L. and Anderson, P. (1986) 'Technological discontinuities and organisational environments', *Administrative Science Quarterly* 31(3), 439–65.

UN (1986) *Transnational Corporations in the International Semiconductor Industry*, ST/CTC/39, United Nations Center on Transnational Corporations, United Nations, New York.

Urban, G., Carter, T. Gaskin, S. and Mucha, Z. (1984) 'Market share rewards to pioneering brands', *Management Science* 32, 645–59.

Uttal, B. (1981) 'The Animals of Silicon Valley', *Fortune* 103(1), 92–6.

Utterback, J. (1978) 'Management of technology', in A. Hax (ed.) *Studies in Operations Management*, Amsterdam: North-Holland.

REFERENCES

Utterback, J. and Abernathy, W. (1975) 'A dynamic model of product and process innovation', *Omega* 6, 639–56.

Vickers, J. (1986) 'The evolution of market structure when there is sequence of innovations', *Journal of Industrial Economics* 35, 1–12.

Walsh, V. (1984) 'Invention and innovation in the chemical industry: demand–pull or discovery–push', *Research Policy* 13(4), 211–34.

—— (1990) 'Inter-firm technological alliances: a transient phenomenon or new structures in capitalist economies', EAEPE conference paper, 15–17 November, Florence, Italy.

Watson, G. F. (1969) 'LSI and systems: the changing interface', *Electronics*, 78–85.

Webb, J. and Cleary, D. (1993) 'Supplier–user relationships and the management of expertise in computer systems development', in P. Swann (ed.) *New Technologies and the Firm*, London: Routledge.

Webbink, D. W (1977) *The Semiconductor Industry: A Survey of Structure, Conduct and Performance*, Staff report to the US FTC, Washington, DC: Government Printing Office.

Weiss, R. (1988) 'Improving the AIDS Test', *Science News* 133, 218–21.

Williamson, O. E. (1975) *Markets and Hierarchies: Analysis and Antitrust Implications*, New York: Free Press.

—— (1985) *The Economic Institutions of Capitalism*, New York: Free Press.

Willman, P. (1992) 'Innovation and appropriability', unpublished paper, London Business School.

Wills, G., Ashton, D. and Taylor, B. (1969) *Technological Forecasting and Corporate Strategy*, Bradford: University of Bradford Press.

Wilson, R., Ashton, P. and Egan, R. (1980) *Innovation, Competition and Government Policy in the Semiconductor Industry*, Lexington, MA: Heath.

Winter, S. (1984) 'Schumpeterian competition in alternative technological regimes', *Journal of Economic Behaviour and Organisation* 5(3/4), 287–320.

Wise, K. D., Chen, K. and Yokely, R. E. (1980) *Micros: A Technology Forecast and Assessment to 1990*, New York: Wiley.

Wyatt, G. (1986) *The Economics of Invention*, Brighton: Wheatsheaf Books.

INDEX

Pasteur Institute 185, 195, 223–4
Patel, P. 211, 215
patent races 13, 14
patent statistics 4, 214–15, 224
Pavitt, K. 9, 11, 18, 22, 211, 215; large
  multidivisional firms 15, 21–2
PCs 211, 224; software *see* software
Perez, C. 107
persistent dominance 2, 6, 9–10, 12–14,
  20–1
personal management software 178, 179
Pertile, R. 150
Petritz, R.L. 30
Pharmacia 192
pharmaceuticals 184–5; *see also* HIV
  diagnostic kits
Philco-Ford 144
Philips 136, 147, 148, 149
Phillips, A. 6, 8, 10, 13, 21
pioneering brands 13
pioneers, business strategies and 213–14
Piore, M. 11
Pisano, G. 17
planar process 139, 146, 147, 153
Plessey 146, 148
polymerase chain reaction (PCR) 202
Pomroy, R. 7, 10, 11, 21
Porter, M. 27
pre-announcements: semiconductor
  industry 87; spreadsheets 162, 165;
  tactical uses 26–7; *see also*
  visions
prices: CMOS SRAMs 135, 136;
  DRAMs 112, 114, 119–20, 121, 122,
  123–4, 124; NMOS SRAMs 128, 131,
  133; and quality 215, 219, 224;
  semiconductor industry 103; TTL
  ICs 149
process innovations 9, 11
product innovations 9, 11
product life cycle: CMOS SRAM 134;
  DRAM 108; HIV diagnostic kits 199;
  innovation and 9, 11, 14, 20;
  integrated simulation model 71–2,
  73–8; memory chips 105–7; NMOS
  SRAM 128
propagation delay 142, 144, 153–4
public good 28–9

quality: price and 215, 219, 224;
  spreadsheets 163–4, 165–7; word-
  processing software 167–70, 171,
  172–3

radical innovations 3, 20; business
  strategies for 213–14; deconcentration
  and 178, 206; entrants and 45, 86–7,
  88; incumbents and 18, 20;
  microprocessors 86–7, 88;
  organisational adaptability 49;
  semiconductor industry 103; small
  firms and 210–11, 224; software
  173–8, 178–80
radioimmunological assays (RIA) 189
Radiotechnique 149
randomness 28, 218
rate of technological change 1;
  econometric studies and data on
  214–15; measuring 4–5, 47–8
Ravenscraft, D. 9
Raytheon 143, 144
RCA 136, 156
RCTL (resistor coupled transistor
  logic) 140, 141, 146, 148
recombinant DNA (rDNA) 183; second-
  generation HIV diagnostic kits 191,
  192, 192–7, 201, 203
reconcentration 96–8; *see also*
  concentration, deconcentration
Reinganum, N. 14
research and development (R&D):
  concentration 9–10; cost of 13, 45;
  measure of technological change 4,
  214–15
Roberts, E. 16
Robson, M. 4
Roche, Hoffman La 191, 192, 195
Rockwell 90, 92
Rogers, E.M. 14, 20
Rosenberg, N. 2, 17, 19
Rothwell, R. 14, 20, 88
routines 14, 15, 20, 21, 24, 206

Sabel, C. 11
Saloner, G. 13, 26, 160, 161, 162
Salop, S. 10
Samsung 120, 121, 123, 138; 256K
  DRAMs 124; IMb DRAMs 125, 126
Saratoga 135
Saviotti, P.P. 5, 17, 18
scale economies 10, 46, 209; in
  innovation 48–9; integrated
  simulation model 52–4, 56–67;
  Moore's law 31; standard logic 32–3
Scheffman, D. 10
Scherer, F.M. 8, 9, 11, 21
Schmalensee, R. 13

Wise, K.D. 30
word-processing software 167–73,
176–8; data used in simulations
170–1; *de facto* standards simulation
model 167–70; rate of vertical quality
upgrading 172–3; simulations 172

Wordstar 169, 222
Wyatt, G. 13, 21

Zegveld, W. 14, 20, 88
Zilog 91, 92